Memoirs of a Maverick Lawyer

(*Be Jubilant My Feet*)

Webster Macdonald

Detselig Enterprises Ltd.
Calgary, Alberta

Memoirs of a Maverick Lawyer
(Be Jubilant My Feet)

© 1993 Webster Macdonald

Canadian Cataloguing in Publication Data

Macdonald, Webster
  Memoirs of a maverick lawyer

  ISBN 1-55059-068-5
  1. Macdonald, Webster.   2. Lawyers—Alberta—
Calgary—Biography.   I. Title.
KE416.M233A3   1993   349.712338'092
KF373.M233A3   1993   C93-091509-7

Detselig Enterprises Ltd.
210, 1220 Kensington Road NW
Calgary, Alberta T2N 3P5

Printed in Canada   ISBN 1-55059-068-5   SAN 115-0324

To my dear wife Sheilah
and all of our sons

Dr. Lloyd Barber, Indian Claims Commissioner, Chief Leo Pretty Young Man, and Webster Macdonald at the time of the ammunition money claim settlement, March 2nd, 1973.

Contents

Preface

Why should the memoirs of a lawyer be any different from anybody else's?

I firmly believe that every person is an island, that we have our own unique lifestyles and philosophies, that each one of us has had particular experiences. I have been a child of the twentieth century and my life span covers what has been one of the most exciting periods in the history of the world.

This is not the story of a series of triumphs or failures, rather it is the account of the doings of an Everyman. I have had a happy life and feel fulfilled. If Oscar Wilde was right when he said, "To love oneself is the beginning of a life long romance," then I am one of the great lovers of all time!

But it's the dance of life itself I find so exciting. Read on, and maybe I can share some of it with you.

A. Webster Macdonald, Sr.
Saltspring Island, B.C.

Foreword

In this informative and entertaining book, you will find a cavalcade of fascinating cases and oddball clients who, to mention just a few, bore such colorful monikers as "Jimmy the Con," "Doc Fingers," "Hurricane Hanne," "One Punch Murphy," and "Mitzi Dupre, the Ping-Pong Queen." (Mitzi's remarkable anatomical feats, which have nothing to do with table tennis, will leave you completely flabbergasted.)

Webster Macdonald recounts several dozen memorable cases from his highly-diversified, 45-year legal career in Nova Scotia, Alberta, British Columbia, Ontario and Manitoba. In the process he introduces us to a motley mob of murderers, rapists, psychopaths, adulterers, accident victims, inventors, oppressed natives and oppressed women, excommunicated Jehovah's Witnesses, a brain-washed "Moonie" badly in need of deprogramming, the Imperial Wizard of the Ku Klux Klan and others too numerous to mention.

With the Treaty No. 7 case, the author recounts a landmark breakthrough in law. For the first time in Canadian history, the federal government was forced to honor the promises of Queen Victoria and pay the Treaty 7 Indians of southern Alberta "ammunition money" owed them for almost a century.

Born in Kentville, Nova Scotia, Webster Macdonald studied law at Dalhousie University in Halifax under my father, Dean Vincent C. MacDonald. After a brief stint in the Navy, Webster practised law briefly in Halifax and for a decade in Kentville. In the late 1950s he set up shop in Calgary, where he logged 31 more years in the profession he loves dearly. Now semi-retired in British Columbia, he takes on the occasional case that excites him.

Words are the stock-in-trade of lawyers, and anyone who has heard this man in court has been struck by how precisely words escape his lips, ever so easily. And no wonder—some guys get all the genetic breaks! He's directly related to Noah Webster of dictionary renown and the legendary American orator and trial lawyer, Daniel Webster.

"It's unbelievable to catch him in action," said a former client whom Macdonald successfully defended on numerous charges, including assault with a deadly bedpan. "He has every precedent memorized and never forgets a significant fact of the case. He hypnotizes the jury with his eloquence and convinces them with his arguments."

Webster Macdonald has always been known as a lawyer who cared deeply about the law and the people caught in its grip. The *Calgary Herald* called him "Calgary's answer to Perry Mason," adding for the record, "The more desperate the circumstances, the more damning the evidence, the more Macdonald enjoys coming to the rescue."

Webster concurs. "I was always a non-conformist and had a burning desire to help people, no matter how heinous their crime or how hopeless their cause. I was a rebel, a maverick who dared to be different. I was a thorn in the side of the legal establishment, but I was not running a popularity contest and I'd take on cases other lawyers wouldn't touch if I felt they had merit and their cause was just. I did it my way and given my druthers I'd do it all over again."

As a chap who practised law myself for 25 years, I say good for you, Webster, and better still for your readers!

Peter V. MacDonald, *Q.C.*
Hanover, Ontario

Publisher's Acknowledgements:

Detselig Enterprises Ltd. appreciates the financial assistance for its 1993 publishing program from Canada Council, Dept. of Communications and the Alberta Foundation for the Arts (a beneficiary of the Lottery Fund of the Government of Alberta).

Disclaimer:

Every effort has been made to ensure that the statements and accounts of trial and legal cases contained in this book are true and accurate. It must be emphasized that the book is not a legal text and no attempt has been made to offer legal advice of any kind.

Neither the author nor the publisher accepts any legal or moral responsibility nor any liability for the material herein contained, nor for any errors or omissions.

Credits:

Front cover design by Dean MacDonald

Front cover photo by Larry MacDougall

Dedication photo by Ashley & Crippen (Toronto and Ottawa)

Inside illustrations by Adrien Town

Back cover illustration by Dave Nicholson

Give me your tired, your poor,
Your huddled masses yearning to breathe free

PROLOGUE

The Wandering Cat of Scarborough

If you practise law for fun, the work is its own reward. Of all the "fun" cases that came my way, I think Laura Crutcher and the Wandering Cat of Scarborough rank near the top.

This was no ordinary feline. This was a Siamese Cat of noble lineage and he weighed 7 kg (15 lb.) soaking wet. Quite apart from his impressive pedigree, he lusted for Laura, and no wonder! Laura Crutcher had come up to Calgary from Oklahoma and was involved by marriage and otherwise with some of the leading figures in the Calgary oil patch. At the time of the incident I am about to describe, she had been a widow for a considerable time. Laura, notwithstanding her advancing years, was an attractive female in anybody's book. She had long golden curls and a full, provocative lower lip, but above all, she was an artist of considerable talent. She did fine landscapes and pastels, as well as such mundane things as painting her own fence and storm windows.

The Scarborough Cat was fully aware of Laura's artistic talents and though never invited, he came to court her and admire her creative endeavors whenever he had the chance. He did not stop at silent contemplation and worship from a distance; he would, among other things, sleep on her peonies and steal the hamburgers from her barbecue. Worst of all, he would walk across her freshly-painted storm windows and leave his footprints there for all to see. These amorous activities only infuriated Laura, who patiently bided her time until she could wreak just revenge on the rascal.

On the night leading to this great case, Laura had spent a whole afternoon painting her storm windows and worn out from her exertions, had fallen asleep on a couch in her basement studio. Just above her was a casement window left open for a little air. At that precise moment, the wandering cat arrived on the scene, unheralded and unsung, and on looking through the open window saw the object of his affections asleep on the cot down below. What an opportunity! He jumped through the window and the full weight of him dropped down on Laura, sleeping far below. He scored a direct hit and landed squarely on the stomach of his *inamorata,* who understandably lost her wind and woke up to look into

And seven kilograms of cat dropped on the sleeping artist.

the baleful eyes of her enemy. Laura was of the stuff of which heroines are made, not one to be frightened by a mere cat. She cried out, "You damn thing! I know how to fix you. Back where I come from this is how we handle cats like you!"

She leaped from the cot and ran to where she had some cleaning cloths she had used on her storm windows that very afternoon. She tore off a large strip of bunting and returned to where her visitor was looking at her with undisguised love and admiration. Hell hath no fury like a woman aroused from her slumbers to find her arch enemy close at hand. She grasped the cat with one hand, and with the other she tied a noose around the poor animal's neck and pulled it tight until the cat's gums turned blue. As her enemy lay throttled at her feet, Laura had second thoughts. "Maybe I've killed him," she said to herself. "Maybe I should call the SPCA." She did call the SPCA, who soon arrived and took the wretched animal away and probably saved its life.

This was all very well, but the authorities felt that remedial action should be taken, and a charge was promptly laid against Laura by the SPCA for willfully causing cruelty to an animal. It was at this stage that Laura Crutcher came to me for legal assistance.

The matter came on for trial in due course before his Honor Judge John Harvie in the Provincial Court of Alberta. Laura knew that the learned judge was a fellow artist in his own right and of considerable local renown. As a colleague, Laura was determined to dress appropriately for the occasion and make the correct impression on the court. She appeared before the judge, dressed in a tattered tam-o-shanter and an artist's painting smock daubed with faded colors of paintings long since vanished. The court, however, was not impressed. To the contrary, Judge Harvie felt that Laura was deranged and ordered her detained over the weekend, so that she could have psychiatric observation. On the following Monday she was found fit to stand trial and at the conclusion of the case was found guilty as charged.

What to do?

"Laura," I said. "We have to appeal. Your honor has been besmirched." And so we launched an appeal in the District Court of Southern Alberta and the appeal came on for hearing before his Honor Judge William Seller. He was a beautiful judge and a very compassionate man. He was quite bald, with laughing eyes and a twinkling expression and he knew all about pain, as he was so crippled with arthritis that he had great trouble in reaching the bench so that he could hear the case. He was on the horns of a terrible dilemma. He obviously wanted to acquit Laura, but there was the suffering of the poor cat to be considered and it was abundantly clear that Laura had put the animal through the wringer. In spite of his sympathy for the accused, Judge Seller upheld the finding of "Guilty" and Laura's conviction and sentence remained in full force and effect.

What to do?

"Laura," I said, "The Court has once again found you guilty as charged. We have no alternative. We must appeal again, this time to the highest Court in the Province, the Appellate Division of the Supreme Court of Alberta."

Laura quietly nodded her approval and off we went to our Court of last resort. The appeal was of short duration. The late Mr. Justice Porter, an environmentalist and an animal lover beyond belief, was presiding that day as the Chief Justice of Alberta.

"Are you telling this Court, Mr. Macdonald," he said, "that your client immediately called the SPCA when she saw the cat's lips turning blue, and that the SPCA came to the scene and attended to the animal's plight?"

"That's absolutely correct, my Lord." I replied, "and I am certain that my client is contrite and penitent for what she had done in a moment of anger and the heat of passion."

The appeal was allowed. Justice was done on the premises and Laura was free of the charge.

Many of my learned friends and colleagues at the bar failed to understand why I should spend my time with such a picayune case as this, but it gave me great pleasure and satisfaction. The artist was vindicated. The wandering cat of Scarborough was free to meander as he pleased. And after this *cause célèbre*, I could carry on with mundane duties that paid the mortgage, but didn't give one-tenth the entertainment value derived from Laura Crutcher and the amorous feline of Scarborough.

Roll Along Wavy Navy, Roll Along

How did I come to my decision to practise law? As with most things, by a somewhat circuitous route.

I speak of my war record in muted tones. It is a trifle embarrassing when any one of my five sons asks his aged parent the pointed question, "Daddy, what did you do during the War?" I smile wanly and try to explain that although I served two and a half years with the Royal Canadian Naval Volunteer Reserve, part of it overseas, I never once saw the enemy nor heard an enemy shot fired. But it was an unforgettable experience for a graduate fresh from the cloistered halls of university.

By the end of May, 1943, Dalhousie Law School was behind me and although only one-third of my term as an articled student was complete, I was anxious to serve my country before the war was over. In the Fleet Air Arm I could hopefully glean some experience in Admiralty Law, as well as see some action. But the powers that be, in their inscrutable wisdom, rejected my application. I turned my energies to the silent service, the Royal Canadian Naval Volunteer Reserve (RCNVR) where I was immediately accepted. I then purchased a great, green book on maritime law called *Marsden's Collisions at Sea* before making my way to HMCS *Stadacona* in Halifax, Nova Scotia.

I shall not forget the morning of June 1st, 1943, when I turned up to enlist. The atmosphere of the place was distressing beyond belief. I announced quite proudly to the regulating petty officer in charge that I was Webster Macdonald, late of Dalhousie Law School, come to join the Navy! Can you believe it? He was singularly unimpressed. In a matter of minutes I became a number (64 832) not a name and was promptly outfitted with the square collars and bell bottom trousers that were my uniform for the next six months.

Even the air seemed dead. I had never been exposed to governmental bureaucracy before and suddenly was part of it. From here on in I would be a tiny cog in a great machine rolling on relentlessly in accordance with the King's Regulations and Admiralty Instructions. Now I knew what socialism was all about.

By this time the Russians were our allies. The Red Army was keeping the Nazis busily engaged on the Eastern front; I could not help but wonder how their war machine could survive if the same socialist morale permeated their ranks as deadened the war spirit in HMCS *Stadacona*. Obviously the Russian *esprit de corps* was quite different, but if ever free enterprise had an appeal as opposed to the collective way of doing things, those opening days in *Stadacona* were proof positive that the dead hand of government kills a man's spirit and initiative.

Our basic training began at once and we were whisked off to HMCS *Prevost* in London, Ontario for six weeks of boot camp drill and the rudiments of seamanship. By the middle of July we were packed off to a sea cadet camp at Minicog Island on Georgian Bay. The Canadian Shield, with its granite rocks and countless lakes, was a land of milk and honey after the burning heat of southern Ontario. There I learned to sail the great whalers, known to the sailors as "Brutal Beasts," and came to know strange characters like Miniature Man Mountain Masloff, who was not very tall but could tie a knot in an eight-inch spike with his bare hands.

And there was Jaybird Martin with a delicious sense of humor and his endless nonsensical queries like, "Why is a mouse when it stands on its tail?" And Gordy Clarke, the greatest sailor of us all, with his ominous observation, "Webbie, beware of the man who knows but one book." By this cryptic utterance he was referring to *Palmer on Company Law*, which he meant to know from cover to cover after the war.

Clarke was one of the shrewdest men I have ever known, and when he made a mistake, and he only made one that I am aware of, he did it on a grand scale. After the war he went to Dalhousie Law School as a veteran. He scored over 80 in Crimes in the Christmas examinations, only to meet his Waterloo in the Spring when the criminal law professor, one Dudley Murray, posed a question on the final paper about the legal situation [there was such an actual case] concerning a man accused of having sexual intercourse with a duck.

This was too much for Gordy Clarke, who implied in his answer that only a sexual pervert would have framed such a question. He was fooling with the wrong man. The professor was enraged and gave the impudent fellow a mark of 20 in Crimes, which cost Clarke his year and there was nothing he could do, try as he might to erase the failure. How were the mighty fallen—from a high of 80 to a low of 20 and all because of a rash remark!

We finished that glorious summer on Minicog Island and were herded down to HMCS *Cornwallis* at Deep Brook, Nova Scotia. By this time I had reached the exalted state of probationary sub-lieutenant, according to some critics the lowest form of marine life known to man. On New Year's day I was posted to HMCS *York* in the old Canadian National

Exhibition building in downtown Toronto. This was hardly the sea-going ship I had expected but it had compensations over and above the call of duty. Here in all her nautical splendor was none other than Lieutenant Sheilah Florance of the Women's Royal Canadian Naval Service, Wren 2 in the whole Canadian Navy, Queen Elizabeth being Wren 1!

Sheilah Florance was a regal beauty with an uncanny resemblance to the Duchess of Kent of that day. In addition, she had what the Navy calls "power of command." I had just purchased my officer's uniform and was broke flatter than a flounder when my superior officer found me in a corner of the wardroom reading the life of that great seaman, Sir Richard Grenville. She immediately took charge and I was a helpless puppet in the play of circumstance.

We planned to marry in Winnipeg. The Great Day finally arrived after a mad week of preparation in which I played an inconspicuous part. After a rainy October morning, the sun broke through for the afternoon and we carried on in glorious autumn sunshine. The Naval Training Ship in Winnipeg was HMCS *Chippewa* and the Captain had very kindly arranged for an officer's guard of honor with drawn swords to provide the proper nautical atmosphere for the first two naval officers to be married in Winnipeg.

The ceremony took place in Winnipeg in All Saints Cathedral and I stood there bravely, all alone at the front, gazing in silence as the church filled to overflowing with Sheilah's relatives and friends. On my side of the church I had only my best man and one of my shirt-tail cousins and his wife to carry me through the wedding. I was arrayed in my number one doe-skin uniform as a sub-lieutenant in the RCNVR. Wren Officer Florance had set aside her naval attire for this great occasion and was resplendent in a chalk white wedding gown, holding an elegant bouquet of calla lilies; a vision of loveliness.

The organ music was accompanied by 12 boy choristers. Their pure and unbroken voices soared like nightingales above the organ loft as they sang "Jesu Joy of Man's Desiring" in a way that would have pleased Johann Sebastian Bach himself. As we went in to sign the registry, one of the choir boys shyly looked up at me and observed that this was the first time he had ever been at a wedding. I smiled reassuringly and told him not to worry, because it was the first time for me too!

But the War was still on and after a few short months I learned I had been posted to HMCS *Niobe* in Greenock, Scotland. After crossing the Atlantic in the great luxury liner *The New Amsterdam*, which had been converted into a troop carrier, we landed at Liverpool and were transported to Greenock at the mouth of the Clyde.

HMCS *Niobe,* my posting, had taken over an insane asylum in Greenock called the Smithton Institute (not to be confused for a moment with the Smithsonian in Washington D.C.). The worthy burghers of Greenock quickly decided that the Canadian Navy was not a great improvement on the former inmates of Smithton. Built high on a hill overlooking the city and the great harbor, it was an embarkation depot to take thousands of time-expired servicemen back to Canada. The sailors had a song that summed it all up:

> *When this bloody war is over,*
> *Oh how happy I will be,*
> *No more church parades on Sunday,*
> *No more sailoring for me!*

The glorious setting, with thick rhododendrons, green humpbacked islands and mountains, sheep everywhere, and white and purple heather as far as the eye could see, was to be my home away from home until the end of the war. I loved the countryside and the little villages with their picturesque place names—Inverkip, Dunoon, Bridge of Allan, the Trossachs, Tail of the Bank, Troon, Alloway, Kilmacomb, Loch Lomond and Linlithgow Palace, where Mary Queen of Scots was born.

Best of all was Dumbarton Castle, perched on a huge rock in the middle of the river Clyde, where William Wallace, the great Scottish patriot, was a prisoner of the English almost a thousand years ago. Dumbarton acted as a safe refuge for Mary Queen of Scots before she was taken to France at the age of three to escape the jealous wrath of Queen Elizabeth I. Nestled below the rock was the site of the Denny shipyards, now a liquor distillery, where the fabulous Cutty Sark was built in 1869. The mighty John Brown shipyards were in a state of decline and the only evidence of their former glory was HMS *Vanguard,* a great dreadnought under repair, so huge that she literally blocked traffic up and down the river. It was a proud but sad moment to reflect on how the unions were pricing themselves right out of the market. Eventually the shipyards of Japan and Germany were to take over the industry from the Clydeside shipwrights.

From time to time there was modest entertainment of its own kind in HMCS *Niobe.* Law and order and strict adherence to King's Regulations and Admiralty Instructions were maintained by one Warrant Officer Thornily, a Cockney from London's East End and an elevator operator for Sun Life of Canada back on civvy street.

For a long time, stoker Danny Skeffington had been a troublemaker on one of the cruisers down in the harbor, HMCS *Haida* to be exact, and he was banished to the confines of HMCS *Niobe* to do Number 14 drill and learn the error of his ways. Warrant Officer Thornily was determined to apprehend a ne'er-do-well like Skeffington, who was unabashed by the discipline of the shore establishment and guilty of many minor peccadillos that would put him on the Executive Officer (XO) report for punishment if only he could be caught *in flagrante delicto.*

When the opportunity to arrest the culprit presented itself, the Warrant Officer could hardly restrain his delight and satisfaction. The Executive Officer, second in command of the base, was one Lieutenant "Curly" Detchen, so named because he did not have a strand of natural hair on his gleaming bald head. As his secretary, he was served by a Leading Wren with a massive bust and generous posterior. One morning following breakfast she left the mess like a galleon under full sail and passed by Stoker Skeffington and his mates, who were sweeping the main deck. Skeffington turned to his pals and in his unmistakable voice called out, "And what do you think of that, boys? All that meat and no potatoes!" Unbeknownst to the garrulous stoker, the Master at Arms was hiding behind the galley door, bent on gathering incriminating evidence of whatever kind against the unsuspecting Skeffington. He quickly emerged from his hiding place and put the stoker under arrest.

"I heard every word you said about the XO's wren and you are on the Captain's report as of now, for committing an offense against good order and naval discipline contrary to KR and AI!"

The wheels of justice ground swiftly and the next day Skeffington appeared before Captain "Daddy" Hunter, duly charged with a naval discipline offense in that he did use unseemly language with reference to the XO's wren, namely: "All that meat and no potatoes."

It was a Gilbert and Sullivan court. Skeffington had no lawyer, Captain "Daddy" Hunter acted as judge and jury and the Master at Arms proceeded to prosecute the case. The facts of the matter were not in dispute. Skeffington had indeed used those obstreperous words, but how were they to be interpreted and what did they mean? Confusion reigned supreme. The Master at Arms would have attached sinister significance to the offensive description but the court was unable to unravel this cryptic puzzle.

The bareheaded stoker stood mute. The warrant officer was pressing for seven days No. 11 punishment with heavy pack, and the captain was bewildered by the whole affair. It was too much for even that kangaroo court and the case was dismissed for "lack of proof." Stoker Skeffington put on his cap, smartly saluted his commanding officer and returned to his duties, as unrepentant a sinner as before. He was transferred back to the good ship *Haida* and the Master of Arms resumed his task as disciplinarian of HMCS *Niobe*, a sadder if not a wiser man.

All that meat and no potatoes!

The country south of the base was stamped with the memory of Robbie Burns. What a man! In a spirit of veneration at Alloway in Ayr, I visited the stone whitewashed farm building where in 1758 the Scottish ploughboy was born. I saw the haunted Kirk of Alloway with its leper's squint and the quaint stone bridge over the river Doon, where Tam O'Shanter's horse lost his tail to the witches. As I was leaving the kirk, I was accosted by a toothless, ragged old man in a dirty green overcoat, who made clear to me better than any book why the author of "Auld Lang Syne" and "John Anderson My Jo" is revered and loved all over the world, even in Russia!

"If I were to die and go to Heaven," the derelict said to me, "and I met Wull Shakespeare and Robert Burns coming through the pearly gates, I would doff my cap in reverence to Shakespeare, but I would throw my arms around Robert Burns and say 'Rabby, hoo's yersel?' And it would be the proudest moment of my life!"

That is why there is a larger-than-life monument to Burns in Dunedin, New Zealand, and why his imposing figure looks down at the Public Gardens in Halifax, Nova Scotia. His memory will live forever with the wind that shakes the barley and the song in the green thorn tree, in the Scotland he bequeathed to the world.

By April of 1945, the war in Europe was virtually over and the return to normalcy had begun. Soccer hysteria was in the air and all of *Niobe* was transfixed with the great game to be played at Hampden Park in Glasgow, when Scotland and England were to meet in the International Cup final. Excitement reigned supreme! On a bleak spring morning, Andy Thompson, the Pride of Ballyshannon in Ireland and later to become the leader of the Liberal party in Ontario, and I, set out for the football stadium to take in the great match.

The whole of Clydeside seemed to be converging on the Park, 120 000 people in all, the strange figures with red and orange tam-o-shanters, topped by enormous pom-poms of every color of the rainbow, a motley throng heading for the game. Back in the U.S.A., Roosevelt was at death's door and I watched a group of these comical figures in their outrageous tam-o-shanters stop at the entrance to a tenement close and make the following enquiry to a little girl about three of four years old.

"Tell me, lassie," one of them said, in a thick Gorbals brogue, "What were Roosevelt's dying words?"

"I dinna ken," the wee tyke replied. "Watch Tommy Armstrong, Scotland's centre half!" Uproarious laughter followed this riposte and convulsed with merriment, they pressed on to the stadium.

At the entrance to the park our tickets were taken by a huge Scottish bobby, most imposing in his blue serge uniform. "Are you not going to watch the game?" I asked.

"Nay, laddie," he replied, "I'll gang awa hame and listen to it on the wireless. I'll hae a glass o' whusky in the one hand and a glass o' water in the other, and every time that England scores a goal, I'll take a wee sip of water, and when Scotland scores a goal, I'll hae a dram o' whusky."

England was unbeatable that day and overwhelmed the Scots 6 to 1, Tommy Armstrong notwithstanding, and I was reminded of the policeman at the gate and reflected upon how he must be spending a very sober time.

Soccer fans are a hardy lot. Apart from the royal box, 120 000 people all stood up to watch the game with newspapers over their heads to keep off the rain. Oh, it was a glum day for Scotland! Under the colorful tam-o-shanters, a great deal of whisky was consumed as the loyal Scotsmen drowned their sorrows.

"Dinna laugh at Scotland, chum," one of the faithful said to me, "We canna win the war and beat the English too." "A disgrace," another was heard to mutter. "A national disgrace."

At half time, the Scottish Youth, all young boys, paraded around the oval. "Where are the girls?" I asked.

"There are no girls in Scotland the noo," said my new Scottish friend, "The Yanks have taken them all!"On this unhappy note the football classic was soon over and the pride of Ballyshannon and I made our way back to *Niobe*, enlightened, if not elated, by the day's proceedings.

Early in November, I, too, returned home on the new aircraft carrier, HMCS *Puncher*. I took with me Beauty, the black-and-white sheep dog I had rescued from a miserable life outside Rothesay on the Isle of Bute. I was anxious and exhilarated to get home to Sheilah and to complete my articles that had been interrupted by events overseas.

The Articled Student

Halifax, Nova Scotia, at the end of World War II was no easy place to earn a living. Some unkind spirits referred to the city as "The Armpit of Canada" (or in terms even more disgusting).

To my wife's dismay, I declined a great opportunity her father had set up for us in Winnipeg and decided to practise law in Nova Scotia. Was this a sound decision? Looking back, I don't think it would have made a great deal of difference. Probably more money would have been made out West, but I am not sure I would have had a more interesting life and which is more important?

Even in 1945, Halifax was very beautiful, with Citadel Hill, whose ramparts were built by Maroons from Jamaica in 1749; the wooded glories of Point Pleasant Park, with its sailors' monument and round Martello Tower; and the sparkling waters of the North West Arm and the Dingle, a huge tower to honor Sir Sanford Fleming across from the City of Halifax. Atmosphere and history—I loved it!

In the Nova Scotia of those days every young lawyer had to serve an apprenticeship as an articled student for nine months and I was now ready for the final six months of "indentured servitude." But who would have me? My first approach was to the legendary Harry MacKeen of the prestigious firm of Stewart, Smith, MacKeen and Rogers. After a few preliminary skirmishes with the great trial lawyer, I was brash enough to ask what salary I might expect.

"Oh," said the leader of the Nova Scotia bar, "We don't pay our articled students anything." My heart missed several beats. I thought of my wife and new child and allowed that as much as I would like to work within the rarefied atmosphere of this outstanding law office, I just couldn't afford it.

With butterflies fluttering in my stomach, I made my way down to the second floor of the same building, where R.M. Fielding *KC* had his office. R.M. was a kind and portly man, an inveterate bachelor, with a gleaming bald head and an extended stomach that indicated he denied himself nothing when it came to the staples of life. R.M. took me on but left me pretty much on my own as an articled student, to sink or swim.

Finally I was called to the Nova Scotia bar and on May 27th, 1946 was admitted as a lawyer to the Nova Scotia Barristers Society. I resolved to make the practice of law a truly exciting profession.

The Fielding office had a broad and varied practice, but I was immediately attracted to the forensic side of the law, to the trial forum, where the life and liberty of the subject were at stake. This was where I first encountered people in trouble with the law, both civilly and criminally, and their problems—of every conceivable kind—were a source of never ending fascination. The contest between the Crown and the people, and the suits between unhappy litigants, were moments of truth.

The academic theories of Dalhousie Law School were all behind me now and there were truly important questions to ponder. Should the alleged thief of sugar from His Majesty's dockyard at HMCS *Stadacona* go to jail or not? Would the Crown's net around the drunken seaman at the Waverley Lakes close tightly enough so that he would be convicted of rape? Was there a reasonable doubt that would enable these miscreants to escape the toils of justice?

These were heady problems and transformed a nine-to-five job into the most wonderful game in the world. Time didn't matter. The task was its own reward, and I began work in my people-in-trouble practice that would hold my attention and consume my energies for the next four decades. I never tired of it. Every day was a new challenge and every case an interesting adventure. Or if they were not, I made them so, and it was a great love affair that never lost its appeal.

Down in the Fielding office I came upon a criminal file that R.M. had overlooked in his attentions to the more engrossing municipal problems of the County of Halifax. The RCMP had preferred a charge of bribery of a public official against a Czechoslovakian immigrant named Sevick. Mr. Sevick had been harassed and tormented, in his opinion, by an inspector of the Food and Drugs department.

What to do?

Back in the looser mores of the Austro-Hungarian Empire, if you were caught poaching for pheasants on one of the great feudal estates in Czechoslovakia, a few kopecks paid to the gamekeeper would cast a blind eye on the wrongdoer. Would not the same solution work in Canada? Mr. Sevick thought so and he made a number of visits to the office of Mr. Kimball, the Food and Drugs inspector, slipping two ten-dollar bills in a brown envelope under the office door, with the cryptic words "A lit. present for you," attached.

It was a different game in Canada. Mr. Kimball alerted the RCMP and in due course Mr. Sevick was caught *in flagrante delicto* pushing his twenty-dollar "present" under the door.

The accused had been found guilty as charged and sentenced to two years imprisonment with the admonition that the kopeck-to-the-game-keeper customs of Central Europe would not be tolerated in Canada. On to appeal! At this point the services of the legendary Harry MacKeen were enlisted and the stage was set to do battle in the Appellate Division of the Supreme Court of Nova Scotia. This is where I came in.

In 1946 the Chief Justice of Nova Scotia was the illustrious Sir Joseph Chisholm, the supreme authority on the "Life and Letters of Joseph Howe" and the *nonpareil* among Nova Scotia judges of his day. His silver tresses cascaded to his shoulders and his bright blue eyes, flashing at you from behind a gleaming pince-nez, went to the heart of the case being argued before him. My mentor was off on the King's business the day of the Sevick appeal, so I stood before the Appeal Court shaking and alone. Opposing me was the mighty Harry MacKeen, *KC*, supported by Irish Dicky Donahue.

What a pair! Between them they made the clandestine operations of the accused sound like the most innocent private enterprise, but the three judges on the appeal court thought otherwise. After long and colorful argument on both sides, the learned judges found that Magistrate Flynn had made no error in law and upheld the conviction and two-year sentence.

In my unbridled enthusiasm as acting Crown Prosecutor for the County of Halifax, I had the temerity to ask that the sentence be increased on the grounds that the integrity of Canadian public servants should be protected, and that the sinister efforts of people like Mr. Sevick would undermine the faith and confidence that the ordinary Canadian would have in our government officials. To no avail. The great Sir Joseph gazed down at me from what appeared a dizzying height and allowed, "No, Mr. Macdonald, has he not atoned for his sins? We are not disposed to alter the sentence imposed in this case." As I sat down, still flushed with the excitement of the appeal, I heard my name called from the bench.

"Mr. Macdonald, would you please stand up!" It was the sonorous voice of the Chief Justice himself. "Young man," the voice continued. "This is your first appearance in this Court and we wish to commend you on the admirable presentation of your case!" I flushed and bowed and resumed a sitting position. *Sic transit gloria mundi*! I was launched on my legal career.

With the Sevick trial and appeal behind me was ready for a joust in the civil courts. One of our most valuable and trusted clients in 1946 was a ruddy-faced young contractor named Laurie Lively. Laurie had a construction company using several three-quarter ton trucks. On a foggy night down along the Eastern shore at Middle Musquodobit, Laurie and one of his trucks were wending their way home when a large black horse loomed out of the swamp and under the cover of fog and darkness, proceeded to attack the Lively vehicle by kicking in the door. The animal turned out to be a one-ball horse, or "blind stallion" as they were colloquially known, with the unfortunate disability of having only one testicle. This malady affected his disposition and brought out vicious propensities not usually found in normal horses. It was a Pyrrhic victory for the stallion. He crashed in the door of the truck, but broke his leg in the process. Eventually his enraged owner, one Mr. Beaver, was obliged to shoot the unfortunate animal and put him out of his misery. A horse is a valuable piece of property in Middle Musquodobit and his loss was not to be taken lightly. Beaver sued Lively immediately for damages and loss of services.

In due course the case came on for trial in the Nova Scotia Supreme Court. Mr. Beaver had engaged the forensic services of a battling lawyer named Johnny Walker (not to be confused with the Scotch whisky of the same name) and my mentor once more sent me into the breach. This time to uphold the honor of Lively Construction, against an unwarranted attack by a "blind" stallion with vicious and unpredictable propensities because he had only one ball. Johnny Walker fought gallantly, but the trial judge sat immovable like a great block of granite and gave the owner of the stallion short shrift for allowing his animal to run at large in the swamp along the Eastern shore, causing damage to persons and their vehicles lawfully using the highway. Case dismissed.

Frank Lima was an Italian immigrant who lived along the South Shore highway west of Halifax at a place called Boutilier's Point. His neighbor across the road was one Boutilier and over the course of time they became deadly enemies. At some stage, Sergeant Yuill of the Royal Canadian Mounted Police alleged, Frank Lima dispatched his neighbor and former friend with unseemly haste, and carried Boutilier over his shoulder to his waiting truck and buried the body in a garbage dump a few miles away where it was subsequently discovered by the RCMP.

A lead-pipe cinch case for the police! But they reckoned without Harry MacKeen, probably the greatest trial lawyer I have even known. I am positive that the interminable work sessions which were his wont went into this case and when the trial took place, MacKeen made mincemeat out of the police, the Crown and everyone connected with the prosecution, including myself. It was a classic case of police bungling, from the production of secret boxes with false bottoms that were used by the defense to show that someone other than the accused had carried out the foul deed, to the inept police cordons around the murder scene and the investigation itself. Poor Sergeant Yuill was banished to the Yukon after the trial.

The One-Ball Horse of Musquodobit

My mentor, R.M., came in with a few skimpy notes written on the back of an envelope and ineffectually argued for conviction. The invincible MacKeen, at the top of his form, addressed the jury for six hours. One of the more memorable lines from MacKeen's jury address went like this, as he contemptuously regarded the vast array of Crown exhibits:

> "Gentlemen of the jury, there is an old Spanish proverb that he who hides can find, and the mountain labored and heaved and made a great noise and brought forth a mouse."

That was it. Lima was acquitted and the unforgettable lesson was driven home, that hard work pays off. There is just no substitute for it!

The legal world of Halifax in 1947 was a busy one. However, R.M. was moving up the legal ladder and his eyes were set on the Nova Scotia Supreme Court. Where was I to go in the legal vacuum that would ensue? The call came from Harold Chase, who had inherited the practice of my great-uncle, to come back home. He needed and wanted me. It pleased my parents that I would be coming back to Kentville and I was not averse to carrying on my legal career in the shire town of King's County where I was born and where my people had been doctors, lawyers and judges for over a hundred years.

Sheilah was to be the "Duchess of Kentville" and in a trice we were on our way to Kentville, Nova Scotia, to start a law practice as a country lawyer in a town that had no more than 5 000 people.

Country Lawyer

Not long after my arrival in Kentville I became embroiled in the Goldie Simmons case, which had been smouldering among the black people of King's County since the end of the war. Camp Aldershot with its jack pines and sandy plains had been a training centre for the Canadian Army for both Great Wars. Outside the camp at the junction of the Centreville and Aldershot roads, lived an energetic black man by the name of Percy Simmons. Percy was the "honeyman" for Camp Aldershot and with his lean, aristocratic features and Van Dyck beard, he looked uncommonly like Haile Selassie, then Emperor of Abyssinia. During his first marriage, Percy begat many children and by the end of the War they had all grown up. Percy had remarried to a woman named Goldie Simmons and brought his new wife to live in the house from where he had carried out his duties for Camp Aldershot during the Second World War.

Rumor had it that Percy Simmons had accumulated considerable wealth as honeyman. Shortly after his marriage to Goldie he came to an untimely end and the interesting question arose as to who would inherit his estate, the progeny of the first marriage or Goldie as his lawful widow by marriage number two. It was soon discovered that Percy Simmons did not have much in the way of cash; his real property across from the Dewdrop Inn on the way to Camp Aldershot was the only valuable asset left behind. There was no will, but Goldie was determined to get her dower from the property before it would be distributed according to law.

The heirs readily grasped the concept that if Goldie's claim to her dower could be defeated, their distributive shares would be enriched. The most effective attack was to show that Goldie was a loose woman who had committed adultery while posing as the lawful wife of Percy Simmons, which if proven could stand as an absolute bar to any claim for dower.

And so there was a trial. There was no jury and the whole question turned on the credibility of Goldie Simmons. Had she committed adultery or had she not? Goldie had come to court from Weymouth Falls, down in Digby County, and in her dark green dress, spangled with gold stars, she sat in the witness box, huge and as impassive as an African queen. She was a niece of the fabulous boxer Sammy Langford, the Boston Tar Baby, whose arms hung to his knees and whom Jack Johnson was afraid to fight. Goldie fought her own fight that day and scoffed with derision at the vile suggestion that she had committed adultery with Jim Lansey, an alcoholic reprobate with an unsavory reputation for perjury and bootlegging. Lansey took the stand and in broken English described his nocturnal misadventures with the pride of Weymouth Falls.

Goldie's lawyer had produced a host of witnesses to prove that Jim Lansey's general reputation for veracity was anything but good. The crunch came when Lansey himself was testifying as to what happened after he had gained access to Goldie's bedroom where she lay in state with only a candle for illumination. I was irresistibly reminded of those lines from Shakespeare: "How far that little candle throws his beams, so shines a good deed in a naughty world!"

In both direct- and cross-examination, Jim stuck to his story as to how he entered the house and approached the sleeping queen.

"And then what happened, Mr. Lansey?"

"And then, Your Honor, I proceeded to have sectional intercourse."

The evidence of adultery was in shreds. The trial judge was not about to accept the evidence of the amorous intruder. The star witness had bombed out and the chastity of Goldie Simmons remained pure and undefiled. Goldie's dower was sustained and after a less- than-generous settlement she returned to her kinfolk in Weymouth Falls, with her sad memories of the Haile Selassie of Camp Aldershot and his heartless and grasping children not quickly forgotten.

Life in Kentville for that ten-year span from 1947 to 1957 was not hard to take. The legal affairs of the County of King's were conducted from a venerable old red brick building known as "The Courthouse" on Cornwallis Street. Legal expertise was supplied by 10 to 12 lawyers of varying ages and abilities.

The King's County bar in those days was a close, almost familial group and I was always crossing legal swords with the same people. The dean of the bar at that time was unquestionably George C. Nowlan. Comparisons are always odious, but he had it over the rest of us like a tent. His constant adversary was W.D. "Stoneface" Withrow, who had come up to Kentville from the hinterland of Hants Country and who for more years than anyone could count was the prosecuting officer for King's County—until they awarded that prestigious position to a younger and more aspiring Liberal like myself. When it came to slipping in leading evidence for the Crown, which was supposedly a no-no, W.D. was an expert.

During all the time I was there, the mighty Nowlan never lost a sex case. Perhaps it was his gigantic stature that made him so appealing to the jury. He was almost 196 cm (6'5") and his innate Irish eloquence was enhanced by a strong lisp that made his most ordinary pronouncements sound impressive and poetic. In addition to these natural assets, he had an enormous carbuncle on the back of his neck, that gleamed like a live coal when he became excited. There he would be, flapping his arms like an enormous vampire bat before the jury, and as he approached the moment critique, did the poor girl consent or did she not, the red appendage above his collar glowed and shone like a Christmas tree, and the worthy burghers of Kentville were mesmerized by this great performance. The unfortunate complainant watched her virtue torn to tatters and "Stoneface" Withrow could only grimace with pain as the Great Defender reduced his beautifully prepared case to rubble. Oh, those were the days!

From time to time we had visits from lawyers outside the county. The most memorable of these itinerant barristers was Norman Blanchard, who would arrive unheralded and unsung from Windsor to defend the denizens of the King's County underworld. To me he epitomized the mark of a top-flight lawyer. Anybody can play a forensic hand when he holds all the cards, but only a truly able counsel can make a silk purse out of a sow's ear, so to speak and turn an absolute loser into a winning case, with nothing really to work on. Such a man was Blanchard.

Some years before he had driven a piece of stone into his eye while repairing his summer cottage and had lost most of his sight. Not that his semi-blindness deterred him very much. He would stand before the star witness for the Crown with a monocle at the end of a long black cord securely attached to his blind eye. He would have the witness floundering and helpless under a withering cross-examination and then at the vital moment he would let the monocle drop from his blind eye to the end of the ribbon and the poor witness would be hypnotized and dissolve in a welter of incoherence and confusion.

Blanchard's sandy hair and dapper bow tie were familiar sights around the courthouse. Years later, after he had become a Crown Prosecutor under the Tory Government, I learned with dismay that he had been felled to the floor of the courtroom by a drunken Micmac Indian, who had leaned out of the prisoner's box and broken a solid oak chair over Blanchard's head. Such a misfortune could hardly be considered an occupational hazard and I am sure it hastened the early demise of one of the most colorful figures in the Nova Scotia courts.

Kentville in the late forties and early fifties was a pleasant pastoral spot, both as a place to live and as a place to practise law. Television had not yet reduced the world to a global village and escape by airplane to fresher and greener fields was the exception rather than the rule.

As a country lawyer with some unusual assignments, such as special prosecutor for the Apple Maggot Control Board, I was a busy practitioner but not so busy as to be completely oblivious to the great world outside King's County. The sad case of William Remington made me painfully aware of the Cold War and its special impact on life in the United States after WW II.

Bill was an eloquent and colorful talker but I had no idea my lanky American friend was a card-carrying Communist. I only thought of him as a leftist thinker of strong opinions, like many other university intellectuals of his day. He was a couple of years older than me and I had more or less lost track of him until I read in the press about his problems with the Loyalty Review Board. The witch-hunting campaign of Senator Joseph McCarthy was at its height and Bill, who had been working with the Office of Price Administration in the American government, suddenly found himself under attack.

He testified before the Loyalty Review Board and was cleared of all charges alleging that he was a traitor to his country. But Bill reckoned without his ex-wife and mother-in-law. No one knows more about you than your wife, and in this instance, his ex-wife and mother-in-law went out of their way to inform the District Attorney's Office that Bill Remington was in fact a card-carrying member of the Communist party and that he had lied under oath when he had testified before the Loyalty Review Board. The roof fell in. Bill Remington was charged with perjury and convicted of this offense and sentenced to five years imprisonment. He was sent to Lewiston Penitentiary in Pennsylvania to serve his time.

At this federal institution, he was considered a model prisoner and was put in charge of the prison library. But that was not the end. His fellow prisoners believed that Bill was a wealthy person and that he had money hidden in his cell. While he was asleep a deranged convict broke into his cell and crushed in his skull with a brick hidden in a sock. Bill died in prison that night at the age of 35.

Of all the characters I encountered in the Kentville of those early days, Fred Huntley was far and away the most entertaining. Fred saved much of his energy for jousts with the federal government. His great battle, with no holds barred, was over the removal of the Sable Island ponies from the graveyard of the Atlantic to the fertile farms and apple orchards of King's County. At one stage, I swear he had promised ponies with names like "Deep Purple" and "Dark Night" to every child in Kentville and he almost kept his word. His *bête noire* at this time was the dashing Bob

Winters, then Liberal Minister of Transport in Ottawa, who controlled the destiny of the little horses. Fred would berate Winters with his "toothpaste smile," and damn the bureaucrats in Ottawa to eternal perdition. The game plan was to transport the ponies from their remote island home to a farm eight kilometres (five miles) west of Kentville, where they would be kept until Fred found a new home for them, at a reasonable profit of course. By dint of great effort the ponies were shipped from Sable Island to Kingsport to be unloaded for the holding farm at Coldbrook, and here the story breaks down.

Fred went over to Kingsport, some 20 kilometres (12 miles) from Kentville, to inspect the horses. As he walked down the wharf to see the animals, he fell off the deep end. One hundred kilograms (two hundred and twenty pounds) of Huntley landed in the soft mud at the end of the wharf. Luckily for Fred the tide was out or undoubtedly he would have drowned. He was discovered at three o'clock in the morning with the incoming tide of the Minas Basin just a few metres from his head. He was taken by ambulance to the Wolfville Hospital and treated for a fractured pelvis. That was the end of the ponies as far as Fred was concerned, though the animals were doubtless given a better home than they had enjoyed on the wastes of Sable Island.

Even in hospital Fred was his incorrigible self. Story has it that in the hospital bed next to him the last rites were being given to some unfortunate person about to go to his reward. As the priest was offering the sacrament, Fred could not resist what seemed to him a golden opportunity to gain redemption of his many sins of omission and commission. In a hoarse whisper he tugged at the priestly vestments.

"Father," he wheezed, "if you are passing out any free tickets to the Great Beyond, please remember this miserable sinner and deal me in!"

As he lay dying at the age of 56 he made one last request.

"When I go, I want all my pallbearers to be bank managers. They carried me all my life and I don't want anything to be different now."

We shall not see his like again!

It was in Kentville that I was made Crown Prosecutor for the County of King's, where life moved at a leisurely pace in the fifties. The Supreme Court Assizes came to Kentville, the shire seat, only twice a year, every May and October, with any attendant appeals being heard in Halifax.

A very pleasant lifestyle, but notwithstanding the demanding work and absence of any strain or stress in my practice, I felt this beautiful microcosm was just a little too narrow and small.

And then the roof fell in. In 1956 the stranglehold that the Liberal party had held on the political life of Nova Scotia for over 40 years was broken and the granitic Bob Stanfield, whose family's unshrinkable underwear dominated the textile world of the little province, brought the Tories into power. My days as Crown Prosecutor for the County of King's were over.

To the victor belongs the spoils, and under the pork barrel system that was the accepted manner of things in that part of the world; my job was gone. In 1957 Maritime rights were being ignored, as always, by Central Canada and it was abundantly clear that the Atlantic provinces were not about to participate in the burgeoning prosperity that Sir Wilfred Laurier had predicted years before, when he prophesied that the twentieth century would belong to Canada. The St. Lawrence Seaway had driven the final nail in the coffin of Halifax as a seaport. Nova Scotia, and the Maritimes in general, seemed to be turned more and more into a backwater.

I was probably going through what is known as "mid-life crisis" and had a visceral feeling that if I was about to make a change in my lifestyle that I should do so before I was 40. Not an easy decision. I had been reasonably successful in my chosen profession. I was a big toad in a small but beautiful pond and yet I felt that there was more to life than being a successful country lawyer. And besides there would be a better future for my boys in a new environment west of Quebec.

So I started to tear up my roots, which is a terrible thing for a lawyer to do, especially one with no friends or connections in high places to pull a few strings or pave the way.

My eyes were really set on the Far West. After listening carefully to a young accountant playing golf at Sandy Hook, who pronounced Calgary the best "legal city" in Canada, I read an article in *Time* magazine captioned "Which Way Canadian Gas?" The section was illustrated by a map of North America, showing the main gas lines—Westcoast Transmission, Alberta and Southern Gas and the Trans-Canada Pipe Line, all based in Alberta and going down to California or eastward to the markets of Ontario and Quebec. Having made a preliminary search into the legal possibilities of Calgary and Edmonton the previous March, I said to myself "Macdonald, you're a fool if you don't do something about this!" The die was cast.

Once the decision was made the rest was easy. We left the boys in Manitoba, made a crate for Buddy the dog and went back to Kentville to wind up my practice. Ensconced firmly in the 1955 Big Blue Buick, we set out on the great trek across Canada to the West and a new life for us all.

City Lawyer

By the first week of September 1957, I found myself part of the California Standard Oil Company team and started my new career in the corporate world. It was a throwback to my days in the Navy. From running a one-man hot dog stand, I was now a cipher in a faceless corporation and one person in a company of 600 employees. It was a tremendous challenge to my ego. From being a trial lawyer of some prominence, I found myself a "landman," one of a team of oil employees whose role as far as I could make out, was to settle damage claims and pacify disgruntled farmers. Every week our little team would sally forth into the hinterland of Southern Alberta and negotiate settlements and rights-of-way with owners, who were unhappy with the encroachment of our company on their lands.

I visited tiny hamlets and sod houses that were at best a geographical expression on the map; places like Gem and Exshaw, Buttress and Joffre, tiny specks on the flat and dusty prairies, and then back to the Buffalo Hotel in Red Deer to rest and play cards after the strenuous activities of the day.

After three days in the field we would return to Calgary, turn in the company car and the keys and make ready for a quiet and extended weekend. It was not for me. As in the Navy, I was again a number, not a name, and could not adjust to the anonymity of it all. It was just too soft. To anyone exposed to the Puritan work ethic, or the great Harry MacKeen, there was something sinful about playing cards at 10:30 a.m. on a work day, behind closed doors so that the head of the department could not see this sloth and inactivity. I stuck it out for two and one half months, and if Sheilah had not been sick and in hospital, probably would not have been there that long.

There was no golden handshake, no severance pay, as I left the corporate labyrinth to find an opening in the legal world of Calgary. The first priority was to be admitted to the Alberta Law Society. Although understandably apprehensive about the bar admission ordeal, I made it, and in the winter of 1958 was called and admitted to the bar. For two long

Down came the fish with a resounding crash.

unemployed weeks I yearned to get back to the life of the courts. It was the only place where I felt at home, where I really belonged.

An opening was not long in coming. Months before, I had met Charles Hetherington, who was the engineering brain for the legendary Frank McMahon and his fabulous gas pipeline, Westcoast Transmission. McMahon's lawyer was the famous hockey player, D.P. McDonald, and between Hetherington and McDonald, they made a place for me in D.P.'s firm of McDonald, Stuart and Prothroe.

As low man on the totem pole in the McDonald, Stuart office, I often had some free time on my hands, and when Julie O'Connor (who had joined the firm just before I did and who is now a Provincial Court judge in Calgary) asked me to lend him a hand down at Bassano, I jumped at the opportunity for my first criminal case in Alberta.

The scene of the crime was the Bassano Hotel, down in the desert country near Medicine Hat. On a hot Saturday night in late 1958, the George brothers and a number of their cowboy friends from Gem, had come in from their cattle ranch to relax and enjoy a few beer, as was their wont.

The George brothers had to be seen to be believed. They were tall and lean and hard. The muscles on their necks stood out like hawsers and underneath their Stetsons they were bronzed and sunburned from their time on the range. Apart from everything else, their hands were their most striking feature, as large as toilet seats and strong and solid. They were not to be trifled with.

As the evening wore on, the cowboys from Gem, which was little more than a crossroad in the badlands of southern Alberta, had consumed far more beer than was good for them. A wrangle ensued between the Ukrainian proprietor of the hotel and his guests. In short order, the contretemps degenerated from an argument to a heated discussion over nothing in particular, and the fight was on.

In a fracas of this kind, the George brothers were never known to take a back seat to anyone, and in seconds the whole tavern was in an uproar. As things started to get serious, the Ukrainian owner brought in his kitchen help as reserves, and soon fists were flashing and bodies dropping like cordwood on the floor. The cowboys added a little zest to the whole affair by hurling steel chairs at the hotel personnel.

The highlight of the evening occurred when the owner of the hotel sank in a bleeding condition to the floor beside the pool table. Overhead was a plaster cast of an enormous sturgeon, a magnificent fish weighing at least 45 kg (100 lb.). One of the steel chairs knocked the plaster fish from its resting place and it dropped down on the unfortunate man as he sat propped against the wall, trying to staunch the wound that he had sustained. Crash! Down came the fish and landed squarely on the head of the unsuspecting innkeeper before breaking into a thousand pieces. It was game over, and the George brothers and their friends from Gem departed into the night before the RCMP arrived on the scene to restore law and order.

In due course eight charges of assault occasioning bodily harm and causing a disturbance were laid against the cow hands, and it was in their defense that Julie O'Connor and I went down to Bassano. The local stipendiary magistrate gave the cowboys short shrift and they were found guilty on seven of the eight charges and fined accordingly.

We applied by way of stated case on a point of law to a judge of the Alberta Supreme Court. For this case we selected the famous Judge Harold Riley to review the matter. Mr. Justice Riley did not attach the same importance to the case that we did, and notwithstanding a voluminous and brilliant written argument that my friend Julie prepared and left in the judge's office, the learned justice never did hand down a decision.

From time to time, Julie would retrieve his magnum opus from the corner to which it had been relegated by the judge and place it in a prominent position on his lordship's desk for his consideration. But it never happened. No decision was ever made. Justice delayed, maybe justice denied, but in this case the ends of justice were well and truly served, and the cowboys from Gem rode off into the sunset.

The firm of McDonald, Stuart and Prothroe had imposing quarters in the Pacific Building on 9th Avenue S.W., and with Frank McMahon as the main client it did not really matter if there were other clients or not. I only saw the great McMahon once, at lunch in the boardroom, when the question of Quebec was being discussed. I attracted the attention of all present by stating that the last hand to wave the British flag in Canada would be the hand of a French Canadian. D.P. McDonald thought this was a very astute remark to come from a "herring choker," as he called me. I mistakenly thought that I was in like Flynn with D.P.'s firm, but such was not the case.

The whole operation was a ship without a rudder. It was patently clear that there was no future for me in that firm with Jack Prothroe in command. He was like a shark in a shoal of herring. Macdonald, the last to arrive, was the first to go. D.P. himself was brought in to deliver the chop. For the second time in my life I was out of a job.

Right around that time I encountered Nick de Grandmaison. He was a friendly little wisp of a man, a White Russian, whose ancestors had fled to Russia after the French Revolution. He had a delightful wife, Sonya (also a White Russian) and five very talented, artistic children. Like most painters, he had had a hard time financially, but was true to his artistic philosophy and, since his arrival in Canada from Vladivostok after the First Great War, had survived from the sale of his paintings and nothing else. During the depression years he would sell one of his beautiful paintings for a bottle of vodka, but carry on regardless in a land that was not too receptive to an artist and free spirit like himself. He seemed to be a sensitive, delicate man, but underneath that soft veneer was a spirit as strong as steel.

By the time I met him in 1959 he had lost some of his early fire, and would much prefer the role of the sidewalk philosopher and international commentator to the demanding discipline of the creative artist. He was a true specialist in the sense that he did only human heads. Nature and sweeping landscapes were not for him. He would paint the children of the rich and famous in Western Canada to put bread upon the table, but his real love was for the native people of Canada.

It was through him that I became really interested in the Canadian Indians and the problems of the aboriginal people of this country. In one of his off-hand moments he described me as "the man with the million dollar mug" and in the next breath, so I would not have a swelled head, would say derisively "and why should I paint somebody like you, when I can paint the Indians of Canada?" And he was really good! His medium was a delicate chalk pastel and his likenesses unique and unforgettable. His wife, Sonya, told me once that she was going to write a book called *The Other Side of the Easel*, but she did better than that. After his death she eventually sold Old Nick's private collection of paintings to the Bank of Montreal. It seems that in North America an artist has to die before he is really appreciated in his own country.

My efforts to fly solo and set up my own practice did not go unnoticed. Calgary in 1959 was going through growing pains, slowly but surely emerging from a cattletown in the foothills of the Rockies to the financial capital of the west. Keeping an eagle eye on the new oil companies and the gas transmission systems springing up overnight in Calgary was one Mike Strong, who had come to Alberta from the oil country of Texas and California. He was a past master of hyperbole and the tall story, and quite possibly the man who invented one-upmanship.

He learned that I was casting about for a place to hang my hat, and he in turn was searching for a Canadian lawyer to head up the Canadian arm of a huge gas transmission company that was to deliver gas from the Fort St. James area in northern British Columbia, down to the gas-hungry markets of California. A breath-taking concept. When he suggested I come and "office" with him in the North Canadian Oil Building, where he would "pick up the tab" and we could put this great proposal together, it was like an answer to prayer. Although the "office" was really more of a hole in the wall, it enabled me to get my foot on the legal ladder and commence the practice of law again.

From Mike Strong's office I tried to build up a legal practice, even though I had no clients to work for, while my oil-and-gas mentor conducted his reportorial operations from an adjoining office of almost regal splendor and opulence. Miss Margie acted as secretary for us both. Her main task was to type the voluminous political reports that he made to his two clients back in the United States. He watched the Canadian political scene like a great bird of prey and pounced on every change in the legislation and regulations affecting the oil and gas industry to pass on to his people south of the border.

The big objective, of course, was to sell the project to Pacific Gas Transmission in San Francisco, and in order to make an impressive presentation, elaborate maps were prepared in Calgary to show the proposed delivery lines from British Columbia down to California. This was to be Big Deal, the last hurrah for Mike, and he spared no effort to convince me that he was the ideal man for the job. Occupying the most prominent place in his office was a huge steel globe of the world.

"You see that globe, Webbie," he would say to me. "During the war I served with the United States Navy as an oil and gas consultant. I was a flower-admiral, a dollar-a-year man, because of my expert knowledge in oil and gas, and after the war, Harry Truman recognized the value of my outstanding services and gave me that globe in appreciation of what I had done for my country."

If I inquired if he were going to the polo match on the coming Saturday afternoon, he would quash that suggestion very quickly with these words:

"No Webbie, I won't be there. I've seen enough polo down in Texas to last me all my life. It was over the crouper and under the crouper, and over the belly, and under the belly all day long, so that I never want to see a polo ball again. I played with Dwight (General Eisenhower) and Doug (General MacArthur) during the war and I've had my fill!"

At this stage he produced an immense photograph showing a great array of polo players, horses, mallets, and all.

"That's Ike there!" he would say, "and that's Doug right there!"

"And where are you, Mike?"

"Over there, my boy!" and he would point to an obscure figure in the background of the photo that indeed bore a slight resemblance to Mike Strong.

It was the same with everything. He had no interest in singing, because he had gone to a parochial school at the age of seven somewhere in

Oklahoma and he sang in a boys' choir from morning till night, so singing no longer had any charm or appeal for him.

He had also studied law, at a night school in Kansas, but his real expertise lay in the field of oil and gas where he had labored for most of his working life.

My American counterpart in the gas transmission project was to be one Ross Chamberlain, a highly successful general contractor out of San Francisco. His only complaint about Mike was that Mike could not even explain the smallest and simplest matter without starting with the Book of Genesis and working through to Revelation to make his point.

In due course Mike and I set out for San Francisco, and met with Ross Chamberlain. We had our interview with the Pacific Gas Transmission people, complete with maps, statistics and supporting data. But all for naught. Chamberlain had no confidence in Strong, the Americans had no faith in the deal and I was ready to move on to other things. As Burns said, "The best laid schemes of mice and men gang aft agley."

By now I was ready for the legal world of Calgary and the forensic problems from which I had been away so long. In my legal work I had come in contact with the brothers Westergaard. They were Danish homeopaths, a pair of bachelors, who put gin in their homeopathic remedies. Their patients swore they were the greatest healers since Jesus. Anton passed on and his brother Chris died of loneliness five months later. Their little house on First Avenue in Calgary was ideal for my purposes, so shortly thereafter I bought their home from the Royal Danish Consulate and was ready to practice law in earnest.

Crime Passionelle, Calgary Style

My people-in-trouble-practice, as I describe my years at the bar in Calgary, began with what was undoubtedly one of the most unusual cases I have ever had. A crime passionelle, it was not the type of case one generally associates with "cold-blooded" Anglo-Saxons, but rather with the Latin people, who take these affairs of the heart more seriously. In Calgary in the early 1960s, there was no legal aid as we now know it, and the practitioners of criminal law were few and far between, and were considered a little *infra dig*. Their more affluent brothers, who lived very comfortably on their fees from oil and gas cases and other lucrative branches of the civil law, considered criminal cases a bit beneath their dignity.

At any rate, quite apart from any mercenary considerations, the case of *Regina v. Patricia Brooks* was viewed by most members of the Calgary bar as a hopeless affair, at least from the standpoint of the defense. It was not even high on the list of priorities of the Calgary police, although as a murder case (relatively rare in Calgary in those days), it had been assigned to the senior crown prosecutor, Mr. Edward P. Adolphe, to be given the attention it deserved.

Why was there a trial at all, they asked? The woman had been caught *in flagrante delicto* hadn't she? Hadn't she admitted her guilt? Hadn't she, and she alone, committed the dastardly deed? Correct on all counts, but the law enforcement officials overlooked one vitally important element—the state of mind of the accused at the time of the killing. It was this ingredient, the "why" of the case, that made the Brooks case so different and so interesting.

The facts were somewhat sordid, to say the least. I interviewed Mrs. Brooks down at the old Calgary Police Station, a red brick monstrosity that must have been erected before the turn of the century. Bail was out of the question, and I spent many long hours in the female quarters of the jail, gleaning from "Princess Pat" as I called her, the unhappy circumstances of the case.

She came from a broken home in rural Ontario, and had married her husband, who was then serving with the Canadian Army, while both were in their teens. At the time of her arrest, Pat was 29 years of age and her husband had attained the rank of sergeant after service outside Canada.

It had been an unhappy marriage, replete with acts of violence and sadistic brutality by Brooks against his wife, but she had stuck it out and kept the pieces of their marriage together. She recounted ghastly tales of his cruelty towards her—how he would kick her downstairs when she was pregnant, haul her around the house by the hair, and throw her from their automobile out onto the pavement at 60 km an hour. Oh, a nice fellow was Sergeant Brooks! While overseas he had learned karate, and he would beat her with judo chops because they left no mark. It was a beautiful picture she painted of her lord and master.

Against such a background and history, the fascinating question immediately arose: why had she killed for this man? And a second and just as interesting a question: why, if she was burning with rage because of her husband's infidelity, had she not murdered him, instead of the mistress? These were just some of the questions I mulled over in my mind as I prepared the case for trial.

The facts were clear-cut and not in dispute. For months the Brooks family had been living in a state of undisguised hostility. The sergeant openly had a mistress, who worked as a civilian at Currie Barracks with the Department of National Defence. Although Princess Pat did not know the full story or exactly who the mistress was, she had her own *affaires de coeur* and was not overly disturbed by the peccadillos of her spouse. She was much more concerned that he was not the good provider he could have been on a sergeant's pay.

As her bus proceeded along 16th Avenue on the way to Currie Barracks in southwest Calgary, imagine her anger and dismay when she looked out the window and saw her husband carrying a huge bag of groceries into an apartment over the Altadore Drugs building. That did it! Adultery was one thing, but failing to put bread on the table for his own family, while providing for his paramour, was more than her flesh and blood could stand.

Princess Pat was in the Non-Permanent Active Militia (NPAM) and on duty that day for 12 hours. While at the barracks she consumed twenty bottles of draught beer, and brooded dark thoughts of what she had seen from the bus earlier in the day. As the hours wore on, she worked herself into a silent frenzy. She would face this woman and have it out with her and Sergeant Brooks would find out all about it in his own good time!

It was the middle of January and the Brooks family were living in Army quarters on 54th Street S.W. It was almost midnight when Princess Pat returned home and changed out of her army uniform. She put on her leopard-skin coat and hat, together with her high-heeled shoes, and strapped her son's sheath and Boy Scout knife around her waist. She then set out through the winter snow to walk from her home on 54th Street S.W. to the apartment of the mistress in Altadore some 38 blocks away.

Arriving at the mistress's Altadore apartment, she quickly made her way to the second floor to find the door to the apartment locked. But the outraged wife was not to be denied.

"Who is it"? called out the mistress, as the injured party sought to gain admission to the apartment.

"It's me, Patricia Brooks," she replied, "and I have come to have a talk with you."

"Go away," answered the paramour, "I've got nothing to say to you."

Princess Pat turned around and went down the stairs, but stopped at the bottom. "I came here to have it out with her," she said to herself, "and that's exactly what I am going to do."

At that point she flew back up the stairs like an avenging harridan, intent on one thing and one thing alone, to meet her rival face-to-face. Outside the flimsy door to the apartment she could hear the mistress talking on the phone.

"Darling, your wife has just been here. What are we going to do?" These words drove Princess Pat berserk. In a frenzy of rage, she charged the door, the only thing standing between her and her adversary. She was not quite 59 kg (129 lb.) and her leopard-skin coat gave her scant protection as she battered against the door with her shoulder. Hell hath no fury like a woman in a jealous rage, and in a matter of seconds Princess Pat had ripped the door right off its hinges and entered the living room, where the sergeant's mistress was still on the telephone. With one hand, Princess Pat hauled the woman off the telephone, and at the same time pulled out her son's Boy Scout knife from the belt around her waist. She hauled the terrified woman out into the public hallway and stabbed her 34 times, leaving her to expire in her own gore. As the poet Milton might have put it:

> *In calm of mind, all passion spent,*
> *Nothing is here for tears.*

At this stage it would appear that Princess Pat regained her composure, for she returned to the living room and made a number of phone calls herself: to the police, to the ambulance, to her husband and to her own boyfriend. She then lit a cigarette and coolly awaited the arrival of the authorities.

When the police arrived a short time later, they found a calm and collected woman who apparently was quite undismayed by the events that had recently taken place. As the police entered the room, she quietly said, "Good evening, gentlemen, I have been expecting you. There's a body in the hall, I did it and I am glad I did it. Here is the knife and I am responsible."

Whereupon she was taken away and placed in jail. She was denied bail and charged with murder contrary to the Criminal Code of Canada.

How to defend a woman in such a predicament? And things were not helped by the fact that the killing had been preceded by a three-day drunken party at her home in Currie Barracks, the highlight occurring when the gas man, who arrived unexpectedly on the scene, imbibed not wisely, but too well, and passed out in her bedroom.

Why would she kill for a man like Sergeant Brooks? He was a wretched, miserable specimen at best, but he was all she had.

She might well have said, "A poor thing my Lord, but mine own." Or was there something masochistic about a woman in circumstances like this? There are no definitive answers to these questions and one can only speculate on her motivation. As in practically all my cases, it was the "why" of the matter that was so fascinating.

In due course, after a brief preliminary inquiry, Princess Pat was committed for trial and a case of this importance was set down for hearing in the Supreme Court of Alberta (as it then was) before His Lordship Campbell McLaurin, the Chief Justice of the Trial Division of Alberta. The words for McLaurin were massive and powerful. He had started his career as a high school principal in Medicine Hat and worked his way up the legal ladder, after specializing in insurance law and lining up the head offices of the big eastern insurance companies as his clients, until he eventually reached the top of the pile and was appointed Chief Justice of the Trial Division of Alberta. He had a preternaturally white face, set in a huge bald head, and he chomped continually on a moist cigar. He had no time for long-winded speeches or histrionics of any kind.

Murder in Calgary in 1960 was a most unusual event. Following a preliminary inquiry and Pat's committal for trial, the Chief Justice McLaurin took the case under his personal wing. The Senior Agent for the Attorney General, Mr. E.P. Adolphe, was the spearhead for the prosecution. Shortly before the trial commenced the Chief Justice summoned me and Mr. Adolphe to his private chambers in the ancient sandstone courthouse (now the Court of Appeal of Alberta) for a briefing on the case. As I watched his beautiful black poodle sleeping by the gas fire, the learned trial judge directed our attention to the task at hand.

Never one to waste time in small talk or airy persiflage, he came right to the point. On the face of it, it seemed like an air-tight case for the Crown. Was there anything left for the Crown to prove? In short order, it was patently clear that the Chief Justice did not think so, nor did the dutiful Crown Prosecutor, Mr. E.P. Adolphe.

"Now, Webster," growled the Chief Justice, as he slid a well-moistened black cigar from one side of his grizzled face to the other, "what possible defenses have you got in an open-and-shut case like this? We all know that everyone is entitled to a defense and that they are innocent until proven guilty, but you can't fly in the teeth of evidence like this. Or can you?"

The late Chief Justice was always an intimidating gentleman, and even in the warmth and comfort of his private chambers he was still a huge and imposing figure of a man. This was no time, however, to be at a loss for words, and out they poured, pell-mell, as I hastened to assure the two symbols of the might of the Crown that my hapless client indeed had a defense and that a properly instructed jury might set her free. Not that the possibility of a jury trial made a deep impression on the Chief Justice. In those benighted days, Alberta still operated with a jury of six good men and true, as a carryover from the frontier days of the Northwest Territories, and Chief Justice McLaurin had only a thinly veiled disdain for trial by jury at all. A jury trial with six laymen sitting as sole judges of the facts was a pack of nonsense. He, as a trained jurist, was the master of the law and far better suited to conduct a trial of this kind, than six local bumpkins off the street. So what could I say?

"At the moment, My Lord," I stammered, "it would seem she has at least two defenses—pathological intoxication and insanity. I also intend to raise the question of her medical condition and suggest that her criminal intent or attitude of mind was deeply affected by a little- known symptom called premenstrual tension. And I shall also refer to the thorny matter of provocation and try to reduce the charge of murder to manslaughter."

Mr. Adolphe was there only as a silent bystander. The pale green eyes of the Chief Justice fastened on me in a baleful scowl and he quickly demolished any hopes that I had for an easy or successful trial.

It was clear that any reference to premenstrual tension was quite lost on a male chauvinist like the Chief Justice. He made no reference to this unhappy condition at all and in a few brusque words he ripped the other "defenses" apart.

"Webster," he said, "you can forget about insanity and provocation. There's just no room for those arguments in this case. But drunkenness, that's different, maybe you've got something there. Five men out of six on that jury will know about liquor and maybe you can make that one stick. It's the only hope you've got." By this time the cigar was burned to an ash. Mr. Adolphe did not participate in this interesting exchange. The pre-trial conference was over and like two schoolboys dismissed by an irate principal, Mr. Adolphe and I went our separate ways.

But the judge was wrong. When it came to the rough and tumble of the trial, all of the defenses I had discussed with the Court were of great importance. Intoxication and the three-day binge, at which the gas inspector played a prominent role, provided a background and set the tone for the whole sordid affair. The premenstrual tension of the accused was probably as much lost on the all-male jury as on the judge, but it was brought to their attention just the same and gave me additional ammunition to argue that an appropriate verdict was really manslaughter, not murder.

As the celebrated George Nowlan, MP (in my humble opinion one of the great trial lawyers of Canada) would have said, "A friend on the jury is better than the first twenty books of the evidence." The late Jim Blake had become my friend, and at the Brooks trial was chosen as foreman of the jury.

The trial lasted three days, as the sad story of Patricia Brooks, her abusive marriage, the drunken party, and everything else were laid out for the jury to see. She took the stand in her own defense and graphically described her visit to the Altadore Apartments, and her blind rage as she destroyed the rival to her husband's affections. I am sure the jury related to her.

My strategy throughout the case was to put her husband on trial. I had arranged for the sergeant to be in court for the entire proceedings, but did not put him on the stand. From time to time, at decisive moments, I would turn to the spectators and say, "Would you please stand up, Sergeant Brooks." At this request the sergeant would rise to his feet and in his lavender tie and with his bulbous lips, he was there in living technicolor, plain for the jury and everybody else to see. He did not say a word, nor did he have to. There was the real villain; and it was he who should have been indicted, not his long-suffering wife. No one will ever know the effect of this change in focus on the jury.

Psychiatric evidence was given on both sides, with the defense striving to bring the accused within the ambit of the McNaghten Rules on insanity, and the Crown stating categorically that she knew the difference between right and wrong, and at all times was fully aware of the consequences of her acts. The finer points of all this legalese was lost on the jury, I am sure. The Crown was convinced it had an open-and-shut case and Mr. Adolphe addressed the jury for exactly six minutes before sitting down, fully expecting a verdict of guilty.

For my part, I dealt with the whole unsavory affair at length, and laid the blame squarely at the feet of Sergeant Brooks. I referred indirectly to pathological intoxication, and premenstrual tension, urging the jury to consider these factors as contributing to Mrs. Brooks's insanity. The trial

Judge summed up the evidence in a matter-of-fact, impartial manner, but left no opening for the jury to conclude that it was a "crime passionelle."

It did not take the jury very long to consider their verdict. After a short deliberation they found Patricia Brooks "Not Guilty" by reason of insanity.

In Canada, and other countries that have taken their criminal jurisprudence from Britain, the guidelines were set in 1843 by the McNaghten Rules. In that celebrated case the accused was found "Not Guilty" on grounds of insanity after shooting Robert Peel's secretary in the mistaken belief that he was the prime minister. The defense basically had to prove that the accused was suffering from a mental defect that made him incapable of telling right from wrong, and unable to appreciate the nature and consequences of his acts. It may well be that the jury believed that the accused acted on irresistible impulse and was temporarily insane.

Who can penetrate the rationale of the good men and true in the secrecy of their jury deliberations, when they strive to do the right thing and true deliverance make according to the evidence?

In any event, the jury returned a verdict of "Not Guilty" by reason of insanity and under the authority of the Lieutenant Governor's warrant, Patricia Brooks was duly incarcerated in the Alberta Mental Hospital at Ponoka. Here she was detained for eight months until a mental review board found that she was really quite sane and was entitled to be released. In no time at all she divorced Sergeant Brooks and when last heard of was a credit officer at the Hotel Vancouver in British Columbia.

Why would such a feisty woman commit the murder of her husband's mistress, after the brutal treatment she had put up with for so many years at the hands of that sadistic man? Why kill the mistress instead of the real villain, her philandering husband? He was indeed a poor thing, but her own, and no one will ever know what stoked the raging fire that burned behind her phlegmatic exterior.

At the moment, the insanity defense is undergoing rigid scrutiny in the United States, where in 1991 homicide deaths amounted to 25 000, the highest in U.S. history. Some bizarre killers like David Berkowitz and John Wayne Gacy went to prison, while John Hinckley, who tried to assassinate the then-President Reagan, was confined in a mental hospital.

This inconsistent treatment in the judicial system has led to outcries for the abolition of the insanity defense. The Supreme Court of Wisconsin convicted Jeffrey Dahmer for the bizarre murders of 15 young men but regardless of the outcome of this trial, the "insanity defense" will undoubtedly take years before the matter reaches the Supreme Court of the United States for final disposition.

In the meantime, Princess Pat, wherever you are and whatever you are doing, you are a very fortunate woman, because an all-male jury in Calgary, Alberta cut through the McNaghten Rules and dispensed some homespun natural justice.

The Road to Jericho

Peter Gerlitz was an unexpected client when he blew into my office on January 2nd, 1962. I remember the occasion vividly because it was the day after New Year's and at 10 a.m. in the morning, he was my first client for the year 1962.

He wore a black felt hat and cowboy boots and a rather sanctimonious expression behind enormous horn-rimmed glasses. He introduced himself and said that Mr. Justice Val Milvain had told him I was a new lawyer in town and that maybe I could help. At this stage he produced a crisp $1 000 dollar bill by way of a retainer and everything proceeded pleasantly from there.

Peter Gerlitz had a most unhappy tale to relate. He had been a prosperous farmer down in Okotoks, where he raised broiler chickens, although he lived in Calgary. He had made so much money that he was able to invest in highway construction projects as a side line. In addition, he had gravel and cement trucks that were extremely profitable.

It appeared that he and Wonderly Construction Company had had a bitter falling out, after embarking on a joint venture in the road construction business. With the assistance of the great Sam Helman, he had sued the Wonderly people, who promptly counterclaimed and ended up with a judgment for $25 000 against Peter Gerlitz. This miscarriage of justice (or so it seemed to him) was more than Peter could stand. He abandoned Mr. Helman and on Judge Milvain's recommendation came over to see me to have things straightened out.

It was no easy task. Wonderly was represented by the mighty firm of Fenerty and Company and their battery of lawyers. Jack Robertson and the late Marvin McDill were not about to forego their judgment for $25 000 dollars and so the fight was on.

It was an uphill battle to find the new evidence that Peter Gerlitz was convinced would prove that perjury had been committed at the trial. The star player was one Bob Stevenson, then languishing in jail over in Okhalla prison in British Columbia. We had to get to Stevenson to obtain the necessary affidavit that could overturn Wonderly's victory on the counterclaim.

Stevenson had held a key position on the highway project but had not testified at the trial. After months of pounding at new witnesses, including Bob Stevenson, we finally mounted an offensive that convinced Wonderly that we might just get a new trial. Grudgingly and reluctantly, and perhaps wisely, they capitulated. The judgment by counterclaim was wiped out and things were restored to normal. For me this was a great forensic triumph, but for Peter Gerlitz it was only a preliminary skirmish in the great war against the forces of evil. The battle had just begun.

By this time I was working on approximately 20 different matters for this strange man and in spite of the victory in the Wonderly case, he was not satisfied. To Peter Gerlitz, success in business and legal matters was largely governed by the powers of the Lord God Almighty, and as a true fundamentalist and evangelical Christian, Peter was sure that he had the inside track in matters of this kind. He would also take the necessary temporal steps to make sure that his legal and business interests would be protected on the planet earth, by giving presents of chickens to the cabinet ministers of the Social Credit government in Edmonton, and chocolate and caramels to the girls in the Bank of Nova Scotia on 17th Avenue and 14th Street S.W. in Calgary, where he banked.

When some of his business arrangements fell apart, he could not very well blame the Almighty, especially when there was a more vulnerable scapegoat close at home—namely me—whom he could find accountable for his business setbacks. Overnight the lawyer became the enemy and a holy war began.

The attack was unremitting and relentless. My former client acquired a printing press and from the basement of his house, churned out defamatory letters about me to the RCMP, the Calgary police, the premier of Alberta and any other public figure he could think of. The defamatory letters were wild and quite bizarre. They accused me of theft and fraudulent conduct, and poured out of his printing press in a virulent stream, until I was at my wit's end to know what to do.

Ordinarily the wisest tactic is to avoid confrontation. As the former Chief Justice McGillvray of the Alberta Court of Appeal once wisely observed, "You don't get into a pissing contest with a skunk."

Another Chief Justice of the Court of Appeal, Bill Sinclair, sagely remarked, "Before you sue for defamation, think hard about it, then think some more, and finally don't do it!"

I remembered these words of advice and tried to ignore the fulminations that roared from the Gerlitz pen in an endless torrent. At last his poison pen letters to the RCMP (of which copies had been sent to me) finally convinced me there was no alternative. If I were to stop him, he had to be sued.

I retained the redoubtable Jack Major, a civil litigation lawyer who had a mind like a steel trap, to sue Gerlitz for defamation. In this cold and analytical fashion, Major was an ideal counsel for the task. The gauntlet was immediately picked up by my old friend Alf Harris, a bulldog in his own right, and the fight was on.

Gerlitz and Alf Harris decided that a civil jury was the way to go, because six persons off the street would not be too friendly towards a lawyer. Gerlitz was a man of considerable means, and the costs of the jury deposit did not deter him in the least. And so we were faced with a jury trial, set down in Calgary before the late Mr. Justice Ted Manning.

Gerlitz, of course, was the defendant, the first and main witness to testify on his own behalf. The civil jury was made up of three men and three women who listened attentively as the defendant poured out his tale of woe. The case lasted several days, and the speech and behavior of the defendant gave an unreal atmosphere to the whole affair, as if it were taking place in Biblical times rather than in a modern courtroom.

Looking solemnly at the jurors, Gerlitz would make strange pronouncements: "Like I say, I was the man on the road to Jericho, who fell among thieves." Who the other thieves were besides myself I was never quite sure and every accusation of theft and dishonesty was prefaced by "and lo and behold," to be followed by disconnected allegations of impropriety that had nothing to do with the case, and only puzzled and confused the jury.

At the beginning of the trial, Gerlitz had sat in the front row of the courtroom, but on the last afternoon, huge black clouds formed over the building. When a great clap of thunder rent the air, Gerlitz leapt to his feet and ran to the rear of the courtroom, where he cowered in solitary silence. Everyone in the courtroom was stunned by this bizarre behavior. I firmly believe that he thought the Lord had spoken in the thunder and deserted him in his time of need. He could no longer look to the Almighty for divine intervention in his secular problems.

After suitable directions from Mr. Justice Manning, the jury retired to deliberate on their verdict. In short order they returned to the courtroom and advised the judge that the defendant had indeed defamed the plaintiff and awarded me damages in the sum of $25 000.

At that time this verdict was the highest award for defamation in the legal history of Alberta and stood as a highwater mark until Peter Lougheed, former premier of Alberta, was awarded damages of $80 000 in his action against the CBC.

The Best Whorehouse in the West

The Rombough case was a *cause célèbre* in Calgary of the 1960s. Janet Rombough was a well-known figure throughout the West, perhaps even across Canada. She trained and ran racehorses with great success, but had really made her mark as the madame of the best little whorehouse in the country.

By the time I became her solicitor, she had been married four times. She ran her business under the name of Babe Yates, after husband number three. The Calgary police had more or less turned a blind eye to Janet's activities and tolerated her business because it was open, well-run and notorious. Over the years she had been convicted approximately seven times and her sentences had ranged from maximum fines of $150 to a term of imprisonment up to three months.

The picture changed for the Babe about 1963. I have it on reliable information that a prominent clergyman in southwest Calgary contacted the Premier of Alberta, The Honorable Ernest C. Manning, who also served as Attorney General, and complained that it was a disgrace that the illegal business of Janet Rombough (Babe Yates) should be carried on with impunity, and the implied acquiescence of the law, in his parish. It should not be tolerated. This complaint did not fall on deaf ears. What happened next can only be surmised, but immediately thereafter, Janet Rombough was arrested and charged with living on the avails of prostitution. She was duly tried in the District Court of Alberta, and ably defended by lawyers other than myself. To the astonishment of all concerned, the accused was found guilty and given the maximum sentence of 10 years in prison.

Her fourth husband, Chuck McCann, was most unhappy with this turn of events and came over to retain me to assert an appeal against her conviction and the Draconian punishment imposed upon her. The maximum sentence was the talk of the town and I was intrigued with the whole affair. I promptly drafted appeal papers, setting out 21 grounds of appeal, to be taken before the Appellate Division of the Supreme Court of Alberta, as it was then known.

The Crown was represented by the same E.P. Adolphe who had conducted the prosecution of Patricia Brooks, and as was customary at that time, as senior crown prosecutor or agent of the Attorney General he was chosen to be in charge of this important case.

The appeal lasted three days. It was a gruelling and unpleasant experience. The case attracted a great deal of publicity, most of it highly unfavorable to the Appellant, and the tense atmosphere in the courtroom made it clear that the Appeal Court was not about to interfere with the decision of His Honor Judge Tavender, who had been the trial judge, nor would they interfere with the maximum sentence imposed.

It was like being in a shooting gallery. For two and one-half days I argued that the Crown evidence was not credible and that the star witness for the Crown, one Susan Robertson, a lady from Toronto, had been brought out to give testimony against my client that was not worthy of belief. Robertson's evidence was to the effect that she had worked as a whore at the Rombough establishment and turned over the money from her nefarious earnings to Janet. Throughout her stay in Calgary she was kept in "protective custody" until she had given her damning evidence and returned to Ontario. Following Janet's conviction, the other ladies of pleasure, who had been incarcerated during the trial as key witnesses for the prosecution, had been released.

Argument after argument, point of law after point of law, were all shot down by the Court of Appeal. Finally there was only one ground left. To use it, or not to use it, that was the question. It was a judgment call and I made what I still think was the right choice, though in the years that followed I may have paid dearly for that decision.

My client had given me some evidence so unusual that I was not sure what course to take. At the time of her conviction and sentence, Janet was locked up in the women's cells of the old Calgary Police Station. On the evening of her conviction, to her astonishment, Mr. Adolphe arrived on the scene with bunches of roses in his arms. They were not for Janet, they were intended for the Crown witnesses, who had been held in "protective custody" in jail, pending giving evidence for the Crown. The roses carried with them small cards of appreciation: "To my little darlings," they read "with thanks from E.P. Adolphe." After this unexpected visit, Janet was able to collect the "thank you" cards from her former friends and employees and turn them over to me.

What to do with them was the question. The Crown in all criminal prosecutions under our adversary system, never wins and at the same time never loses a case. It is expected that Her Majesty will at all times conduct herself with a fine impartiality, and merely present the evidence without fear or favor to anyone. However exacting it may be, she is supposed to be like Caesar's wife, above reproach, so that justice may not only be done, but may abundantly be seen to be done.

In my final argument, in what was a harrowing appeal, I produced the cards that Mr. Adolphe had taken to the jail that night and submitted to the three-man Court of Appeal, presided over by the late Chief Justice Bruce Smith, that the Crown had been guilty of gross impropriety and that at the very least, my client was entitled to a new trial.

The air was thick with tension and for the first time in three days, they really listened to me. It is common knowledge that in a British country, the office of the Crown Prosecutor has almost an aura of sanctity about it, enshrined in the centuries old adage, "The Queen can do no wrong." (It must be remembered this was long before the repatriation of the Canadian Constitution and all that went with that historic change.)

Their Lordships were on the horns of a most unusual dilemma. The visit, the roses, the cards, the whole incident was bizarre and highly suspicious. The Court retired to deliberate on this unusual situation and resolved the problem in a unique and practical fashion. The Court ruled that inasmuch as the inappropriate act had not taken place within the precincts of the court house, they had no jurisdiction to deal with the matter! And so argument 21 was laid to rest. It might appear to some that on the highly-acclaimed principle of justice being abundantly seen to be done, there was an aberration of justice on this point, and that Janet Rombough should at the very least have been granted a new trial.

There was no new trial, and Janet went to serve her 10-year sentence at the Women's Penitentiary in Kingston Ontario. She was released on good behavior, after serving three years of her sentence, and shortly thereafter died of cancer while looking after her race horses. Her houses of ill-fame in southwest Calgary, by the Stampede grounds down along the banks of the Elbow River, were shut down forever.

The Rombough case, quite apart from the incredible publicity it engendered, was unusual in a number of ways. The 10-year sentence for what in effect was keeping a common bawdy house was most difficult to understand. The Babe was not a well woman, and in spite of everything it was held she was not entitled to bail. Reasonable bail is a fundamental tenet of our judicial system, and on Janet's behalf, I went from judge to judge in the Supreme Court of Alberta (before the name was changed to the Court of Queen's Bench) in a vain attempt to have bail set for this unfortunate woman. Three times I tried and three times bail was denied. The third attempt was almost successful and it changed the criminal procedure for the Province of Alberta for all time. I checked the court documents authorizing her incarceration, and to my astonishment I found that no Warrant of Committal had been taken out authorizing her imprisonment, as provided by the Criminal Code of Canada.

Janet Rombough was behind bars in a Canadian prison with no official document to support this step other than what for countless years had been known as a Calendar of Sentence. I argued that the Calendar of Sentence was merely a clerical document that was a record of her incarceration, not a valid order as envisaged by the Criminal Code. This final bail application was heard by that wise and compassionate jurist, Mr. Justice Harold Riley, and on the slimmest of legal technicalities he ruled that his hands were tied by an adverse ruling in the Supreme Court of Canada and that he was unable to release my client.

This was 1963, almost 20 years before the Charter of Rights and Freedoms would have almost certainly altered the whole situation. It was some satisfaction to note that following the Rombough case, Calendars of Sentence became obsolete in Alberta and all prisoners are now covered with a warrant of committal authorizing their imprisonment.

I was to meet Mr. Adolphe again a few years later, under quite different circumstances, at which time I wondered whether he had forgotten about the roses for his "little darlings." Time heals all wounds—or does it?

Frosty the Snowman and Applied Science

Around the time I opened my office in the little house in Calgary (where the brothers Westergaard had carried on their thriving osteopathic business by giving their patients a little medication spiced with vodka), Lloyd McSorley made me aware of his new ideas for agriculture.

His china-blue eyes and mop of prematurely snow-white hair gave him the cherubic look of someone who has just stepped off the farm with some unusual tales to tell. Here was a man who had all of nature as his teacher. His curiosity knew no bounds. Were you interested in playing 18 holes of golf in your living room? Lloyd McSorley had designed a machine to do just that. Or perhaps an ultrasonic dishwasher to eliminate the chores of washing and drying dishes by hand? Frosty had the answer for that one too, long before dishwashers as we now know them were on the market. Interlocking building blocks that dispensed with mortar and cement were his answer to the housing problems of the Third World.

But his great love was a plan to save the citrus crops of North America from frost damage by sowing the clouds with chemical particles that would act as a blotter and screen the ultraviolet light that causes millions of dollars of damage to the citrus crops of Florida and California. Because of his interest in protecting growing crops from frost damage, Lloyd took on the nickname "Frosty the Snowman."

Frosty the Snowman was a beautiful human sponge. Although he did not have an inventive or completely original mind of his own, he saw unlimited possibilities in the practical application of other's ideas. He took over these ideas and made them his own. In a way it was like putting old wine in new bottles, but it was his approach to those matters that was so different.

Some years before he and I met, he had been gored by a bull on his father's farm near Brandon, Manitoba, and was sent to the Mayo Clinic in nearby Minnesota to recuperate. As he lay flat on his back at Mayo's he found himself next to the great meteorologist, Dr. Crick. This was the weather prophet who had told Dwight Eisenhower that on June 6th, 1944, the English Channel would be as smooth as a millpond—and conditions would be perfect for the allied invasion of Europe. Dr. Crick found a willing and understanding ear in the farmboy from Manitoba, so the learned weather forecaster carefully outlined his methods of suppressing hail by sowing the clouds with silver iodide to modify the weather.

Frosty became the Canadian representative for his new friend. Soon he was crisscrossing the western provinces, educating grain farmers about weather forecasting and how to suppress hail which could destroy an entire crop in a matter of hours.

I listened carefully to Frosty's plans. It did not really matter that for the most part the inventions emanated from other people. His gift lay in seeing the practical application of these new approaches to daily living. He could bring them down from the rarefied atmosphere of abstract thinking to the basic problems of the here and now.

As we were awaiting his arrival at the office, I said to my Hungarian secretary, "You know, Gizelle, Lloyd McSorley is a highly intelligent fellow, but in some ways he is like a magpie. He picks up other people's ideas, like a magpie steals other birds' eggs."

The next day my client came in to see me about his inventions. As he entered the office, Gizelle looked up from her typewriter.

"Hello, Mr. McSorley," she said, "Mr. Macdonald says you are just like a magbird, and that you go around picking up other birds' eggs."

There was a pained silence for a brief moment. Frosty and I quickly moved on to other things, such as an offer from the Italian-Swiss Colony people near San Francisco. They wanted Frosty to tell them of his plans to screen ultraviolet light and save their 20 000-odd hectares (50 000 acres) of grape vineyards from frost destruction. We had sent out hundreds of letters to people who might have been interested in this revolutionary proposal, but the only invitation of a concrete nature came from California.

By this time Lloyd and I were fast friends, as well as solicitor and client, and at the invitation of Louis Petri, the president of the Italian-Swiss Colony, we set off for California.

Previous attempts to ward off the frost menace had been primitive in the extreme: using windmills at night to keep the air in circulation around the citrus trees; burning old tires to lay down a cloud of smoke against the ultraviolet light that Frosty was convinced caused the damage.

Under the watchful eye of Louis Petri himself, we gave a full briefing session at the head office of the Italian-Swiss Colony in San Francisco. While there, we learned that at that very moment the motor vessel S.S. *Petri* was stuck on a reef at the entrance to San Francisco harbor, en route to France, with a cargo of 18 million litres (4 million gallons) of wine from the Italian-Swiss vineyards for use as a base for famous French products in the international champagne trade. Frosty presided over the in-house meeting like a university professor as the California wine growers listened with rapt attention to his gospel message on the evils of ultraviolet light.

We then moved into the Napa Valley, where equipment was supplied by the Petri people for a demonstration of the McSorley plan. Technicians drilled a hole in the manifold of a tractor and a gaseous smoke was produced to float over the vineyard like a blotter, soaking up suspect ultraviolet rays. Alas, a wind came up and the protective layer of gas fumes dispersed. Although the experiment could not be called a success, no one has yet been heard to say that the process would not work under proper conditions.

And so I watched the inventions of my client with the keenest of interest, as over the course of 30 years he grappled with the problems of weather modification. The fact remains that citrus fruit at certain stages in the ripening process is damaged by frost and drops in temperature. Could the screening of ultraviolet rays be an answer to this age-old agricultural question? Probably no one really has the answer for the weather modification conundrum; Lloyd McSorley's plan may well be a positive, if inconclusive, step towards a solution to the problem.

For a number of years I lost track of Frosty, who went to Winnipeg in pursuit of his endeavors. Always a resourceful fellow, at some stage in his Winnipeg period he discovered fascinating business opportunities in Liberia, on the west coast of Africa. In true McSorley fashion, he spent a lot of time in that country and became friendly with the prime minister and the attorney general and other persons in top government positions. He pursued his interest in the gold and diamond fields of Liberia but then unfortunately came down with malaria and was forced to return to Canada.

Perhaps the bout with malaria was really good fortune in disguise, for almost immediately after his departure from Liberia the country became embroiled in a virulent civil war that toppled all of Frosty's friends and connections in the government and led to their violent execution by decapitation, drowning and other similar barbaric measures.

Lloyd was in Calgary when he read in the newspaper of this devastating turn of events. To his horror he learned that his best friends in Liberia had been turfed from office and murdered without trial. While he was still convalescing from malaria and in a weakened condition, this appalling news was more than he could bear. He was in a shopping mall in southwest Calgary and as the frightful news stories from Liberia sank in, he became temporarily deranged and acted in a bizarre manner completely out of character.

Although he had ample funds in his wallet, Frosty proceeded to help himself to clothing that did not fit him and for which he had no need. He neglected to pay for the merchandise and was promptly arrested outside the store and charged with shoplifting. This is something that happens to many upright citizens, who in a moment of forgetfulness neglect to pay for their purchases. Out on bail, and completely bewildered by the whole affair, Lloyd came to me.

In due course the matter came on for trial in Provincial Court before His Honor John Harvie. By this time the judge, having been on the bench for over 20 years and having heard the stock defenses over and over, had become inured to them all. He invariably convicted for shoplifting and imposed a fine of $100, but he had never before heard a defense quite like this one. We of course had entered a plea of "Not Guilty."

The judge had three widely different accounts before him as to what had happened on the day Frosty was apprehended with the outsized jacket in his possession. To the store detective it was a straightforward case. As far as he was concerned, the accused had been caught *in flagrante delicto*. Period. I called Lloyd in his own defense and he explained to the court that when he had learned of the terrible things that happened to his friends in Liberia, how their decapitated bodies had been thrown in the sea, he lost all contact with reality and quite literally did not know where he was or what he was doing.

His testimony was supported by psychiatric evidence which corroborated Lloyd's own story that his mind was unhinged and he was incapable of forming the necessary *mens rea*, or criminal intent, required to prove a criminal charge. The court accepted this argument and dismissed the case. A triumph for Frosty!

The civil war continues in Liberia and shows no sign of abatement. Lloyd McSorley is busily engaged in turning out interlocking building blocks for houses in the Third World. He has a revolutionary plan, along with the National Research Council of Canada, to trap neutrons from the sun in an abandoned nickel shaft in Sudbury, Ontario. It is interesting to note that the walls of the mine shaft that are to receive the neutrons from the sun will be made of McSorley's interlocking building blocks. The magbird has landed!

In his off hours, which are rather infrequent these days, he is still working on his invention which lets you play 18 holes of golf in your living room for a nominal price. Indoor golf, anyone?

The Imperial Wizard of the Ku Klux Klan

A strange case came my way one hot summer afternoon in the early 1960s, down in my little office by Buffalo Stadium. From first to last it was a fun case, and like so many cases I have encountered, probably never should have come before the Court at all. It involved the Imperial Wizard of the Ku Klux Klan, or so he said he was.

I looked at this unusual fellow and was quite impressed by what I saw. He was in his mid-twenties and was just over 183 cm (6' tall), with a pink and white complexion, enormous black eyes and a goatee beard to match that gave him an imposing appearance. He said his name was Charles MacPherson, but if I did not mind he preferred the Gaelic version of Tearlach Mac-a-Phairson. He claimed to be the Imperial Wizard of the Ku Klux Klan for Alberta and he had just been charged with the unusual offense of "watching and besetting."

"How did all this come about?" I asked.

I was informed that the Wizard lived at home in northeast Calgary, with his foster parents, who had adopted him in Prince Edward Island and brought the Wizard as a young boy west to Calgary. He was unmarried and an evangelistic minister in his own church, where he was authorized to perform marriages and carry out his ministry whenever the spirit moved him.

Only the day before, Tearlach's foster father, Mr. Dunsford, had called a rug-cleaning company, Ram Carpet Services Ltd., to come to his home and clean the carpets. A contract order form was drawn up, but when the Ram Carpet people learned that this was the home of the Imperial Wizard of the Ku Klux Klan, they refused to clean the rugs of Mr. Dunsford.

Needless to say this harsh and incomprehensible approach incensed the Wizard. After conferring with a one-quarter Cherokee Indian, who was the only other Klansman in Alberta, the Ku Klux Klan decided to take appropriate action of their own. They thereupon donned Klan regalia, complete with great white pillowcases, and marched down to the Ram Carpet premises. So that there would be no mistake as to their identity, each of them carried a pole with a banner bearing the inscriptions

Watching and besetting, Wizard style.

RAM CARPET UNFAIR TO KU KLUX KLAN
RAM CARPET REFUSES TO HONOR KLAN CONTRACT

Up and down 11th Avenue S.W. they marched, in front of the Ram Carpet premises, telling the world about the perfidious conduct of the cleaners. This two-man picket was not cordially received by the merchants and neighbors of Ram Carpet. Hoots and jeers were levelled at the Wizard and his friend, and at one time, buckets of water were poured over the Klansmen from a second-storey window. Such unfriendly behavior did not deter the picketers, who persisted in their denunciation of what they deemed to be the unfair business tactics.

At last a hairdresser across the street could stand the performance no longer and summoned the Calgary police. When the police arrived they were not quite sure what action, if any, they should take, and what charge under the Criminal Code would be appropriate in view of all the circumstances. Notwithstanding their uncertainty, they quickly dismantled the pickets and took the two Klansmen off to the police station. There a puzzled magistrate released the pair on bail and a bizarre charge of "watching and besetting" was drawn up against the Wizard and his friend.

In due course the case came on for trial before the late Magistrate Verne Reid, who was not noted for his acquittals, no matter what the charge. This peculiar set of circumstances, however, was too much, even for Verne Reid, and at the conclusion of the Crown's case, the charge was dismissed inasmuch as no one was quite sure if an offense of any kind had been committed or if a proper charge had indeed been laid.

After the hearing the Wizard regaled me with the history of the Invisible Empire, as the Ku Klux Klan used to be known. He informed me that in years gone by such eminent personages as Mr. Justice Hugo Black of the United States Supreme Court and a former Lieutenant Governor of Alberta had both been members of the Klan in good standing, and that the Klan was a cyclical organization that ebbed and flowed with the social needs of the day.

I knew the Wizard was an evangelical minister of some obscure sect or cult called the Church of Positive Thinking and the Calgary police were firmly convinced that he practised black magic when the moon was right. I was equally convinced that this was sheer speculation on their part for they never prosecuted him for anything as *outre* as that.

It may be that I was the only lawyer in Calgary who would listen to the Wizard, but over the years I found him to be a highly intelligent fellow. If the great North American crime is to be different, he was indeed guilty, but that didn't bother me in the least.

He next came to my attention in a legal sense some years after his contretemps with the Ram Carpet people. He had been apparently carrying his gospel message to Mexico, and after that was over had brought home with him to Calgary a young Mexican servant boy who he thought could be of some assistance to his aging father.

Unfortunately for the Wizard things did not work out too well. There were shotguns in the house, and two weeks after his arrival in Canada, the young Mexican arrived home after a night out on the town to find the Wizard asleep in their downstairs bedroom. Tearlach woke up upon his friend's arrival and after a while the talk between them turned to military service and the use and handling of guns. To illustrate a point, the Mexican lad picked up a 12-gauge shotgun from its rack on the wall and proceeded to march up and down the bedroom with the shotgun resting on his shoulder.

"That's not how we do it in Canada," said the Wizard. "Here, let me show you how to shoulder arms." At this point he took the gun from his Mexican friend who lay down on the bed, the better to watch the Wizard in action. At this point the story gets a little blurred, with the Wizard making further attempts to explain to his friend the workings of the trigger and the cocking mechanism of the Canadian shotgun. Unknown to either of them, the gun was loaded, as they always are. Suddenly the gun exploded and the Mexican boy had a large, gaping hole over his heart and died within seconds. The Wizard, of course, was horror-stricken by this unfortunate turn of events and immediately called the police.

The defense was lack of criminal intent and the police were unable to provide any alternative to death by accidental means. There was one puzzling factor about the whole affair that mystified the homicide detectives investigating the case. At the centre of the breast-bone of the deceased, there was a round blue tattoo, surrounding what the police conceived to be a raven's claw. The police attached great significance to this tattoo mark which was proof positive to them the Wizard and the dead boy had been practising black magic together and had a falling out which ultimately led to the Mexican's death.

The mystery on this point was quietly, but firmly, put to rest by the coroner, Dr. Butts. In his considered opinion he had seen these marks many times, and the blue tattoo on the breast of the deceased was the international peace symbol, worn by thousands of people who were protesting nuclear rearmament.

We were successful in the defense of "death by accidental shooting." The Court imposed a fine of $2 000 on the Wizard for shooting his Mexican friend, which under the circumstances was a most fortunate outcome for the leader of the Ku Klux Klan.

Tearlach Mac-a-Phairson, as he kept assuring me his name was spelt in Gaelic, was a most ingenious fellow. He would spend countless hours striving to gain legal recognition for the Midwives Association of Alberta, or trying to set up schools of all kinds to promote his oddball causes. He would have clandestine meetings with motorcycle gangs—for what purpose was never clear, and work with the leaders of the Jewish Defense League, like Rabbi Lewis Ginsberg, to show that in Alberta at least the Ku Klux Klan had no anti-Semitic prejudice.

At the peak of his missionary efforts in Alberta, the Wizard had been able to attract only a mere handful of recruits to his ranks; the part Cherokee Indian from Oklahoma, and a lone black named Louis Proctor, who were the only known members. When anti-Semitic extremists threatened to kidnap Harold Milavsky, the Wizard offered to co-operate with the Calgary police to frustrate the plan, but his offer was rejected. At the time of the Calgary Olympics in 1988 he proposed a Klan convocation to which Klan leaders from the United States were asked to attend. None of these efforts amounted to anything and in the end result, the American Klansmen labelled the Alberta Wizard a "whacko" and a "crack-pot." With the advent of David Duke on the American political scene, however, it was plain that the neo-Nazis and the Aryan Nations were far from dead and that the sinister people who carry the fiery cross were still a force to be reckoned with.

As fortunes of the Invisible Empire wax and wane, there is little doubt that the much publicized activities of the Klan in Alberta are very puzzling to the Klansmen south of the border. Mac-a-Phairson insists that in the Klan, as originally constituted, there was no intent to harbor or show discrimination against any person because of race or religion. Says the Wizard, "It was originally meant to be a fraternity like the Masons, just a simple benevolent organization. But over the years big money, graft and the growth of Naziism in the 1930s twisted many sincere members' aims and tarnished the Klan's image."

This was all highly interesting, but it was difficult to see how the Wizard could earn a living from his offbeat pursuits. Where the Wizard is at the moment no one knows. He has probably left Alberta for fresher and greener fields, where he marches to a different drummer from the rest of mankind.

Murder Most Fair

Struggling to assemble a law practice in the early sixties was no easy task, as I had no clients to look to for fees. It was all very well to fly solo and operate a one-man show, but it did not matter how much law I knew or how much experience I had: if there were no clients to work for it was almost impossible to earn a living.

Early on, for some unaccountable reason I found I was attracted to people in trouble, and gravitated towards this kind of work. Looking back, I must have had a Messiah syndrome of some kind, with a burning need to help those unfortunates who found themselves in trouble with the law and with nowhere to turn. (This was in the days before Legal Aid and the new constitution, when a mere handful of lawyers at the Calgary bar did criminal work.)

It was sometime during the year 1962 that Lance Miller, who was lodged in Calgary cells on a charge of murder, called for help. What made the whole affair unusual was that the alleged killing had taken place in Seattle, Washington. It was only a matter of time before the American authorities would take steps to extradite Lance Miller to the U.S.A. for trial.

What was it all about?

An interview with my new client at the Calgary cells filled me in. Lance was a sturdy young man in his early thirties, with an attractive square face, curly hair and a cleft dimple in his chin; a most engaging-looking fellow who did not look at all like a murderer. But there it was. He was charged with killing a waitress who had been working at the World's Fair in Seattle and the District Attorney's office had already applied for his extradition to Washington.

The whole matter proceeded by way of affidavit evidence. The Americans made out a damning case against my client. They claimed he had shot a waitress at her downtown apartment in the early hours of the morning and thrown the body in a gravel pit as he fled to sanctuary in Canada.

Lance was a man of considerable artistic talents and a painter and musician in his own right. After the war he had left his native Toronto to work as an illustrator with the Walt Disney Studio in California. Somehow, he made his way up to Alaska, where he acquired a pistol (affectionately referred to as "The Blue") for $20 from an inebriated Eskimo. This weapon was with him when he moved into an apartment in Seattle with the World's Fair waitress. Because their relationship was more than platonic, on her return to her apartment one morning at 4 a.m. Lance felt his trust had been betrayed and promptly accused her of infidelity.

"Where the hell have you been?" he asked the waitress.

As a girl of spirit who did not feel bound to him she replied, "None of your goddamn business," or words to that effect. The fight was on. In short order, Lance had "The Blue" in his hand. He fired the gun and there was "the broad" dead at his feet, her brains all over the floor. Lance knew that his plight was desperate. As morning broke, he threw the girl's body over his shoulder and headed for his Citroen automobile in the parking lot below. Unfortunately, the morning newsboy in the stairwell witnessed Lance's precipitate descent. Lance stuffed the body in the trunk of his little car and headed for the Canadian border *tout de suite*.

One hundred and twenty kilometres (75 miles) out of Seattle, at a deserted gravel pit at Sedro Woolley in Skagit, he stopped long enough to bury the body. He eventually arrived in Calgary, where he felt safe from the wrath of the American police, who he knew would soon be hot on his trail. A young Sioux woman harbored him and Lance hid out as a fugitive at her house while he waited for the storm to blow over. It did not occur to him to change his Alaska licence plates, so it did not take the Calgary police long to discover his whereabouts and arrest him for the alleged killing in Seattle.

Things moved expeditiously and the preliminary inquiry was conducted before Mr. Justice Milvain of the Alberta Supreme Court, as it was then called. Under the provisions of the Extradition Act, the State of Washington merely had to make out a *prima facie* case for an extradition order to be granted. The court did not have much difficulty on this score. On the strength of lengthy and detailed affidavits, the court ruled that a *prima facie* case had been clearly made out, and ordered the extradition of Lance Miller to Washington State.

The Extradition Act, however, gave Miller the right to apply for a review of proceedings. We had everything to gain and nothing to lose by this manoeuvre, so we applied immediately for an order by way of *habeas corpus* (produce the body). The matter came on for hearing almost immediately before the late Mr. Justice Harold Riley, one of the judicial giants of Alberta.

The first time around, the State of Washington had relied on the affidavits themselves to support their application for extradition. On the *habeas corpus* hearing, officials appeared on the scene from the District Attorney's office in person. Mr. Justice Riley cut their affidavits to ribbons (figuratively, not literally) and found in effect that the Americans had overplayed their hand. He ruled that the affidavits were too detailed and entered into areas beyond the knowledge of the affiants, who had sworn to the truth of their contents. In addition he found that some of the affidavits had not been sworn before the proper authorities and had not been completed in compliance with the provisions of the Canadian Extradition Act.

The legal effect of all this was that he overruled the decision of Mr. Justice Milvail. Lance Miller was a free man. But not for long! We had reckoned without the resourcefulness of the police. As Lance Miller walked out of the Calgary courtroom he was met by "Butch" Roberts, one of the ablest detectives in the Calgary Police Department. Butch waited for Lance with open arms and a warrant for his arrest on a charge of defrauding Air Canada airlines of a travel ticket. Off Lance went to the local prison.

Back in Washington, the District Attorney in charge of this *cause célèbre* was the subject of considerable ridicule for not having prepared the extradition papers to the satisfaction of the Canadian courts. This time the American authorities took no chances with documentary evidence and were prepared to send up their witnesses by busload, if necessary, to testify.

I had worked for many months on the Miller case as a learning experience, but just could not afford this latest ploy from Washington. Throughout the months I had been ably assisted by my first articled student, Timothy Davis from Prince Albert, Saskatchewan, but we both agreed we had gone as far as we could without funds. We now had to trust the mercy and decency of the American legal system.

"Will you give him a fair trial?" I asked the D.A. That worthy gentleman solemnly assured me this would be the case, and transported a handcuffed Lance Miller back to Seattle to meet the ends of justice. The wheels of the gods sometimes grind slowly but exceeding small, and when the dust had settled, Lance was found guilty of murder in the second degree and sentenced to 20 years imprisonment in Walla Walla penitentiary in Washington.

I was his only correspondent while he was in jail. After five years, Walla Walla released Lance on good behavior and he made his way back to Canada. No one would employ him, but I finally got him a job in a music store in downtown Calgary. After eight months he bit the hand that fed him and ran off with $800 worth of musical instruments. He has not been heard of since. And he was such a pleasant-looking fellow, too.

The Robin Hood of Calgary

By the middle of the 1960s, Calgary was emerging as the financial metropolis of Western Canada. Long renowned as a centre for grain and cattle, the big oil discovery at Leduc in 1947 had made Calgary the undisputed oil and gas centre of the country. Along with this industrial fame had come countless American companies, large and small, to take part in the economic bonanza.

At the beginning of the decade, there were hardly any gourmet restaurants in the city, and theatre and the liberal arts were just starting to come alive. Calgary appeared to be free from organized crime, and the police force was relatively small and extremely efficient. It was against this quiet background that the Talbot case burst upon the Calgary scene.

White-collar crime was not unknown here and the stock market manipulations of the notorious Solway Mills case had been the subject of a number of fraud trials that had rocked the legal fraternity for years in courtrooms all across the country. Compared to the Solway Mills trials, the peccadillos of Bob Talbot were on a much smaller scale, but closer to humanity.

Talbot was a one-man operation. There was no corporate umbrella to protect him, except the charitable organization known as the Canadian Cancer Society. He was a tragic figure, standing all alone, which made his decline and fall so pathetic. He was a complex personality—a strange mixture of good and evil, generosity and greed, inseparably intertwined. This was the man who retained me to defend him on charges of theft and forgery amounting to $191 000. In actual fact it was probably a much larger sum, but the authorities settled on that figure as the amount they could positively prove.

It was a heinous allegation. Stealing from the Cancer Society was worse than stealing from a blind man, or so I thought. But then it was not for me to judge. If you believe in the system, as I most whole-heartedly do, then every person charged with a criminal offence is innocent until proven guilty beyond all reasonable doubt, and it was my task to defend these unfortunate people, as best I could, until they were either convicted or acquitted.

On a late autumn evening in 1964, I was down at my office on 1st Avenue S.W., where the brothers Westergaard had once made their homeopathic remedies, when the telephone rang and an unfamiliar female voice informed me that Bob Talbot had been arrested and had asked me to act as his lawyer. Bob Talbot was completely unknown to me—I was unaware that he was the chief executive officer of the Cancer Society in Calgary. It made no difference. Here was a man in serious trouble, who needed help. I dashed over to the police station and there behind bars was the morose figure of Robert Neville Talbot, facing charges of theft and forgery from one of the most esteemed and prominent charitable organizations in Canada.

As might be expected, he was glum and despondent. His eyes were shielded by a pair of dark glasses. A stocky, almost portly man of medium height, he had tousled blond hair with a wind-blown look and a smile which was broad and boyishly engaging. He was obviously glad to see me and briefed me as to the uphill task confronting us. It was apparent from the outset that bail was out of the question.

I met with the bonding people right after my interview. They explained the magnitude and enormity of the crime that had been perpetrated on a hapless charitable organization. This unpleasant interview took place in the dining room of the Palliser Hotel and it was abundantly clear that the bonding company was going to leave no stone unturned in their efforts to recover the stolen money. I faced the cold black eyes of the investigator with all the equanimity I could muster and tried to placate him.

"Mr. Talbot," I said, "is very contrite and penitent about this whole affair and I am sure he will want to make full and complete restitution."

"Never mind his penitence. Never mind his contrition," snarled the investigator, "Where is the money?"

That of course was the $64 000 plus question. The bonding company engaged Mr. Sam Helman, *QC*, the dean and elder statesman of the Calgary bar, to seize and impound every item of Talbot's property, and with incredible swiftness, injunctions and preservation orders were put in place to freeze everything he owned, until the Cancer Society could be recouped for their loss.

Bail had been set at $50 000, far beyond the reach of Talbot or his family. With the preliminary inquiry over and done with, Talbot anxiously awaited his trial, as ugly rumors and half-truths about his hidden assets flew around the city. How could this man, earning $10 000 a year, have lake-front homes at Windermere in British Columbia and a palatial condominium in Hawaii? And how much money had he concealed in numbered bank accounts in Switzerland? And how did he come by a stamp collection of incomparable value? And were there really platinum faucets in his bathroom? And how could he afford several expensive automobiles on such a modest salary? These, and other penetrating questions, created an atmosphere of hostility and doubt that was anything but helpful to his defense.

For four months, Talbot languished in jail at Calgary's Spy Hill Prison (now more euphemistically termed Calgary Correctional Institution) until at last his trial date arrived. Ready to face his accusers, he had already been tried in the court of public opinion and been found wanting.

Was there any question of his guilt? There was no doubt at all on the faces of the citizens of Calgary, who had come to see punishment meted out to this evil doer, and to most of those present there was only a certain sense of satisfaction and poetic justice in watching this felon being sent to his doom.

To the onlookers he appeared a smooth, slick con man of the deepest dye. He has had the temerity to plead "Not guilty" to the charge of theft of $191 000 and to the added nine charges of forgery. He even had the audacity to elect trial by judge and jury; but as the black-robed clerks, like medieval monks in some ecclesiastical monastery, wheeled in the Crown exhibits and the mountains of forged cheques were piled high on the prosecutor's table, it looked like a hopeless and untenable position for the portly figure in the prisoner's dock.

Over the years I witnessed many criminal trials, but I have never felt the latent hostility that this case aroused. Prominent in the audience were the doctors' wives, who flocked to this case in unparalleled numbers, along with the female hangers-on who attend any trial of public interest. To me they were no different from the women who flashed their knitting needles before the guillotines of the French Revolution, or who congregated outside Newgate prison at the time of a public hanging.

The trial is about to commence before His Lordship Mr. Justice Kirby, who like Talbot had been a cub master at one time. The judge has mounted the bench and opened his thick book with the red covers in which he will write down the salient points of the evidence. The sharp but kindly face of the judge and his pallid skin and prematurely snow-white hair are in sharp contrast to his flowing black robes. Canadian judges do not wear wigs like their English counterparts, but otherwise the court moves with the same even-handed tempo that is the hallmark of British justice from Hong Kong to the Old Bailey.

A rumor has gone abroad that Talbot is about to change his plea to "Guilty" and all eyes are riveted on the man who is alleged to have committed the unspeakable crime of cancer theft, as he stands uncertainly before the court. The accused has a brief conference with me and then looks falteringly at Arthur Godfrey, the Clerk of the Court, who massive and erect, holds the indictment in his hands. The Clerk commences to read the formal charges in a stilted, almost melodramatic manner. He has obviously at one time studied for the stage, and the time-honored phrases "fraudulently" and "without color of right," and "convert said money to your own use" roll fruitily off his tongue as if he were a character in a Shakespearean play.

"On these charges you have the election to be tried by a judge and jury, but you may with your own consent be tried by a judge without the intervention of a jury. How do you elect to be tried?"

Softly, but firmly comes the answer."My election is trial by your Lordship."

"And how do you plead to these charges?"

In a resonant, hesitant voice, Talbot replies,"The plea is guilty to all charges."

At this point in most trials everything is over, but there is a sense of drama in the Court today and all present have the feeling that now the case is really about to begin.

The disconsolate figure in the prisoner's dock looks querulously at the bench. It is now his turn and at long last he is to have his day in Court. I look at the sheafs of documents, the cancelled cheques, the records of his incredible bank deposits, in spite of the net take home pay of some $800 a month, and at the clever rubber stamps that he used to dupe the banks and the auditors. I ask myself, "What is there left for him to say?"

It is plain that this is a most unusual case. The Crown is obviously determined to expose this charlatan for the white-collar thief and trust violator that he is. For some years now, Edward Adolphe has been the senior Crown Prosecutor and agent of the Attorney General in the Calgary area. He has prepared his case against Talbot with meticulous care and has no intention of letting the prisoner off the hook, with the customary terse comment that the accused has no record and a brief outline of the facts for the court. He solemnly recites the charges of theft amounting to $191 000, together with the nine counts of forgery, and the ominous tones ring like a death knell in the crowded courtroom.

The prosecutor has a massive, domed forehead, under a taut, jaundiced skin that shines with a parchment-like pallor. His deep-set eyes are angry and brooding as he reflects on the enormity of the crime he is about to describe. He resembles some Jesuit before the Spanish Inquisition, ready to recount with almost religious fervor and intensity the *modus operandi* of the man, who has looted funds, ear-marked and subscribed for cancer research. After some bobbing and weaving on the part of counsel, as to who should open first to the court, Mr. Justice Kirby resolves the issue by directing Adolphe to proceed, and the trial begins.

This ruling is pleasing to the defense, because not only does it give me the last word, but it provides my client ample opportunity to call all the friends and supporters he can draw upon to tell the Court what a great humanitarian he really is, and of the services he provided to the Cancer Society over and above the call of duty. The Court is generally disposed to allow considerable latitude when hearing submissions in mitigation of sentence, and here is a glorious chance to describe the crime itself in colors as favorable as possible to the accused, and to show that he is far from being as black as he has been painted.

At the back of the Court, craning his thin neck like an ostrich, I see the pallid pasty face of Fred Schultz, the man who has blown the whistle on Talbot, and turned his boss over to the Calgary Police. I wonder what thoughts are running through his mind at this juncture? It is Schultz who felt that Talbot's gifts of chocolates and flowers to the ladies of the society, when the board met in Lethbridge, were not authorized expenditures, and reported his boss's generosity to the police and thereby set the whole investigation in motion.

Schultz is doubtless displeased by the action of the directors, who rewarded his informing tactics with a speedy dismissal for having their dirty linen laundered in public. Talbot would have branded his former employee as a sneak and a liar, but all his efforts in this direction come to naught. To the contrary, it appears that Schultz, before arriving at the Cancer Society a year before, had a distinguished record as a pilot in the Royal Canadian Air Force, followed by an honorable discharge at his own request, before entering the services of an ungrateful charitable organization. It would appear that he and Talbot had no rapport right from the beginning. Talbot resented his new assistant and made a point of mispronouncing his name, by calling him "Schlitz," which would have been quite different if Schultz had been in the beer business, but under the circumstances only made him bitter and revengeful.

"My Lord," the Crown Prosecutor begins, "this is perhaps the most serious matter of its kind that has ever been before these courts." In a voice strident with righteous indignation the Crown outlines Talbot's *modus operandi*, described as "a studied and systematic scheme of forgery and fraud designed to deceive the people he worked with and to enable the prisoner to feather his own nest." The litany of heinous crimes goes on and on and looking at the paper mountain of forged cheques and illegal bank deposits, there seems to be nothing left to add.

But the accused is not alone in his time of trouble, and friends and well-wishers from every quarter have assembled to pay tribute to a remarkable man. Approximately 30 credible witnesses have come forward to tell the Court that the accused is really a great humanitarian and that he would go to any lengths to see that the victims of cancer received the financial help they needed. It is patently clear that it did not concern the accused at all that many of the cases he helped were not strictly within the jurisdiction of the Society, or that the proposed assistance had not been authorized by the directors. In Talbot's eyes, they were deserving cases. They needed help and he would see that they got it!

And now, after months of waiting, Talbot's moment is at hand. We have heard from numerous Boy Scouts and the priests from his church, all of whom have extremely high praise for the accused. Dr. Hanley, the psychiatrist, has described his acute depression and his "Messiah syndrome," with a compulsive urge to give beyond his means and help the underdog. But it is Talbot himself who will be his own best witness.

The "Talbot story" as he tells it, is a pathetic and moving narrative. He describes his work with the volunteer workers, known as "the Daffodil girls," with the daffodils becoming a symbol of hope in the battle against cancer. There is now before the Court an image of a truly good man, working with almost superhuman energy to fashion the sinews of war against an insidious and dangerous enemy. The prisoner is making a valiant effort to justify his unauthorized actions with case histories that fall outside the program of the Cancer Society and to explain how he spent public funds on a never-ending stream of cancer patients.

It is a poignant story of Herculean effort, but unfortunately he cannot come up with much chapter and verse to substantiate his behavior. He has created a Frankenstein monster that makes insatiable demands upon his time and energies, and as his peculations mount, Talbot finds himself in a mood of suicidal depression and despondency. He becomes burdened with an non-sharable problem, but it is not clear whether the problem arose from the responsibility of his duties, or whether it was due to the fact that he was short-changing a charitable organization of huge sums of money. By a strange twist of logic, he shows a latent hostility to his board of directors for permitting him too much latitude and freedom. He finds their indifference bewildering and frustrating and their readiness to leave everything to Talbot he finally interprets as a *carte blanche* invitation to help himself to the funds of the Society and to do with them as he pleased. He even makes an oblique suggestion that the accountants for the Society have not been too perceptive or they would have discovered his peccadillos long ago. He seems to have an almost guilty feeling of wanting to be caught, but he has no qualms or pangs of conscience about his efforts to give these people a new lease on life and a chance to become human beings again, even if it takes theft and forgery to do it. His compassion for these wretched derelicts, and a burning desire to help them, are still there, even in his present helpless predicament.

It is crystal clear by now that to Talbot the end justifies the means, and that the constant contact with the malignancies of cancer has warped his personality and caused his moral fibre to disintegrate and decay. He finally describes himself as almost a cancer patient, not so much a victim of the disease, but a victim of the problem. After he had been on the job four or five years the enormity of the cancer problem got to him, and he realized that he was acting in an unprofessional manner and that he should have left. In dramatic fashion, he describes his years of sleepless nights and his bizarre nightmare, always the same, in which he is swept down the turbulent rapids of Marble Canyon, with the directors running along the river banks, jabbering among themselves and paying no attention to poor Talbot drowning down below. His evidence comes to a dramatic conclusion with a sweeping and categorical denial of hidden assets and secret bank accounts anywhere in the world, and the trial has now reached the stage for counsel to sum up their respective positions and await the sentence of the court.

As might be expected, the Crown labors long and hard on the breach of a sacred trust, and asks for the maximum penalty of 10 years imprisonment. I in turn, make as strenuous an exculpatory statement as I possibly can on behalf of my client, who will now throw himself on the mercy of the Court. But before Mr. Justice Kirby can impose sentence, Calgary's Robin Hood has a few final words to say. The learned judge has made it abundantly clear that he regards Talbot's behavior as a gross breach of trust and that he feels the accused has not made any real efforts towards restitution. Nor is the good judge impressed with the psychiatric evidence presented by the accused, nor with his uncontrollable compulsion to help people in need and distress. Most upsetting of all to the Court is the attempt of the accused to pass off the blame for his misconduct to the directors and the accountants, which the judge feels is unwarranted and unjustified. He looks at the accused and asks him if there is anything else he wishes to say.

It is the final hour of the trial and the prisoner has a swan song to sing the like of which has probably never been heard in a Canadian courtroom before or ever will again.

This is what he said . . . . .

My Lord, I knew that you would possibly ask me if I had anything to say before you pronounced sentence. I did prepare a few words during the past few weeks in my cell which I revised from time to time.

I don't feel entitled personally to ask for your merciful consideration in making your verdict. I believe that my actions have precluded this. However, I am deeply grateful to my counsel and my friends, and my shame as I heard them give testimony in my behalf was very great, because I feel I forfeited the right to their friendship and their favor when I first indulged in the actions which brought me here today.

As I look back over these offenses to which I have pleaded guilty, this deep feeling of remorse is qualified by a question I have asked myself many times: "Is it remorse at being caught, or is it remorse because of the crime itself?" Well, I do not think my remorse stems from the day of my arrest, it stems from, oh, about six or seven years ago, from what my counsel has called the beginning of this non-sharable problem. It has haunted my days, and my waking nights until today. My remorse stems from the terrible thing that I have done to these men and women, the volunteers of my organization who have trusted me. They knew, they were completely confident that I would not let them down.

My remorse stems from watching my wife, who has aged 10 to 15 years during the past four months, give evidence at the trial this morning. My remorse stems from a letter I received in the RCMP cells late last evening, a letter from a little girl that said, "Dad, no matter what happens, you are the best," little knowing that the man she thought was the best had feet of clay.

During the 16 weeks preceding my trial I have suffered more than the normal pangs of every man or woman awaiting trial, because of the unusual publicity given to this case. I had to endure some rather extra refinements of punishment, even of torture that I know weren't dreamed of when our laws were made. I refer to trial by news media, or rather trial and punishment and conviction by news media. In the Middle Ages when a man sinned, more often than not he was summarily executed; in modern times, and certainly in my case, he sins and he dies a little bit every day, as the prison radio, at full blast, blares out on the hour every hour the story of his delinquencies, real and imaginative, ad infinitum on and on. The news media have also gone beyond the point of publishing the facts as heard in evidence before the court when they tell of me secreting or squirreling away vast hordes of loot in unknown foreign parts.

I have a document, it is rather an important document to me. It is the commission I received as an officer in the Canadian Army. I can't quite recall how it reads, but it is something like,"His Majesty the King reposing special confidence in your integrity and loyalty." Her Majesty the Queen is against me today, and yet I am not believed when I say that right from the beginning I have in every sense and with every power at my command volunteered to make complete restitution. I still shall do so, but it is impossible to do more than I have done from a prison cell. Before God, I say to you that nowhere in the world, in Canada or any foreign country, have I any assets, in my own or anybody else's name, of which the Crown or the counsel for the Canadian Cancer Society are not aware. The only remaining assets I have and they are probably my greatest ones, are my wife and children, and as long as I have them I will never be completely destitute.

I often think of the overworked truism of there being one law for the rich and one for the poor. I must confess that during the past four months this has made itself rather apparent to me. Although testimony was never given at any hearing about my hidden assets in foreign countries, nevertheless that did appear in the news stories about my case right from the beginning, and it was repeated so often that it became a permanent fact in my trial, and I cannot but help feel that this influenced the setting of my bail which was finally fixed at $50 000. If I had been the crook I was supposed to be, My Lord, I would have had that bail money, but to me it was no bail at all. I have spent 16 weeks in custody, most of it in Spy Hill prison, and because of this, it has been absolutely impossible to give my counsel any assistance whatsoever in making restitution or in the preparation of my defense. In fact, those in custody awaiting trial at Spy Hill are in maximum security and are far more closely guarded than those undergoing sentence. I know this full well and I know that had I been free on bail during these past four months I would have been able to prove my claim that I have given many, many thousands and thousands of dollars to cancer patients by producing the actual bodies to substantiate what I am saying.

May I say just one or two things more, My Lord? There is one aspect of my crime that I would like to emphasize. I was privileged to serve the Cancer Society for 17 years, and during this time I was fortunate, as few men are, to see human kindness and true philanthropy at its finest. In a hundred fields of endeavor, many, many men and women have given their time and the best talents they have to this great cause, that of trying to find the answer to the age-old riddle of cancer. They are trying to do something about it, and they are succeeding.

It is true that I did have certain criticism of the support given to me by my officers over the years, the men and women to whom I have been directly responsible. As I said, I have been a servant of this organization for 17 years and I know so well that much of my service has been worthwhile. I know, despite all my wrong doings, that I have been dedicated to this cause.

You might say, "What, you are looting the Society and yet you claim you are devoted to its cause?" Yes, I believe that to be true. I believe I was, and yet since the day of my arrest, 16 weeks ago, my officers and directors have never bothered to listen to what story I might have to tell. Never have they said, something is terribly wrong here, let's ask Talbot what happened. They chose not only to believe every word of testimony submitted at my preliminary inquiry, most of which was the truth, but a great deal of other scandal and rumor and lies fed to them from irresponsible sources. I feel, My Lord, that the officers and directors of my organization did let me down. They failed me when times were good, and they failed me when I needed them most. Even a simple word, "Talbot, you made an awful mess of things, but over the years you did some good," would have helped me immeasurably— but they never came. Nevertheless the Canadian Cancer Society is the general public. It is the community itself. The officers and directors, the ones that I perhaps have mildly criticized, are merely citizens with a more active sense of responsibility than most. They have taken on the thankless job of giving direction to the wide program that they are carrying out so well. Because of this, the Society itself cannot become tarnished nor discredited by the actions of an unfaithful servant like me. They have got rid of me, now this all-important job remains to be done.

Just a few minutes ago I jotted down some figures about this great work. Since the sun rose on New Year's morning, 1 500 people in Canada have died of this disease. Well, I didn't spend the whole of my service looting this organization for which I have lasting esteem and respect, and this respect and dedication will continue. I helped in a humble way to build it, my heart is with it always.

I have just been thinking that a man is supposed to be composed of a little bit of everybody with whom he has come in contact. If this is so, I will go to my punishment as a convicted felon with some components of devotion, loyalty to the cause, the inspiration of hard-won skills and knowledge, and all of these have been gained from working with some of the finest people I know. These are not the people who should be made the targets of criticism and censure from the press and the subject of scathing editorials; rather these people should be helped to rise above everything that I have done to them and to fulfill their destiny.

I can expect, My Lord, to receive a heavy sentence from you. I expect a scathing verbal castigation from you, and as much as I will take it to heart, as much as I will try to endure the punishment that awaits me, I know that nothing can exceed in severity the pangs and living hell of my own conscience. As I face the future without a friend or a ray of hope, and also I feel, although I probably will have it, without the entitlement to the love and respect of even my own family. Perhaps God in his own good time will forgive me for all of these things, but I wonder if they will?

My Lord, whatever sentence you give me, will at my age and condition, and in the light of what awaits me afterwards, be a light sentence. I do thank you for the consideration you have given to the presentation of my side of the case, and I would like to thank sincerely my counsel, and also my counsel for the prosecution who I believe has been most fair. Thank you, My Lord.

The moving, solemn requiem has ended and pushing back the blond locks of hair from his sweating forehead, Talbot looks expectantly at the judge. He has started to sink down in the prisoner's dock when in terse, succinct words the presiding justice bring the proceedings to a close.

"Mr. Talbot, would you please remain standing. The offense of theft is the more serious charge in this case, because of the large amount of moneys involved. The various offences of forgery you have committed were all part of means by which this theft was affected."

"You are sentenced on the charge of theft to eight years in Prince Albert penitentiary, and on each count of forgery to three years in Prince Albert penitentiary. All sentences will be served concurrently. This is all."

For Bob Talbot the wheel has come full circle. Flanked by the two young constables in scarlet tunics, he weaves his fumbling way out of the courtroom, a broken, ruined man. He has had his day in court and justice has not only been done, it has abundantly been seen to be done. To the worthy citizens of Calgary, this has been an unprecedented case, with the main point still left unanswered: What happened to the money? I still do not know the answer to that one, nor does anybody else, except perhaps Bob Talbot.

If Bob Talbot's answer as to where the money went were accepted at face value, then he was Calgary's Robin Hood, and in his own uncontrolled discretion merely detoured countless thousands of dollars to hopeless recipients who would not otherwise have received any help from the Society. This facile explanation was not accepted by the court, and it was readily apparent that by criticizing the directors, Talbot's sentence was increased from seven to eight years. Maybe it was only human nature for Talbot to reach out for a scapegoat. Behind the boyish smile, perhaps there lurked an arrogant aristocrat, who knew what was best for his liege subjects. For my part, he has satisfactorily resolved my query as to "Why did he do it?"

It would seem he not only had the Messiah syndrome, but as the middle brother of five, he had the middle-child syndrome as well. In many ways he was like Willy Loman in "The Death of a Salesman," or "The Fat Boy" at the circus. He not only wanted to be liked, he wanted to be "well-liked," and he was not deterred at all by the fact that he was buying his reputation for generosity with other people's money. And so the curtain fell on Robert Neville Talbot, a forlorn and broken man who was whisked away to serve his time in Prince Albert penitentiary. Beware of pity was the lesson for us all!

The hellhole of Prince Albert, a maximum security prison, was no place for a man like Bob Talbot, and within two weeks I was able to arrange his transfer to a minimum security institution at William Head Institution, a former quarantine station 24 kilometres outside Victoria.

A year or two later I was in this area, and I drove into the prison to see how my ex-client was weathering the storm. There he was: a stocky, solitary figure coming up the roadway to the main gate. His wavy blond hair was blowing in the wind, and his skin was fresh and ruddy, as if he had spent a lot of time in the out-of-doors. I could see inmates heading for the ocean with fishing rods over their shoulders, and the whole place had the atmosphere more of a country club than a prison.

"Hello, Bob," I called out, "and how is everything going?"

"My," he replied, "am I glad to see you."

He had the expansive, boyish smile on his face I so well remembered, and his great chest swelled with pride as he told me his news.

"Guess what happened today," he said, "I've just been given a new job."

"Doing what"? I asked.

"Well, you know how it is," he went on, "I am now the sports supply officer for the whole jail. I buy golf balls by the gross, tennis shoes by the dozen, all the sports equipment that they need around here. It's a very important job, a position of trust. They trust me with everything. Everything except the money!"

I did not know whether to laugh or cry at this ironic remark, and I just let things carry on their normal course. I never saw him again. He was shortly after paroled on good behavior, and was living in Victoria with his family. In time he obtained a job with the Provincial Treasurer's office of the B.C. Government and has since passed away. One can only speculate as to what he is doing now!

The Trial of Webster Macdonald

One hundred kilometres west of Calgary on the road to Banff there lies a guest ranch known as Rafter Six. Nestled in the foothills of the Rocky Mountains and surrounded by the Stoney Indian reserve, it is a magnificent spot. In the mid-1960s the charms of Rafter Six had gone as far afield as Oregon and Saskatchewan, and competing groups of investors from the prairies of Canada and the west coast of the United States were striving to acquire this great tourist attraction. The Oregon group was based in Portland, and they had deposited $160 000 with the Canadian Imperial Bank of Commerce in Calgary as a down payment on the property and an indication of their intentions to buy the land.

Most of the ranch was made up of Crown grazing leases, but at the centre of Rafter Six was a 20-acre tract of land owned and occupied by Alvin and Eva Gwynn, who had managed the ranch for many years. Options were granted to prospective buyers and down payments were taken from rival investors who were seriously interested in buying the ranch.

By late 1965 the legal position of the Gwynns was by no means clear, and heated and emotional meetings were held at the ranch house to determine which of the various options, if any, was enforceable, and whether or not the Gwynns were obliged to sell and to whom. Following the last of these meetings I was retained by the Portland group to protect their interests and the legal battle was on. In due course, the Gwynns decided that none of the options were enforceable and that they were not obliged to sell to anyone. The gentlemen in Portland felt that they should have their money back and perhaps invest in Hawaii, where things were not as contentious as they were in Alberta. By this time, things were coming to a head and various Calgary firms and lawyers were acting for the different clients involved.

The Portland group, quite understandably, were most concerned about the return of their money, and they came up to Calgary from Portland to get it back. They brought an Oregon attorney with them and attended at the office of the Canadian Imperial Bank of Commerce on 8th Avenue and 6th Street S.W. in Calgary to complete the necessary documentation for the release of their $160 000. All papers were prepared by the bank's officers and duly signed by the president of the American company and the Portland attorney, who was the company secretary. The bank released their money to the men from Oregon, who departed for the United States. I have not seen them since.

I carried on with other matters, and was quietly working in my office on the morning of Saturday, March 5th, 1966 (I can see it now, as if it were yesterday) when I was arrested. It was 10 a.m. and the electric fire was burning in the grate. Buddy, my black-and-white collie, was resting quietly at my feet, when to my astonishment there were four burly policemen in my office, unheralded and unsung. I had been hoping to get away for a winter holiday to Portugal or Mexico and it may well be that they believed I was about to flee the jurisdiction, although for what reason I was not quite sure. One of the three policemen blocking the doorways to the office was Sergeant Frank Van Gastel of the morality squad, whose main occupation in those days seemed to be the pursuit of con men and "paperhangers" and other perpetrators of frauds on an unsuspecting public.

The officer in charge, however, was Police Sergeant Ernie Reimer, who years later became the Chief of Police for Calgary. It was a terrifying moment. Reimer stood across from me with eyes like cold green glass, and prematurely white hair, the perfect model of a Calgary policeman in action. In the corner of his jacket, I could see a stiff white document that I presumed was a warrant for my arrest.

"Well, gentlemen," I looked up and said, "to what great honor do I owe this visit?"

"We're here on business," said Reimer and his voice was hard and stern, as he leaned over my desk and reached for the warrant that was protruding from his pocket.

"You know," I replied with a jocularity I did not really feel, "I did not think it was a social occasion that brought you here!"

"This is a warrant for your arrest on eight counts of forgery. We're taking you to jail."

There was no idle persiflage about the right to engage counsel without delay or constitutional matters of that kind. This was 1966 and the new charter was many years away.

With Calgary's finest barring all the exits, there was no escape for me—not that I had anywhere in particular that I wanted to go. This was a command performance and I was all alone and very much on centre stage.

I reached for the telephone book and dialed the number for my friend and colleague Milt Harradence, who is now a justice of the Alberta Court of Appeal. At that time Milt was the doyen of the Calgary defense bar and I was amazed that I should catch him at home on a Saturday morning, where I gathered he was reading the morning paper. "Webbie," he said, "just be quiet and go with them. You've got yourself a boy [meaning himself]. I'll meet you at the jail."

Without further ado, they took me away, collie dog and all. In 1966 I had been at the Nova Scotia and Alberta bars for 20 years and this whole performance was not really something to which I had become accustomed, and besides it was my son Roger's eighth birthday and we were planning a great celebration for that afternoon.

In short order we arrived at the new police station and I was handed over to the constables on duty, who were ready to book me in. Before that intimidating event took place, one of the arresting detectives approached me .

"Mr. Macdonald," he said. "What are we going to do with your dog? He's over in the parkade and we should let your wife know where he is and what has happened to you."

"Don't worry," I answered. "He'll be alright where he is, and I don't intend to be here that long!"

I was really whistling in the dark and I did not actually feel as courageous as the remark sounded.

Off to the booking office we went, where I was to provide the police with all the vital particulars they needed, such as birth, residence, identification etc., as part of my "criminal record." With great dispatch I was brought before a plain-clothes detective, who was preparing the necessary documents before I was taken off to the cells.

I can see him now. He was a huge man completely bald, with dark horn-rimmed glasses and a blue business suit that seemed somewhat out of place in the Calgary police station. He was right out of the pages of Dostoievski and *Crime and Punishment* was very much on my mind.

I made sure that he had spelled my name correctly, Macdonald with a small "d" as prescribed by Lord Ranald of Clan Ranald, the Chieftain of the Clan Macdonald, and prepared to answer his questions.

We soon got down to my physical characteristics and he asked me the following questions:

"Any marks?"

"No."

"Any scars?"

"No."

"Gentlemen, you are looking at the perfect specimen!"

"Any tattoos?"

"No."

And at this point I made a cheery interjection that I did not really feel. "Gentlemen," I said, "You are looking at the perfect specimen!"

The bald one's eyebrows hit the top of his head, and for the moment he really did look like the lead character in *Crime and Punishment*, and on this happy note the interrogation concluded.

It was Saturday morning and there were not too many bail magistrates to be found anywhere. By this time Milt Harradence had arrived on the scene and for the longest time we paced up and down waiting for a bail magistrate to arrive.

Eventually the Crown found His Honor John Harvie of the Provincial Court of Alberta. It was arranged that the bail hearing should be held before him. As I walked over to Judge Harvie's courtroom, I saw a horde of newspaper reporters rushing off to the bail hearing for this was big news in Calgary. It was not every day that a lawyer and officer of the court found himself under arrest and facing eight counts of forgery. Among the journalists was the snow-capped figure of Tom Moore, a veteran crime reporter with the *Albertan*, who broke all speed records that morning to get a front row seat for this unprecedented hearing.

Fortunately for me, Milt Harradence had brought his chequebook with him. Judge Harvie, in his inscrutable wisdom, set my bail at $8 000, $1 000 for each of the eight counts, and with the banks closed on a Saturday morning and not being in the habit of carrying $8 000 on my person, I had visions of spending the weekend in jail as an unhappy guest of Her Majesty the Queen. Harradence and his chequebook, however, were prepared for this turn of events and I was sprung from durance vile in a matter of minutes. There was no time to lose. We had to prepare for the defense at once, and so poor Roger's birthday party was held notwithstanding, but under sombre circumstances.

What had I done?

I was charged with eight counts of forgery. My clients had taken their own property back to the U.S.A. and I had signed absolutely nothing. So what was it all about? As a lawyer, I had worked with my clients to preserve what both they and I felt to be their legal rights, and somebody, somewhere, felt that this was highly illegal and that the lawyer should be punished. I am sure that if the Portland people could have been extradited, these steps would have been taken, but forgery was not an extraditable offense and the whole Rafter Six matter was so mixed-up and uncertain that no action of any kind was taken against my clients. I was left to face the legal ire of disappointed Calgarians and the would-be investors in Rafter Six.

It was not an easy time. Old friends and fellow lawyers were puzzled by these unusual proceedings. "You have made us uncomfortable and put us in a very awkward position," some of the more charitable spirits would say. "Where there's smoke there's fire," was among other canards, and these were only some of the surface remarks, so I could imagine the things that would not be put to me directly. It was not very pleasant for my family either. On being accosted on the schoolyard of Elbow Park School, little Roger would stand up for his father and say, "He didn't do anything wrong. His clients were the ones who took the money!" He was only eight years old, but he understood.

Nor was it easy as a sole practitioner trying to carry on the practice of law with that great dark cloud hanging over my head. Forgery was one of the most serious crimes in the Criminal Code and carried with it a maximum term of imprisonment of 14 years. Luckily for me, my wife and boys, and my father, who had come out from Nova Scotia to spend the winter with us, knew that I had done nothing wrong and that the whole affair was a nightmare that would soon be over.

With a speedy disposition of the case foremost in our minds, we pushed on for trial. Because of the gravity of the charges and because I was a prominent member of the criminal bar, the case aroused a tremendous amount of interest in the legal fraternity in the city, to say nothing of the various clubs and organizations to which we belonged. We all knew about the presumption of innocence, but when it struck so close to home, the presumption became somewhat academic.

"What a rascal! He must have done something terribly wrong or the police would not have arrested him!"

We have a beautiful legal system in Canada, and the entire process is designed to give an accused person a full and complete defense, and a fair trial. In Alberta one can waive his right to a jury trial, and my counsel and I thought that under all the circumstances it would be best to proceed to trial with a judge alone. And so, even though I had single-handedly enlarged the petit jury in Alberta from six to twelve persons, we elected trial by judge alone without the intervention of a jury.

It worked out very well. We began with a preliminary inquiry before His Honor Frank Quigley, who was to determine whether there was enough evidence to have me committed for trial. The courtroom down in the police station was packed with young lawyers and members of the press. My wife was there every day, as well as friends of mine from the oil patch who took detailed notes of the entire case. A preliminary inquiry is not a trial and there is no plea. The Crown does not have to call all its witnesses. If a *prima facie* case is made out, then the court will commit the accused to stand trial at the next competent court of criminal jurisdiction, when the accused will plead to the charge and be given every opportunity to defend and answer the charges brought against him.

Judge Quigley directed that I remain in the prisoner's dock and would not permit me to sit at the counsel table. A number of witnesses made out a *prima facie* case against me and I was committed for trial on the same bail as had been set by Judge Harvie. As he passed me at the conclusion of the preliminary inquiry, Judge Quigley wished me "good luck," and I got ready to face my accusers.

The toughest part was trying to carry on my law practice as usual, until the trial could be heard the following June. Potential witnesses were scattered across Western Canada and the United States and the logistical problems in assembling our evidence were formidable indeed. The star witness for the defense was myself. It was not a prospect that I anticipated with relish, even though I had done nothing that even remotely resembled forgery.

The prosecutor was the senior agent of the Attorney-General, Mr. E.P. Adolphe and the trial judge was Chief Justice Val Milvain. I was in good hands, but I knew if the evidence was there and I had broken the law, that I would pay the price for my wrong doing, the same as anybody else, and the fact that I was an officer of the court would be of no assistance to me—rather it would be to my disadvantage.

The trial lasted a whole week and the prosecution labored and heaved and brought forth a mouse. I took the stand in my own defense and it was not a happy experience to look down at that crowded courtroom and justify my behavior. I explained to the court that the clients from Oregon had merely released their own money and had taken it back to the U.S.A., in the process signing their own names and at no time resorting to forgery. This evidence, along with the testimony of the manager of the Canadian Imperial Bank of Commerce and the bank's solicitor, Jack Johnson, were more than sufficient to result in my acquittal.

The moment of truth had arrived and it was an intensive and frightening experience for me. At that point in time I was 48 and my career and reputation hung in the balance as I looked up at the wise old judge who held my fate in his hands. His decision was not long in coming. There was an empty feeling in the pit of my stomach, as I leaned forward in the prisoner's dock with my head clutched between my hands. My attention was riveted on the little judge, who gazed down serenely on the packed courtroom. Before he summed up the evidence of the week-long trial, the judge asked me to leave the prisoner's box and proceeded to deliver his decision:

> At the outset I wish to make it known now that I have not the slightest hesitation in acquitting the accused. The accused stood charged on three counts of forgery. As was made clear during the course of the

argument, and admitted very frankly by Mr. Adolphe, in order to attach the accused with forgery it would be necessary, even if a forgery was in fact committed, to attach him with that offense through the force of Section 21 of the Code as an accessory, an aider and abettor, and to do that he had to be fixed with guilty knowledge, because it is absolutely clear that he had nothing whatever to do with the physical making of the documents in question. So that the whole case, in the final analysis, comes down to a scrutiny of what took place with a view to finding whether or not there has been established, beyond a reasonable doubt, that Mr. Macdonald had knowledge.

Now I think it would be a very terrible conclusion if courts were to draw an inference of guilty knowledge on the part of the solicitor because he happens to act for the crook. There are no lawyers who have practiced for any length of time who have not, on occasion, had the misfortune to act for crooks, but that doesn't make the lawyer responsible for the conduct of the client. To draw such an inference would make orderly, decent social life impossible, because I think that the public should know and realize that the most precious thing that we all enjoy is the right of living under the law.

The law of this land is a good law. It is imperfect, of course, because it is a mechanism made by imperfect human beings. It is a thing that must slowly improve and get better. But life under the law would be absolutely impossible were it not for the presence of lawyers in our society. It is lawyers and their interaction on behalf of citizens—just people within the mechanism of the law—that makes social life possible. The duties and responsibilities of a lawyer are high and tremendous. He is placed in an extremely vulnerable position because of the fact that he deals with the secrets of his clients, he deals with the everyday affairs of his clients, he has deep trust placed on his shoulders and he cannot be charged with criminality on the mere suspicions of people.

I find from my observations of the evidence in this case, that not only is there a reasonable doubt, and more than a reasonable doubt, as to Mr. Macdonald's complicity, but I am satisfied beyond any possible shadow of doubt that he had no guilty knowledge whatsoever. He was in the unfortunate position of a lawyer who happened to act for a crook, and because of the fact that the crook got into trouble, we have a professional man charged with these offenses and dragged through a criminal proceeding. It is a matter which society, and those who have charge of these matters should scrutinize with the greatest of care. This idea of prosecuting professional men on suspicion is to me a very, very reprehensible course and one that should not be embarked upon loosely.

At long last my ordeal was over and the agony had abated.

As Jack Major, one of the leading members of the Calgary bar and now a judge of the Supreme Court of Canada said to me, "Webster, he just didn't find you 'Not guilty,' he found you 'Innocent.'"

It will be a long time before the Crown office in Alberta makes a mistake like that again.

After the trial my wife and I and the Commanding Officer of the Canadian Armed Forces in Calgary, my old friend Ned Amy, were walking past the court house. General Amy looked up and said, "There's Adolphe looking out the window and he is crying!" I looked up and it was true. Why was he crying? It was surely not that I had been acquitted, for in English law the Crown never wins, and never loses a case. The Crown merely presents the evidence regardless of the outcome. So why the tears? Speculation on such a question would perhaps be improper and after all these years, the least said, the soonest mended.

The time between my arrest and acquittal was a harrowing time for me. I carried on with my career as if nothing untoward had happened, but I was hurt and deeply angry that any member of the bar could be treated this way. And after it was over I sued them all; Adolphe, the prosecutor, Bill Code, the complainant, who had put the machinery of the criminal law in motion for reasons best known to himself, Judge Harvie for setting what I conceived to be excessive bail and Sergeant Frank Van Gastel, and anybody else who took part in my prosecution. There was only one problem—I could not find a lawyer in Calgary to take my case, until finally Reg Gibbs, who is now a judge of the British Columbia Court of Appeal, agreed to act for me. He issued a Statement of Claim, but shortly thereafter his firm merged with another prominent Calgary firm and pressure was exerted on him to drop the case.

If time heals all wounds, I suppose I have recuperated from this unpleasant experience. I think I have, but I still think that prosecutors and police have no right to hide behind the discretionary provisions of the Public Officers Protection Act, and remain immune and inviolate for their behavior. Bad faith is almost impossible to prove, but it existed in my case, of that I am sure. Or, perhaps the Rombough appeal only three years before, and the disclosure to the Court of Appeal that the Crown had given roses to vital Crown witnesses while they were in "protective custody," had something to do with my prosecution. Maybe that's all part of the game.

Murder at the Turf

By the middle of the 1960s, Calgary was coming into its own as a financial capital, fast becoming the hub of the Canadian oil and gas industry. Ever since the Province of Alberta was carved out of the Northwest Territories in 1905, Calgary had been a city of boom and bust and waves of real estate hysteria were invariably followed by deep recessions. In spite of the recessions, the city had moved steadily forward and was about ready to take off as one of the major financial centres of Canada.

Since the beginning of the century Calgary had been a cattle town, not too different from other prairie cities. All this had changed forever with the oil strike in Leduc in 1947. Calgary's future was assured. It soon had one of the largest concentrations of American citizens outside of the continental U.S.A. and with a fortunate location geographically on the mainline of the Canadian Pacific Railway and the newly constructed Trans-Canada Highway, there was a buoyancy and confidence in the Calgary atmosphere that set the city apart from its western neighbors.

Even to a new arrival in Calgary like myself, it was very soon apparent that there was no organized crime in the city and the criminal element, such as it was, had not yet become a major problem. In those days Calgary was still a cowtown, with the Calgary Stampede, as the greatest outdoor show on earth, the highlight of the year. But the usual forms of metropolitan entertainment, such as good hotels and restaurants, were in short supply, apart from the mighty Palliser Hotel.

Against this backdrop, and not too far from the city jail, was the once palatial Turf Hotel. In its salad days the Turf had been a gathering place for cattle buyers and horsey people, who followed the sulky races with enthusiasm and to whom thoroughbred horses and pari-mutuel betting were a way of life. But the Turf had fallen on evil days. The high rollers and horse-trainers were all gone, and the Turf was inhabited by the halt and the lame, old age pensioners and social welfare recipients who could find nowhere else to go. The Turf was owned and managed by an absentee landlord, who had placed my client Ernie Raymond in charge of the day--to-day operations.

Ernie Raymond was a reticent, soft-spoken man and, generally speaking, not given to violence in any way. He ran his little kingdom in a laid-back, efficient way, and it was no doing of his that the covetous eyes of the Trudel brothers were seeing his domain as a prospective takeover and investment with no down payment required.

The Trudels were small time hoods from the boondocks of Saskatchewan. They found the booming prosperity of Calgary extremely attractive when compared to the austerity and bleakness of their native province. Word had reached Ernie Raymond that unknown persons from out of town were planning to pay him a visit and that shortly there would be a change in ownership. These rumbles filled my client with concern and misgiving.

Calgary in the middle of January is often bitterly cold. The warm chinook winds that float down from the nearby Rocky Mountains can lift temperatures in hours from sub-zero conditions to balmy weather. The night the Trudels planned to visit the Turf, as the first step in the hotel takeover, the ancient structure was paralyzed with freezing temperatures.

The Turf was a very narrow, red-brick building that had been hastily thrown together during one of the real estate booms that had been all too frequent in the life of Calgary.

At Ernie Raymond's behest, a large group of Turf inmates had gathered in the front room of the hotel and a party was in progress. For want of a better name it was christened the Lemon Pie party, as that culinary delight was the *hors d'oeuvre* of the celebration. The stellar attraction of the gathering, however, was a battered old twelve-gauge shotgun, on hand to ward off unwelcome visitors. There must have been more than lemon pie for this festive occasion, and refreshments took the form of a liquid and alcoholic nature. As the evening wore on, various members of the group would take up Raymond's blunderbuss and march up and down the front room like soldiers on parade to demonstrate their military prowess.

Suddenly, to the consternation of all concerned, except Ernie Raymond, who somehow had been forewarned and was expecting trouble, a thunderous knock was heard at the main door. Gary Trudel entered the room, an uninvited and quite unwelcome visitor. Only Raymond knew why he was there, and as Trudel lounged against the open door, Raymond took charge of the shotgun and the party carried on. By this time the celebrations were in high gear. The lemon pie was all consumed, but there was no shortage of beer and wine to enliven up the proceedings. Trudel silently watched the party with a baleful eye. Suddenly and without warning of any kind, there was a violent explosion from Raymond's ancient firearm.

Gary Trudel, with a gaping wound in his hairy chest, fell dead on the floor. The room was packed with eye witnesses to this unfortunate event, and the Calgary police arrived on the scene in short order to apprehend Ernie Raymond and charge him with murder.

The case came on for hearing before Mr. Justice Kirby, a soft-spoken, sympathetic judge and a jury of six, as it was then before the Jury Act was changed. There was no question about the killing, so I put the gun on trial. When it was proven that the murder weapon had a hair-trigger and was a dangerous and obsolete weapon, the jury returned a verdict of manslaughter. Ernie Raymond was sentenced to 18 months imprisonment for an accidental shooting with no criminal intent.

Once again the question of legal fees became somewhat important. There was still no Legal Aid and it was readily apparent that Ernie Raymond had no money to pay for his defense. The owner of the Turf interceded at this point and offered to pay me with the shotgun, which of course was quite out of the question as the gun was the Crown's prime exhibit in court. Money was in short supply and the owner's next gambit was to again offer to pay me in kind, but of a different nature.

"Webster," he said, "How would you like to have a monkey? Not just an ordinary monkey, but a blue monkey that has been beautifully trained by the Hudson Bay store people and is housebroken and a great family pet?"

I was nonplussed and at a loss for words. Over the years I had been paid in barter with household rugs and provender, and such like, but nobody in all my years at the bar had offered me a blue monkey for my services.

"Thank you very much for your kind offer," I replied, "But I will have to consult with the War Office, and see if she would consider your proposal."

The thought of a monkey in the house was just too much for my long-suffering spouse. Five sons, my father, a male dog and an incompetent husband she could handle, but a monkey, even a housebroken blue monkey, was straining my luck to the breaking point.

The rejection of the monkey was clear, firm and unequivocal.

"Webster," said the Duchess of Kentville, tersely and to the point, so there was no room for misunderstanding. "There are enough monkeys around this house already and we don't need any more. It's the monkey or me!"

Guess who won out?

The Queen Can Do No Wrong

For centuries in English law, it has been difficult to take legal action against the Crown. Constitutional prerogatives have protected the monarch from civil suit, and it has been virtually impossible to penetrate the royal veil that throws a cloak around the sovereign, especially in the field of tort.

Witness the problems that confronted the mighty Sir Edward Carson, who wanted to act for the Winslow boy, charged with stealing from HMS *King Alfred*. For years Carson was thwarted by his inability to obtain the necessary fiat from the Admiralty before he could have his case tried in an English court.

Or closer to home, consider the unhappy plight of the British Columbia Indians of the Naas Valley, who after years of litigation, were tossed out in the Supreme Court of Canada in 1974 because they had failed to obtain the necessary fiat from the Lieutenant Governor-in-Council of British Columbia. Millions of dollars and thousands of square hectares of aboriginal territory were at stake in this *cause célèbre*, and all for naught, because of a constitutional requirement that had been part and parcel of the common law for a thousand years.

The two cases I am now about to discuss were heard in Alberta during the period 1965 to 1975, almost 10 years before the new constitution and Charter of Rights and Freedoms became the supreme law of Canada. Although they were both provincial rather than federal cases, they show that the ancient prerogative,"The Queen can do no wrong," and the necessity of a fiat from the Crown were on their way out.

Indeed in Alberta the Proceedings Against the Crown Act of 1959 had dispensed with the necessity of obtaining a fiat under certain circumstances and rendered the doctrine of sovereign immunity virtually obsolete. Nevertheless, to prove the Crown had erred was still a very difficult matter.

In the early sixties I acted for an enterprising gentleman by the name of Fred Hickey, who was manufacturing a type of insulation by heating up native limestone to 1090° C (2000° F), until it flowed like buttermilk before it hardened into a building material known to the trade as "rockwool." For many years energetic Mormons from the south country of Alberta had been quarrying limestone rock for rockwool from pits west of Exshaw on the eastern slopes of the Rocky Mountains. Fred Hickey had taken over their crown leases and was busily churning out rockwool insulation to be sold to the Alberta government as well as to the private sector.

Always operating on a shoestring and hard up for cash, Fred found that his rental payments owing to the provincial government were constantly in arrears. When he came to me, the Crown in right of Alberta was about to move in on him and his rockwool company and take back their crown leases. Working on the principle that the best defense is offense, we sued the government under the Proceedings Against the Crown Act without the necessity of a fiat, and tried to prove that it was the government who was really in default with their respective leases, and that if they would only leave Foothills Rockwool Limited alone, the company could go into production and with the support of huge international building companies in the United States, like Johns Manville, be a great financial success.

This position was vigorously resisted by the provincial government, and they appointed Mr. Blair Mason to defend the case. The matter came on for hearing before Chief Justice Milvain, who during the course of the trial remarked to Mr. Mason that when you are fighting a prairie fire, sometimes the best course is to let it burn. This interjection by the court set the tone of the trial, and at the end of the case, the plaintiff's claim was dismissed.

Mr. Hickey was never one to back off from a fight, legal or otherwise, and in no time we were off to the Court of Appeal. The issues that had seemed so vital to the Chief Justice were not considered of the same importance by the Court of Appeal, and at the end of the day, after much blood, sweat and tears, the Milvain decision was reversed and Fred Hickey was allowed to hold on to his crown leases, including the all-important quarry lease.

After much sheer, unrelenting hard work, and several heart attacks later, Fred Hickey was able finally to go into production. All of this legal manoeuvering and battling took years to complete, but at long last Alberta was in a healthy position economically, due in no small part to the energy crisis and production of oil by the OPEC countries.

A rootless person himself, my erstwhile client was finally able to dispose of his rockwool company and made enough money so that he could set up a sanctuary for the wandering nomads of North America and their huge recreational vehicles. Which proves one important point: you should never let the government—federal, provincial or municipal, push you around. Resist, resist, and resist some more. In the long run, you can wear them down, even if they do hold all the cards. Fred Hickey and his rockwool company were proof of that.

Who can say that the struggle naught availeth?

My other court case with Her Majesty the Queen, as represented by the provincial government, was the incredible case of Anthony Arnold, against the Provincial Treasury Branch of Alberta. Tony Arnold at one stage in his career, had actually worked for the Government of Alberta in the Department of the Attorney General. Tony was a free spirit. He left the security of a civil servant's job to search for precious metals in the wilderness areas of Alberta and British Columbia and live the exciting but uncertain life of a prospector. By good fortune and hard work, Tony was in on the discovery of the fabulous Craigmont copper mine near Merritt, B. C. As a reward for his efforts, Tony was allotted a block of Craigmont stock, and as time went on, he returned to Alberta and settled down in Medicine Hat.

Always an entrepreneur at heart, he was soon developing an unusual coat hanger with quite remarkable attachments. He had been living off the sales of his Craigmont shares, and used much of the money to finance the promotion of his coat hanger. He lodged his last block of Craigmont stock as collateral security with the Provincial Treasury Branch in Medicine Hat, to secure his advances from the bank in order to finance his coat hanger.

His promotional work took him far afield. In the late sixties he left Medicine Hat for Mississippi, knowing that his block of Craigmont stock was safe in the hands of Mr. Manning, the local manager of the Provincial Treasury Branch. He knew that his stock had only been pledged as collateral security and that he would be notified through regular banking channels before any steps would be taken to dispose of it.

Imagine my client's consternation and dismay when, on his return from the United States, he was met at the airport by his friend and banker, Mr. Manning, to learn that his stock had been sold.

"I've got bad news for you, Tony," was the greeting he received. "I thought your Craigmont stock was going to drop in price and as you were away, I unloaded it for you."

Tony was dumbfounded by this news. "But," he replied. "How could you possibly have done that? That stock hasn't gone down at all. To the contrary, it has gone up in price. What are we going to do now? You should never have done what you did and especially without my permission. You've cost me one hell of a lot of money!"

"I'm sorry, Tony," said a contrite Mr. Manning. "I didn't think there was anything else I could do, I was only trying to help you and really believed I was acting in your best interests."

Tony had no choice but to sue, which he did forthwith, and brought action against the bank, known as the Provincial Treasury Branch, under Proceedings Against the Crown Act, and he was not required to obtain a fiat, which at other times and in other circumstances might have proved an insuperable obstacle for him.

The trial came on before Mr. Justice Harold Riley, one of the greatest lawyers and trial judges that Alberta has produced. Judge Riley had an unerring sense for prevarication and he felt somehow that Tony was not telling the whole story. He found against my client and dismissed the case.

Nothing daunted, Tony appealed and in an incredible turnabout, the Court of Appeal of Alberta ruled that the trial judge had erred on a point of law, and in a unanimous judgment awarded Tony damages of $125 000 for the loss of his stock. Tony of course was elated. The provincial government detailed the outstanding Edmonton lawyer, Carl Clement, to come to Calgary and offer Tony $45 000 to settle the case. In hindsight, he should have taken it. Tony rejected the offer, and on the afternoon of the last day of the appeal period, the Provincial Government filed a notice of appeal and we were off to the Supreme Court of Canada.

This time the Crown was represented by Mr. Howard Irving, now a judge of the Alberta Court of Appeal, like his Edmonton colleague, Carl Clement, who had also been appointed to that court. The Supreme Court of Canada, the Court of last resort, restored the judgment of Mr. Justice Riley and dismissed the decision of the Alberta Court of Appeal, which establishes once and for all the truth of the axioms, "Half a loaf is better than none" and "Never look a gift horse in the mouth." There was much weeping and wailing and gnashing of teeth in the Arnold camp, but it was all over, and Tony could only retire to British Columbia and carry on with the promotion of his wonderful coat hanger.

Deep down in the heart of every lawyer, or at least in mavericks, there must be an inborn desire to resist governmental authority—what the late Lord Hewart so aptly termed the New Despotism, the creeping and pervasive growth of the bureaucratic power that destroys individual initiative until you become a cipher, not a name. In that first year at Dalhousie Law School in 1941, our contracts professor was "Gorgeous

George" Curtis, who went on to become the first dean of law at the University of British Columbia.

Professor Curtis once described the role of the lawyer in a few pithy words that have remained with me always.

"Gentlemen," he said. "Never forget a lawyer wears no man's collar."

From that weighty remark, he moved on to discuss the finer points of the law of contracts, like past consideration is no consideration, and similar principles of great importance in commercial transactions. The remark about "the collar" stayed with me long after *Anson on Contracts* was forgotten, and is alive and vital to this day.

This precept attained practical importance for me when our landlord Austen Ford came to me in a distraught condition about the arbitrary arrogance of the federal government as to the way he was running his beautiful summer resort at Lake O'Hara in Yoho National Park. "O'Hara," as Austen Ford called his mountain paradise, was an alpine jewel. You came to it after a 11-kilometre (seven-mile) trek through the mountains from the Trans-Canada highway, and when Austen came to me with his governmental problem, he was low and despondent.

He had just received an edict that his toilet disposal system did not comply with the standards of Parks Canada and that henceforth his sewage waste would have to be taken by truck across the mountains to Field in British Columbia, some 24 km away, at a cost prohibitive to his whole operation. There was no alternative.

"Transport your sewage by truck to Field," they said, "or we'll shut you down." And that was that.

Who ever argues with the Federal Crown? Austen felt that no-one, but no-one ever takes on City Hall, and the park officials were not disposed to discuss the matter further. They had the power to close his operation and if Austen did not respond immediately they intended to exercise that power and brook no delay.

The whole situation was like waving a red flag at a bull. I made my way up to the Lake O'Hara resort and assessed the toilet situation, which had been operating adequately for Austen's company for 35 years or more. We finally engaged engineering consultants, who came up with an alternative solution and introduced us to new equipment just out on the market: a Swedish chemical toilet that could handle all the sewage problems on the spot, and obviate the problem and expense of trucking the waste from the resort over the rugged mountain terrain to Field.

The chemical toilets were quickly installed. After our numerous meetings with the officials of Parks Canada, their arbitrary stand was modified and the bureaucratic insistence that the waste material be trucked into Field was thrown into the discard as if it had never been thought of.

That's what a lawyer can do for you. You *can* beat City Hall and you can beat the Federal Crown too, if you try. All it needs is a certain amount of intestinal fortitude and a modicum of hard work and right and reason will prevail.

A Predatory Tomcat

ꙮꙮꙮꙮꙮꙮꙮ

One of my more memorable cases in Calgary as the sixties drew to a close was *The Queen v. Lionel Llewellyn Staples*. Staples was a thoroughly bad man, a villain of the deepest dye. There is no question he was a criminal sexual psychopath and it was my lot to defend him. Not once did I believe in his innocence, but it was not for me to be his judge. There were Crown prosecutors, homicide police officers, social workers and the judiciary, to maintain law and order and see that lawbreakers were well and truly punished and not allowed to escape the toils of justice.

But who was left to defend the indefensible? It may be an arguable proposition, but I have always believed it is better that 99 guilty men should go free than that one innocent person should be convicted and punished. That is what the system is all about. That is what has made English common law, with its adversary system, a model for the whole world, with its trial by jury and an insistence that all criminal charges be proven beyond all reasonable doubt before a verdict of guilty is pronounced.

It is the defense bar, firmly based on such a system, which stands between the despotism of the modern state and the freedom of the individual. A lawyer who truly believes in these principles has no difficulty in defending the most heinous criminal. It is not for defense counsel to pass judgment on the accused, who has turned to him for help. To the contrary, his duty is crystal clear. He has only one obligation: to defend the accused to the best of his ability, to give him a full and complete defense according to law.

It was on that basis that I strove to defend the accused, Lionel Llewellyn Staples, on the serious charges that the Crown had preferred against him, no matter how overwhelming and damning the evidence appeared to be.

I had come in contact with Staples early in 1960, after first opening my office. He was a rather prepossessing fellow, in a strange sort of way. He told me he was a mulatto, half Welsh and half black, and that his mother's people had come up to Saltspring Island in British Columbia just before the American Civil War by way of the "underground railway."

A dapper little man with close-set eyes and a jaunty imperial beard, he wore a dirty yachting cap which perched on his oversized head like a crown. It was readily apparent he had a fetish for cars, and indeed anything mechanical, and while he worshipped these inanimate things with a blind adoration, he was quite amoral insofar as people were concerned—especially women.

Above everything else he had the small man syndrome, and with a quiet contempt he knew that he could do anything better than anybody, and that in his own way he was a king and born to command. He was barely 153 cm (5') tall with gnarled, thick hands. His physique was slim rather than burly, but on a Harley Davidson motorcycle, or in a Twin Otter Cessna airplane, he was monarch in his own right and the law was a matter of no importance.

With respect to women, and his need for sexual satisfaction, he had a *modus operandi* all of his own. In his huge automobile of the moment, usually a long white Lincoln or Oldsmobile, he was a hungry wolf on the prowl. Always a loner, he roamed the streets of north Calgary in the early hours of the morning, looking for young girls or women, who would be standing patiently at a bus stop waiting for public transport to wherever they were going. Along these deserted streets, in the dark hours after midnight, would come Staples, complete with yachting cap and a long limousine.

The pattern was always the same. At Staples' request, the young lady accepted a lift and stepped into his car so that Staples could take her to work at the hospital or some similar destination. In a matter of minutes he had driven to some deserted field outside the city. There the hapless female would be bound up with cords, gagged and raped and left to her lonesome fate by the ungallant Staples, who drove off into the night.

He was not always successful in escaping capture. When he first came to me in 1960 he had been apprehended at work by the Calgary police at 7 o'clock in the morning, immediately following his sexual assault, when his victim was still able to identify him with ease. As usual, the complainant was a nurse. She had been standing by the curb on the way to the Calgary General Hospital when she accepted a ride from Staples. At this time he was a relatively young man and the Crown did not have a lengthy record to produce against the accused. After the nurse had described her harrowing experience, Staples was found guilty and sentenced to eight years imprisonment in Prince Albert Penitentiary.

The years sped by and I had no word from Staples, until the year 1969. Can a leopard change his spots? I had almost a feeling of *déjà vu* when a call came through from Spy Hill jail and once again I was listening to Staples telling me the same story I had heard almost ten years before, to the effect that he had been illegally arrested and was completely innocent.

This time it was even more serious, for the victim of his sexual attack had died and Staples was facing a charge of capital murder.

It is true, I guess, that the evil that men do live after them. The facts were grisly indeed and the whole *modus operandi* was hauntingly familiar —a throwback to the dark night of 1960 and the crime for which Staples had been previously convicted. Now, however, the victim was dead and Staples was looking at a long term in the penitentiary.

The half-naked body of Robin Banyon had been found by the Calgary Police in a deserted field in Canyon Meadows in southwest Calgary. She had been raped and strangled and shot in the face with an airgun, and it did not take the homicide squad of the Calgary police very long to make an arrest. Staples' love for things mechanical quickly led to his undoing. Some time after his return to Calgary from Prince Albert, he had acquired not only the long-white Lincoln car with expensive Michelin tires, but also an airgun that could fire deadly pellets for the sum of $17.

On the morning of the killing, he got up at 6:30 a.m. to wash the blood stains from his car, his pride and joy. He could not bring himself to destroy or throw away the airgun used to shoot Robin Banyon so he stowed it away in the trunk of his car.

The day after the murder, he was working as a mechanic at a tractor plant when the Calgary police arrived during the lunch hour with a warrant for his arrest for the murder of Robin Banyon. Imagine their surprise and delight when they opened the trunk of his car and found the airgun they were looking for. Staples just could not part with the murder weapon. It would have been so easy for him to have tossed the gun into the Bow River or down a drain, but to have preserved it for the Calgary police was even more than they had hoped for. It explains perhaps why the police generally win in their fight against crime and how the idiosyncrasies of the evil-doers so often play into the hands of the police.

Regina v. Lionel Llewellyn Staples was one of the last criminal trials to be heard by that great jurist, Harold Riley. When Staples learned that Riley was to be the judge, he reelected his mode of trial from judge and jury to judge alone, and consented to trial by a judge, sitting without a jury. With his vast experience behind him, and realizing that the client is sometimes the enemy of his own lawyer, Mr. Justice Riley advised me in private to get written instructions from Staples on this point. I am pleased to report I did just that.

In spite of a spirited attack upon the time of death and the tread of the tire marks in the field, Judge Riley found the testimony of the accused to be a tissue of lies and convicted him of murder and sentenced him to life imprisonment according to law. Staples expressed no remorse over the whole affair and seemed mainly concerned with the effect of his imprisonment on his pilot's licence from the Department of Transport.

While locked up in Prince Albert penitentiary, he made a daring escape through a bathroom ceiling of the prison, but was shortly thereafter apprehended in the hay loft of a farmer's barn outside Saskatoon and returned to jail, where he is presently serving the balance of his sentence.

At the time of Robin Banyon's death, a number of young women in Calgary either disappeared or were found dead on the outskirts of the city, showing signs of mutilation that looked like the handiwork of Staples. After his conviction by Judge Riley, Staples was a patient in the forensic ward of the Calgary General Hospital. With his consent, he was given a truth serum by the prison psychiatrist. While under the influence of the drug, he confessed to several baffling killings and gave directions that enabled the police to discover where the bodies of the women were concealed.

The Staples conviction, following a full, fair and public trial, resolved many unanswered questions about sexual offenses in Calgary. For many years thereafter, the women of Calgary led lives free from the fear of bodily harm and rape that had plagued the city as the 1960s came to an end.

Romania Remembers

When I tore up my roots in the Annapolis Valley and headed for the West, in many ways I had committed professional suicide. I intended to start afresh in Vancouver, so when I took the job with California Standard (now Chevron) in 1957 in Calgary, it was to be a stay of brief duration. As it worked out, I was like the man who came to dinner and stayed six months. No matter how much he knows, a lawyer must have clients to work for. By sheer good luck, the neighbor at my back door in Elbow Park was a wonderful man named Chas de Chastelain.

The name was French, and the accent upper-class Cantabrian, but in actual fact he was a Scot and never let me forget it. He was a man of indefatigable energy. He did all the domestic chores around his own home and was the dutiful secretary-treasurer of every social organization (and they were many) to which he belonged. He promptly dragooned me into service with the Kanukeena Club, a vigorous group of old sweats from World War II, as editor of their monthly newspaper.

The editorial task did not consume too much of my time and was a wonderful entry to the legion of colorful personalities who were Chas's friends. Calgary was a clean, dynamic city and Chas opened all the right doors for me. At that time I had no specific clients, and instinctively gravitated towards criminal work and the trial world, where I conceived all the action to be. Chas and his company, Eastman Oil Well Survey, were my first clients.

Chas and I were kindred spirits and became fast friends. He seemed to know everyone; like Michael Wilding, Elizabeth Taylor's second husband and the top officers from the innumerable consulates set up in Calgary. His closest friends were in the Romanian community. Before the outbreak of World War II, Chas had been working in the Romanian oil fields and the Romanian expatriates who had come to Calgary looked to him as their mentor.

Chas had been captured by the Germans when he bailed out over Italy during the war and was a P.O.W. for eight months in Romania, where he did hand-stands every day in his cell to keep himself in top physical condition. He was small but mighty and with his gleaming bald head and expansive smile, a benevolent Buddha to all. He took me on fishing trips down to Balboa, California and then on a flight up to Yellowknife where his bosom crony, Sandy Cross, had been jailed for drunken driving. We were to bail him out. On our arrival, we found that the bird had flown and our trip was in vain.

Yellowknife in 1959 was a fascinating place where golf had to be played with a closed stance, or the ravens would steal your balls! Where else except in Yellowknife would you find a golf course with no fairway between the tee and the green, and hazards like huge boulders and clumps of bulrushes right in the middle of the course. Chas introduced me to his friend, Jake Woolgar, who Chas claimed was the only man in Canada who could work underground at a temperature of -60° C (75° below F).

And then suddenly my relationship with Chas de Chastelain changed and the idyllic picture was shattered. What had happened?

In 1959 Calgary was casting off the image of a cowtown and emerging as a powerful financial centre, the focal point for 40 000 expatriate Americans who were to make Calgary the oil capital of Canada. As the natives put it to me so succinctly, Edmonton was the warehouse centre for blue-collar workers, and Calgary was the city of the fountain pen. But underneath the oil facade, Calgary was still the red-necked cattle town it had always been. There were only two restaurants of any renown, Hy's Steakhouse and the Palliser Hotel. Four clubs, the Ranchmen's, the Petroleum Club, the Calgary Golf and Country Club and the Glencoe Club, dominated the social scene.

It was a red-necked Wasp-oriented milieu and I quickly sensed I was rocking the boat by taking on the petty criminals and social outcasts I found so intriguing. These were people in trouble, and completely outside the mainstream of the powerful clique that really ran the show in the city.

Poor Arthur Martin lost his job as general manager at the Country Club, when he inadvertently permitted the brothers Viner—Jewish to the core—to come to a gathering put on by the Calgary Chamber of Commerce on their return from a good will visit to the Orient. It reminded me of a sign in Scotland some years back: "No blacks, no women, no Campbells need apply."

In Calgary the Campbells were all right and socially acceptable, but no blacks, no Jews, no Indians, and no petty criminals were tolerated. It was a hard-nosed tightly-knit lot. They did let Ron Ghitter, a high-profile Jewish lawyer, into the Glencoe Club, but he was such an outstanding tennis player they made an exception for him.

And my good friend Chas de Chastelain was an integral part of this invisible social network. My father once said to me, "Remember, Webster, a sober man's thoughts are a drunken man's words."

He was right on the money. It came to a head one night at a cocktail party in my own house in Elbow Park. Chas, his bald head gleaming and eyes misty behind enormous horn-rimmed glasses, took me quietly aside. With no preliminary introduction, he immediately launched into a subject that was obviously causing him considerable distress.

"Webster," he said, "when are you going to stop defending all this human garbage?" I was dumbfounded at this inquiry from such a sophisticated and urbane gentleman like de Chastelain. I could not believe my ears. It seemed that the oil fields of Romania, or perhaps the playing fields of upper-class Britain, were not familiar with the principle of reasonable doubt, or that every man is entitled to a defense and presumed to be innocent until the contrary is proved in a court of law.

From there on it was never quite the same. We had great times together, but I could detect that Chas's reaction was only the tip of the iceberg. By lending a sympathetic ear to the plight of the underdog, I was cut off from the powerful inner circle. Chas would come to my house and play the mouth organ while his son John (who was to become Commander-in-Chief of the armed forces for Canada and Canadian ambassador to Washington) paraded through the house skirling on the bagpipes, but the hurt had been done.

Overnight from being the golden-haired boy, I was suddenly *persona non grata*. Quickly and quietly all the doors were shut. It was unspoken social ostracism, quiet and deep. In those red-necked circles my behavior was unacceptable. When I had the temerity at one social function to speak out in favor of a national flag for Canada, I was taken to task by the host and never invited to his home again! I had some difficulty in adjusting to all of this. After all I was one of the "endangered species" myself. My mother's people had been United Empire Loyalists. We were faithful attendants at Christ Church, that centre of Anglican ecclesiastical establishment in southwest Calgary. To be sure, I was inclined to be pro-American and felt that the U.S.A. was the hope of the world. But was all that terribly wrong? In short order I became an Ishmael from the Far East (Nova Scotia in fact!) who went his own way, defending the down-and-out and anybody else who needed help in their time of trouble. Maybe I had a touch of the Messiah syndrome, and was indeed a loner; like everything in life it had its price.

I saw less and less of Chas and his interesting friends as the years went by. One dark day in the fall of 1973 it came to my attention that Chas had died, and that a funeral service would be held for him at Grace Presbyterian Church. I dropped everything and went over to pay my last respects to my old friend.

The church was filled to overflowing. The Presbyterian clergyman did not know Chas personally and could not do him justice, but Ernest

Watkins, a former writer for the BBC and a local lawyer of great renown, gave the most stirring eulogy I have ever heard. Chas's widow, who had worked with Churchill and the CIA, and his two children were there, as well as a host of Romanian friends he had helped and befriended since World War II. Most moving of all was a great red banner strung across the church below the pulpit. It bore only two words, which are etched indelibly in my memory: ROMANIA REMEMBERS.

Law Professor On Trial

The strange case of Keith Latta came down to me from Edmonton, where all of the main events in the case had taken place. I first conferred with the ex-law professor when he was a prisoner in Drumheller penitentiary. His criminal trial and appeals were over and he was about to start serving a life sentence for murder.

Apart from his professional duties and his inventions in the field of legal computers, Latta found time to be a dormant partner in the travel business in Edmonton with a flamboyant gentleman named Robert Neville. By 1968, or thereabouts, Latta had wearied of the Edmonton scene and moved himself and his family to Queen's University in Kingston, Ontario, where he had accepted a position as a full-time professor of law.

It was a grisly case. Latta had been born and raised in east Edmonton and for a number of years was a professor of law at the University of Alberta in that city. A dapper, soft-spoken little man, he was obviously highly intelligent, and long before the day when computers and memory banks were just emerging to revolutionize every aspect of the business world, the law professor and his friends at Queen's University were working on a pioneer legal retrieval system that was eventually turned over to the Department of Justice in Ottawa.

Back in Edmonton, Neville was running a travel business, with incursions into local politics and following the horses at the local race-track. He also found time to make frequent gambling junkets to Las Vegas and Hawaii. Latta would come back to Edmonton from time to time to see how things were going in the travel business and to check on other matters that were of interest to him in his home town.

Things fell apart one Sunday morning in November of 1971. The travel office was in the Corona Hotel building at the corner of 109th Street and Edmonton's main thoroughfare, Jasper Avenue. According to Latta, he had arranged a meeting with Neville that Sunday morning to straighten out a few business problems and around 11 o'clock was in the photocopying room making copies of some business documents to show to Neville. As he was hard at work on the photocopier, Latta heard shots in the outer office and rushed out to find his partner dead on the floor. The killer or killers fled from the scene, and in their haste left behind them a key to a locker in the Edmonton bus depot. For some inexplicable reason Latta did not call the Edmonton police. Instead he picked up the key and, realizing that it was for a locker in the Edmonton bus depot, just a short distance away, made his way to the terminal and opened up the locker. Inside he found a Michelin map of Italy and a street directory for the city of Edmonton, all of which convinced Latta that the killer or killers were professional hit men, and that the fine hand of the Mafioso was involved in the slaying.

Instead of advising the police that his old friend had been murdered, as most people would have done, Latta quickly made his way back to Kingston and within two days was at the office of the London Life Insurance Company, requesting that the proceeds of the double indemnity insurance policy be paid over to himself.

All of these manoeuvres aroused the suspicions of the Edmonton police, and in a matter of days, Latta was arrested and brought back to Edmonton for trial. Latta and his counsel, the late Mr. Justice Cameron Steer, elected trial by judge and jury, before the then Chief Justice Val Milvain. When the smoke finally settled, the former law professor was found guilty as charged and sentenced to life.

For some unaccountable reason, Latta had declined to take the stand in his own defense, which would have provided him with the opportunity to tell his version of what had happened. No person is obliged to incriminate himself or to testify, if he does not wish to do so. Was he afraid of the merciless cross-examination of the Crown Prosecutor, Bill Stainton, who committed suicide almost immediately after the trial? Or did he abstain on advice of counsel?

I have spoken to them both on this pivotal question. Latta would have you believe that he wanted to testify in his own defense, but that his counsel urged and persuaded him not to do so. Mr. Steer's position was that he strongly requested Latta to testify, but for reasons best known to himself, Latta refused to take the stand. Perhaps these are might-have-beens of history at this late date, but in any event the accused chose to remain mute and one can only speculate on what impact the testimony of the accused might have had on the outcome of the trial.

Still, Latta yearned to have his day in Court. His strategy was to sue the London Life Insurance Company for payment under the double indemnity provisions of the insurance policy, which would provide him with the opportunity to give the evidence he wished he had given at his criminal trial—notwithstanding the well-known common law principle that no one can profit from his own crime.

And so I took up the cudgels for Professor Latta. The case proceeded along the ordinary channels of a civil trial with pleadings and pre-trial discoveries, and eventually the matter came on for trial in the Supreme Court of Alberta in Calgary. This time Latta, as the plaintiff, did testify and at length. He was on the stand for some six hours, during which time he described in full and complete detail the fateful events of that Sunday morning when Robert Neville was shot to death.

The whole case turned on the credibility of the law professor, and Mr. Justice Ken Moore just did not believe him. The plaintiff's case was dismissed and an appeal to the Appellate Division met with a similar fate. The last legal step was taken in an application for leave to appeal to the Supreme Court of Canada, which was also refused.

When the application came on for hearing before a panel of three judges in Ottawa, the hearing which ordinarily took about 15 minutes lasted three-quarters of an hour. Finally, Mr. Justice Ron Martland, who was acting as Chief Justice, looked coldly down at me and tersely remarked, "The trial judge heard him at length Mr. Macdonald, and did not believe him." That was the end of the lawsuit. It was game over, indeed!

During the course of these legal proceedings, Latta was a serving prisoner at William Head Institution, a minimum security institution outside Victoria on Vancouver Island. I made several visits to see him while he was in prison and found him to be a most unusual person. Among other things he was busily causing a book to be written protesting his innocence, entitled *A Matrix of Evidence*, as well as laying out a golf course for the benefit of the inmates of William Head.

Shortly before my last visit to see Latta, someone had driven a golf ball through the warden's window. Latta was the most likely suspect, inasmuch as the golf course was his project, so in due course he was brought before the warden to give his explanation for this unfortunate event.

On being asked directly whether he had been responsible for shattering the warden's window, he replied, "No, Warden, I don't know who did it, but it wasn't me. That hole is 249 metres (272 yards) long and I just can't drive that far!" This time he was successful and it was case dismissed!

Win, lose or draw, Latta was a fighter to the end. Fresh evidence, in the form of testimony unknown at the time of the criminal trial, was proffered by unexpected witnesses, but was not accepted by the court. An Edmonton bus driver was prepared to give evidence that he had seen two swarthy men, running down Jasper Avenue from the Corona Hotel shortly after 11 o'clock the morning of the shooting. The court felt that this evidence was too far fetched and flimsy to be worthy of belief. A woman from Edmonton, who had married the foreman of Latta's jury, wanted to tell how by an incredible chance she had overheard conversation in a Las Vegas gambling casino that pointed conclusively to a gang plan to kill Robert Neville. Her proposed evidence was rejected as hearsay.

And in Hawaii there was the strange shooting of Hymie Garshman of Edmonton's Garshman's Travel, which Jack Moxam, a private eye hired by Latta's wife to investigate the case, felt was vitally connected with Neville's gambling debts in Las Vegas and his travel business in Hawaii. Once again this was long on speculation but short on proof and the conviction of Keith Latta on circumstantial evidence remained unshaken. Long after the case was over, I met the chief of the Edmonton homicide squad, who had been in charge of the Latta investigation. He summed the whole matter up quickly and succinctly. "We knew that Latta didn't pull the trigger, but he had set the whole thing up and as a party to the offense he was equally guilty."

Time marches on. The last I heard of the Lattas, his faithful red-haired wife, who had stuck to her husband through thick and thin and years of tribulation, finally obtained a law degree for herself from Queen's and divorced the professor.

Latta had been released on parole after serving 10 years of his sentence. I have it on reliable information that while on parole he was caught forging travellers' cheques in Port Alberni, British Columbia, and is now back in prison serving the balance of his sentence.

This leaves nothing more to be said.

The Loss of Spiritual Paradise

I did not quite know what to make of the Zebroskis when they first came into my office in 1976 but soon realized they had no ordinary story to tell.

From the outset there was no doubt that for many years the Zebroskis had been faithful adherents to the religious tenets of their church. Their belief was unquestioning and deep. Indeed, it was their disagreement with the interpretation of Holy Writ, as laid down by the church elders, that led to dissension with their spiritual leaders.

The tiny sect the Zebroskis belonged to had been embroiled in legal battles about their faith since the turn of the century. They had stood firm on what they felt to be revealed truth, regardless of the consequences, as they waited for Armageddon and the Last Judgment to arrive.

Their central organ of truth was the Watchtower Tract and Bible Society, based in Pennsylvania. The fact that there had been fallacious predictions in 1914, 1915, 1918, 1942 and 1975 that the world was coming to an end did not affect the hard-core believers, who were certain that they would be among the chosen 144 000 souls to escape eternal damnation when the fateful day arrived.

It was plain to see that the Jehovah's Witnesses were a people with a very unusual background. Ever since their church was founded in New York state about 1875, they had been stubborn non-conformists standing apart from the main stream of religious thought in North America, always ready to do battle for what they felt were their constitutional rights and liberties. In many ways they conceived themselves to be the special guardians of the freedom of unpopular causes and fought with outstanding success for their beliefs.

This was the case towards the end of World War II in the province of Quebec, where the Witnesses had resisted the formidable power of the Roman Catholic Church and the political might of Maurice Duplessis, who had ruled the province as his own private fiefdom for decades. In Quebec, where religious intolerance was the norm, the Witnesses had been granted the right to worship as they pleased, to distribute their proselytizing pamphlets at the street corners of major French-Canadian cities and to hold onto a restaurant license when it had been wrested from one of their followers for specious reasons. They had made "bail" and "habeas corpus" living symbols of justice at a time and in a place where they were generally overlooked or ignored.

The Witnesses were freedom fighters on the ramparts of justice. One could only admire their courage and tenacity as they fought for the principles in which they so deeply believed. They were convinced, for example, that blood transfusions were against the Word of God, and that under no circumstances should a Witness resort to a practice of this kind.

Such unorthodox and unconventional beliefs did not endear them to the general public and the news media. But then, public approval was not a governing concern as far as the faithful were concerned, who apparently never felt involved in a popularity contest. Looking back at the bloodletting practices of nineteenth century medicine, and the present day fears and hysteria about AIDS and the HIV virus, who can say the Witnesses were wrong?

The factual context of the Zebroskis' case was neither complex nor difficult. For many years after the end of the Second World War, Michael and Helen Zebroski, as a husband-and-wife team, had worked tirelessly to construct Kingdom Halls for the Jehovah's Witnesses and to spread the teachings of the church throughout Alberta, as laid down and approved by the elders of the governing body. The Zebroskis for the most part concentrated their efforts on their own church, known as Kingdom Hall in Tuxedo Park, Calgary.

It was a two-way street. In return for their physical labors and evangelical work, the Zebroskis entered into what they felt was a spiritual contract with their church whereby at the time of Armageddon they would be among the 144 000 chosen souls to enter a celestial paradise and receive their heavenly reward.

As true believers, the Zebroskis further undertook to remain childless until Armageddon arrived. Throughout this period of dedication, the Zebroskis had been supported and uplifted by the teachings of the Bible as revealed by the scriptural interpretations from the Watchtower Tract and Bible Society in far-off Pennsylvania.

It was at this point that the confrontation between the Zebroskis and their spiritual mentors took place. The Zebroskis steadfastly maintained that the ministerial servants and circuit supervisors of the Tuxedo Park congregation had lapsed from grace and fallen into spiritual error. This, they claimed, was manifested in misinterpretation of Holy Writ and the teachings of the Bible.

Who was telling the truth?

The Zebroskis interpreted and followed the word of God according to their own knowledge and beliefs and refused to accept or abide by the precepts and directions of the governing body.

The wrath of the elders was swift and deadly.

The Watchtower Tract and Bible Society, as the supreme governing body of the Jehovah's Witnesses, through the elders of the Kingdom Hall in Tuxedo Park in Calgary, moved quickly to expel and excommunicate these troublesome apostates. In short order the Zebroskis were disfellowshipped from the church which was the be-all and end-all of their lives. In a matter of moments, in a kangaroo court without benefit of counsel, the two faithful and tireless workers were found guilty of heinous sins against the teachings of the church and were immediately ostracized by their fellow parishioners and former friends. In effect, they were spiritually condemned and hurled into outer darkness. And all without a fair and impartial hearing of any kind.

Was this not a denial of the most elementary principles of natural justice? But what remedy did they have, since all of this took place before the repatriation of the Canadian Constitution and the Charter of Rights and Freedoms?

After months of examining Scottish and American precedents that shed some comforting light on their unhappy predicament, I issued a Statement of Claim in the Court of Queen's Bench of Alberta on the Zebroskis' behalf.

The fight was on! And lasted for years!!

To the Jehovah's Witnesses, the Zebroski's claim was serious business indeed. The allegations went to the heart of their religion. If these threats were left to go unchallenged the effect could be far-reaching and have serious impact on a religious body which was attracting millions of converts and followers all over the world.

At that time the unquestioned legal champion of the Jehovah's Witnesses in Canada was the renowned W. Glen How, *QC*, in Toronto, who had won a number of contentious lawsuits for his church over the years.

Under the watchful eye of their eminent counsel, the church moved with dispatch to strike out the Zebroski's Statement of Claim. Expert ecclesiastical lawyers were brought down from Edmonton to assist Glen How and a full-scale attack was mounted to blow the Zebroski case out of the water. On a sultry afternoon in the summer of 1980 the Zebroskis faced their moment of truth in a special hearing in the Alberta Court of Queen's Bench before his lordship Mr. Justice William Medhurst.

Various allegations were submitted to the court, ranging from libel and assault to loss of property rights and excommunication. But to the

Zebroskis there was only one issue, the proper interpretation of Holy Writ as enunciated by the Watchtower Tract and Bible Society. Nothing else mattered. Degrading assaults, humiliating defamation, denial of children, social ostracism, kangaroo court hearings, and disfellowshipping were all incidental.

To the Zebroskis the only matter of substance was the gospel message and its alleged subversion by the Tract and Bible Society through the elders of the Tuxedo Park "authorities" in Calgary.

The Zebroskis' complaints fell on deaf ears. Though he did not say it in so many words, the learned judge seemed to feel there was a separation of church and state in Canadian jurisprudence and that the proper forum to deal with the excommunication and disfellowshipping of the Zebroskis was in the ecclesiastical tribunals of the Jehovah's Witnesses, rather than the secular courts of the land.

As the Jehovah's Witnesses church expands around the world, it is interesting to watch the power struggles and changes of goals taking place within the church. There are countless Witnesses, of course, who are anxious to be among the 144 000 true believers who will escape damnation at the time of Armageddon, in spite of the false prophecies announced about the imminent end of the world and the Last Judgment that is at hand. And then there are the Witnesses who are more concerned about the proper interpretation of Holy Writ and related matters like blood transfusions. It appears that the number of disfellowshippings and lawsuits against the church are on the increase and there are many more disenchanted Witnesses now than some years ago.

And against all odds, financial, emotional, and otherwise, the Zebroskis have battled on with their legal crusade. Whatever damages have been awarded them for personal injuries sustained, they are no solace or answer to the complaints that have tortured them for years.

- Have the Jehovah's Witnesses in Pennsylvania properly interpreted the gospel message?
- What would be adequate compensation for the loss of a spiritual paradise?
- Can there be a monetary value placed on a failure to procreate children?
- Is Armageddon at hand?

These fundamental questions, posed by the Zebroskis, remain unresolved.

The Fall and Decline of Billy Freek

His name really was Billy Freek and he came from Pincher Creek, down in the foothills of southwestern Alberta. I well remember the beautiful October day in 1977 when he walked in off the street to tell me his bizarre story.

Although his name was rather unusual, there was nothing very imposing about his appearance. Mousy and nondescript, he was just under average height and slightly stooped, with sharp black eyes peering out from a great pair of horn-rimmed glasses. He looked like a scientist a little out of touch with the problems of the everyday world. His voice was high-pitched and almost effeminate.

Our interview began in a very ordinary way. He wanted me to draw a will for him, and this, of course, I was quite prepared to do. He explained that he was a science and math teacher in one of the high schools in Calgary, up from the ranching country near Pincher Creek. The Freek family was of Dutch ancestry, which accounted for his rather peculiar name.

It became evident that Billy Freek was obsessed with a hidden anger. His fixed goal in life was to clear his good name from the vile accusations and calumny heaped upon him. Childless and now living alone in a small bungalow in north Calgary near Confederation Park, he had married a Hungarian nurse late in life, from whom he was divorced and on bitter terms. This lady, according to my client, had been married four times, and by the time he came in to see me she was living in eastern Canada.

An interesting challenge. The drawing up of the will was straightforward, but as far as I was concerned, an exercise in futility. Billy wanted me and his psychiatrist to be co-executors of his will but in view of the disparity in our ages (Freek was 51 and I was 58) I did not see any likelihood of being called upon to act as his executor in the event of his death.

As it turned out, eight months later Billy Freek was dead.

I immediately probated the will, but found that his proposed co-executor was not interested in the problems of Billy Freek. In short order this gentleman filed a renunciation of probate and I was left alone with an intriguing problem on my hands. How can you clear anyone's good name? The lines from Shakespeare's *Othello* came to mind!

> *Who steals my purse, steals trash . . . but he*
> *that filches from me my good name robs me*
> *of that which not enriches him and makes me poor indeed.*
> *(Othello, Act III, Scene III.)*

It was a very modest estate, less than $35 000 and by the time the mortgage had been paid off on his house and a release obtained from the surviving members of his family, there was very little money left to work with.

It seemed to me that the only way open to clear the reputation of Billy Freek was to have a story written about him and make it known to the public. That was not going to be an easy task. In cold fact, there was very little out of the ordinary in Billy Freek's life as a schoolteacher, and all in all, he had led rather a humdrum existence.

He was a Mr. Everyman in the blackboard jungle where he aspired to be an avant-garde teacher. It was a formidable task to turn a rather lacklustre career into an exciting story that would hold the interest of the general public and clear his good name in the process. The problem was to find a first-class free-lance journalist who would take on this assignment.

I felt that I had an obligation of trust to my deceased client to do everything I could to clear his good name, so I searched far and wide to find competent writers to tell the story of his life. I finally found two people who felt they could do the job. One was a free-lance journalist and the other a Moravian Minister.

Both tried to tell the Freek story in a compassionate way, portraying him as an educator before his time, and as the kind of man who just did not fit in to the Calgary public school system of 1977. I provided these two writers with all his papers and correspondence, as well as his tapes, and between us we tried to reconstruct the unhappy story of a lonely, driven man.

When the pieces were put together, a picture was formed of a man in the eye of a storm raging against him from every quarter. He was the centre of attack from his students and his fellow teachers and his ex-wife, or so he thought. He was probably paranoid about the whole thing, but it would appear that there was some evidence to support the phobias he developed about his enemies.

In the classroom he was harassed and taunted by obstreperous teenagers who would ask impertinent questions like, "Please sir, what is a queen sir?" or, "Please sir, how would you like to lay me, sir?" and many obnoxious remarks in a similar vein.

At teacher meetings, he felt that although he was the object of snide and derisive remarks, in reality they were jealous of his avant-garde techniques that made his students highly successful and leaders in their classes.

His tapes were eerie and depressing. They took the form of long rambling monologues, for the most part directed against his ex-wife in which he described her as that "viper in my bosom." Undoubtedly this provided him with emotional release and satisfaction, as he hurled his diatribes at an unsuspecting woman who neither heard the accusations nor was given an opportunity to reply.

As his persecution complex became more acute, he included the Calgary police as part of his delusions. This aspect of the matter would seem to have been mostly in his mind and there was no hard evidence that I could see to support his belief that he was the object of police observation or attention.

He was quite irrational about the Calgary police and felt that they were hounding him unmercifully. In particular he complained about a police X-ray machine with a blinding light they focused on him. This gave him splitting headaches for days afterwards. Needless to say there was no evidence of any kind to support this bizarre allegation.

The two stories produced by the free-lance journalist and the Moravian Minister as to the sad demise of Billy Freek were not entirely to my satisfaction. So with only a few dollars left in the estate, I cast about to find some biographer who could do justice to my client.

I interviewed countless writers in Alberta and British Columbia to find someone who would take on this virtually impossible task. Finally I discovered a feature writer in Calgary named Suzanne Zwarum and she agreed to write a play about my client's life that might be suitable for television. I was delighted at the prospect and for two months Zwarum closeted herself with the Freek files and wrote a play in two acts which she called "The Rise and Fall of Billy Freek."

It was a first-class effort and I was sure at last that I had a production which might have satisfied Billy Freek if he were still alive. By this time funds had run out, but I shipped the manuscript to the Canadian Broadcasting Corporation in Ottawa, where it still remains as far as I know.

Game over, but it had been a fascinating task just the same. Who killed William Freek? The official death certificate would have you believe the cause of death was a heart attack. I believe he died of a broken heart, the victim of his own persecution complex and all the factors, both real and imaginary, that eventually led to his breakdown and death.

He really was a Mr. Everyman of Calgary, an unprepossessing school-teacher, a kindly, talented, decent man, who just could not measure up to the stresses of modern society and who cracked up when he could take no more.

God bless you, Billy Freek.

The Therapeutic Abortion of Amy Mang

By 1979, the whole question of abortion or no abortion was a serious problem in Canada and the pro-life, pro-choice factions had drawn their battle lines and taken up immovable positions from which there was no retreat. The abortion clinics of Dr. Morgentaler were springing up across the land. The crusaders on this emotionally charged issue were prepared to serve time in prison rather than tolerate a law that they felt was contrary to the will of God.

In Canada, this frightening problem had been answered for the moment by the provisions in the Criminal Code of Canada which provided for a therapeutic abortion if the medical condition of the woman warranted an operation. I had never had a medical malpractice case before and was deeply interested when Harry Mang, a one-time policeman from Hong Kong, consulted me about the circumstances surrounding the therapeutic abortion of his wife Amy.

The Mangs and their two children had come to Canada in 1977, and when Amy, a former model, found she was pregnant with her third child, she wanted to have an abortion. This decision did not meet with the support of her husband, who apparently opposed the whole matter for reasons never fully disclosed, but in due course Amy Mang applied to the Calgary General Hospital for a therapeutic abortion as permitted by the Criminal Code of Canada.

The application was reviewed by the Therapeutic Abortion Committee as a routine case, when it was examined at the Tuesday luncheon meeting by the medical officers of the hospital. Based on a psychiatric report that Amy Mang was a fit and suitable candidate for a therapeutic abortion, and with the other preoperative tests apparently in order, the application was approved and she was admitted to the hospital. After being carefully examined by an anesthesiologist prior to the operation, she was given a clean bill of health. Neither the nursing staff or the gynecologist noticed anything unusual about her condition and yet something went terribly wrong. When the abortion was completed, a healthy Chinese female, 32 years of age, had become a vegetable with symptoms of irreversible brain damage.

What had happened?

Were the doctors at fault?

Was the hospital negligent in any way?

It was a medical conundrum with no answers of any kind forthcoming. The lovely model from Hong Kong could now barely lift her head. Her eyes were glazed and she could only talk in a whisper. Something inexplicable had gone wrong, and what should have been a routine operation had turned into a horror story, leaving Amy Mang a cripple for life.

The hospital authorities were as baffled as her husband. The patient's chart became thicker and thicker as doctor after doctor examined Amy Mang. No one could explain what had happened to her.

Harry Mang reviewed the whole situation with almost stoic impartiality. He did not show anger toward the doctors or the hospital for what had happened to his wife, but he was adamant in his determination to find out why a normally simple operation was not successful.

The great Mr. Justice Porter of the Alberta Court of Appeal once said, "Mr. Macdonald, every trial is a search for truth." How profound those simple words were. On the surface, the case of *Mang et al v. Moscovitz et al* was a medical malpractice suit, in which the Mangs were seeking to establish negligence against the medical establishment of Calgary, with enormous damages flowing therefrom, resulting in the pitiful plight of Amy Mang following her surgery.

Harry Mang was determined to solve the medical conundrum. It was transparently obvious that his wife had suffered a terrible trauma, but his overriding concern was to unravel the medical cause for her suffering, and the legal ramifications of medical malpractice were of secondary importance to him. The nursing reports told him nothing. The post-operative reports by the medical doctors gave him no help.

It was clear beyond any doubt that Amy Mang had sustained permanent and irreversible brain damage which was not related in any way to the gynecological procedures performed during the course of her abortion. The case was a mystery to the entire medical profession. None of the specialists consulted could throw light on the matter. And while the experts examined Amy Mang, and gave learned opinions as to the cause of her injury, she became thinner and weaker until her life hung on a thread.

Harry Mang desperately needed an expert of his own and did not know which way to turn. In the first place he was penniless, and could not have afforded a specialist, if indeed one could have been found. Quite apart from the financial problem confronting him, the medical profession had closed ranks—no local doctor was prepared to come forward and criticize the skill and competence of his fellow physicians. To have brought in a qualified surgeon from the United States or outside Alberta was too great a monetary hurdle for Harry Mang to surmount.

A medical malpractice case is difficult enough at the best of times, but without an independent expert on our side, the battle was virtually hopeless. I glumly explained to my client that in Canada only 15 percent of the cases against doctors and hospitals had been successful in the past, and that the future for our lawsuit was anything but promising.

At this precise moment a glimmer of hope broke on the horizon. It came to my attention that a learned medical doctor east of Calgary had heard about our case and was prepared to testify on Amy Mang's behalf. There was only one drawback. He was an experienced surgeon, true, but he was serving a life sentence in a Drumheller penitentiary for murder. As Sherlock Holmes once remarked to the faithful Doctor Watson, "When a medical doctor becomes a criminal, he is the most dangerous criminal of all."

Undoubtedly Dr. Glen Stewart would have qualified for this description. After seven years as a surgeon in the Toronto General Hospital, he had gone west to British Columbia to carry on his medical practice. While on Vancouver Island he locked horns simultaneously with the Royal Canadian Mounted Police, the Department of the Attorney General and the Roman Catholic Church, any one of whom would have proven a formidable adversary.

Guess who lost?

The energetic doctor abandoned his wife and relocated at Smithers, a remote village in the mountain fastnesses, 1 000 kilometres (600 miles) north of Vancouver. Stewart was a man of considerable personal charm, and shortly after his arrival in Smithers he became more than friendly with the hospital dietitian. Under suspicious circumstances, the doctor and his lover returned to Vancouver Island en route to San Francisco. But tragedy lay in his way. While bivouacked at an abandoned logging camp belonging to MacMillan-Bloedel, the doctor had a violent argument with a young hippie, who was acting as caretaker for the camp. Words led to blows and in the ensuing struggle the doctor split the young man's skull open with an axe and then proceeded to dismember his body with surgical precision.

The star-crossed couple fled to Nanaimo, where the doctor drove his vehicle into the harbor to escape detection. They then stole a boat and set out for the United States. A storm arose and the lovers were rescued by the U.S. Coastguard and turned over to the Canadian authorities. In due course, the doctor was convicted of murder and sentenced to life imprisonment.

While serving his time in Drumheller penitentiary, Dr. Stewart had learned of the unhappy fate of Amy Mang and volunteered his medical expertise to help her.

In due course the case came on for trial in the Alberta Court of Queen's Bench before Mr. Justice Russ Dixon, sitting without a jury, and lasted for almost two weeks. Amy Mang's doctors were represented by the redoubtable Jack Major and the Calgary General Hospital by Jack Smith, now deceased. The learned trial judge felt that "in all conscience" he could not hear evidence from Dr. Glen Stewart, and the willing doctor's application to testify as an expert in this bewildering case was politely but firmly rejected.

The gynecologist and the anesthesiologist satisfied the Court that the entire operation had proceeded with the fully informed consent of Amy Mang. The judge accepted the expert testimony of an eminent neurologist that the injuries had been caused by an embolism no one possibly could have foreseen or detected.

A short time later, Amy Mang was dead.

The Lion of Red Deer

I was never quite sure how Bob Sayers discovered me. For many years he had been a professional litigant, bouncing back and forth between the courtrooms of Calgary and Red Deer in pursuit of the elusive dollar, but he never lost sight of the fact that there was real money to be made in fighting oil and gas fires, like Red Adair was doing down in the oil fields of Texas. When he walked into my Calgary office, having gone through a number of lawyers in Calgary and Red Deer, I was only mildly excited about his claim against Shell Canada Resources.

Shell was one of the Seven Sisters, as they were known in the oil patch, and a giant in the industry, not to be taken lightly. After Sayers presented his bill for services rendered to them, Shell took the position that he was an unprincipled rogue and circulated defamatory reports about him all over the world, to the effect that he was deceitful and a liar and untrustworthy and incompetent.

I listened to this burly fellow, with his strong handsome face and ingenuous smile and the more he described the facts of the case, the more I felt he had a valid claim, if we could only get on to trial. For an uneducated man, he was beautifully articulate, with all of the facts and figures of his claim at his fingertips. He was quite winning in his way, but it was very plain to me that this was a man of steel, who would press on for years if necessary to prove his point. By the time the case reached my desk, it had been before the courts for almost five years and he was not about to give up, even for a moment.

In his own way he was a very ingenious gentleman. Although he was perennially broke, and he knew that a civil jury was an expensive procedure, he was determined to have a jury trial, as he felt that a jury would be more receptive to his David-and-Goliath claim than a judge sitting alone. On this point he was dead right.

The backing and filling between the Shell lawyers and myself over the jury problem went on for months, from the chambers judge to the Court of Appeal and back again. Finally Sayers, the man of iron, wore the oil company down, and it was resolved that there were questions of fact eminently suitable for a jury to decide.

Sayers was off to a good beginning now that he had secured trial by jury, but he was far from home. The trial took place in the Court of Queen's Bench of Alberta, before Mr. Justice Peter Power, sitting with a jury, and required approximately ten court days to try. Counsel for Shell Canada was Don Sabey, a Mormon advocate from the south country, and a dogged little man of enormous energy and ability. He was assisted by a young lawyer, Roddy Wilkinson, whose Aberdonian accent enlivened the proceedings. Bob Sayers had only me, but his incredible grasp of detail and knowledge of the drilling industry made it quite unnecessary for him to have a second counsel.

My client was no ordinary man. He had, over his colorful 50 years, done a host of interesting things. In brief summation, he told Mr. Justice Power and the jury of six good men and women about his innovative inventions and the high-risk and dangerous work he had been engaged in since he was a boy.

He had been a rodeo cowboy and worked on nuclear submarines for the U.S. Navy. He had applied for an international patent on the use of liquid nitrogen for a method of freeze-branding cattle. He was experienced in heavy-industrial equipment and had perfected a fire-capsule system for putting out fires on tanker ships which was of more than passing interest to the Greek merchant marine. He had built cattle corrals for Air Canada in Toronto and been involved with offshore drilling operations in the Gulf of Mexico. After working with firefighters in Texas and Alberta, he set up business in Red Deer, Alberta, as a blowout specialist.

The case turned on the interpretation of a loosely-drawn contract that had been hastily prepared by the Shell people when they learned there had been an explosion leading to an oil-and-gas fire at their Shell Randell well site, some 208 km (130 miles) outside of Edmonton, near Slave Lake at a spot called Wabasca. An oil and gas fire of this kind could be extremely dangerous and expensive to handle. The more quickly the fire could be brought under control the better.

Red Adair, the acknowledged king of firefighters, was somewhere in Texas and could not be located. Firefighters in Alberta were few and far between. The Shell people elected to request Bob Sayers to douse the fire. Sayers responded to the call without delay and flew to the scene of the blaze in a Shell airplane. He was actually at the scene of the fire for less than 48 hours, and while he was there he was given an open-ended contract which engaged him to extinguish the fire on Shell's account, but neglected to provide any details as to how much he was to be paid for his services or how long his term of employment as a firefighter was to last.

"What would Red Adair have done in a situation like this?" Sayers asked himself.

"No problem," he decided. "It will probably take two days to bring this fire under control and Red Adair would have charged $100 000 a day, which comes to $200 000. Now maybe I am not as well known as Red Adair, so I'll only charge $90 000 a day, and give them a bill for $180 000, and cheap at the price." And he went to work with a will.

The fire must have been an awesome and terrifying spectacle. The flames were mountain high and the roar of the blaze could be heard for miles away. But Bob Sayers was a fearless man. Like Daniel in the lion's den, he would walk into the raging inferno, alone and unafraid.

On that bleak night in February 1979, dismay and consternation reigned as the Shell people awaited the arrival of the blowout specialist from Red Deer. What was the best way to attack the raging monster and "kill" the fire before any more damage was done? All hands gathered together in the makeshift office building in the small hours of the morning to debate the matter.

The key player for the multinational company was Dan Dane. He had many years experience as a production manager, but had never been confronted with a gas fire like this before. Charlie Arndt was there to protect the interests of Cactus Drilling Company, who actually owned the drilling rig that had already toppled into the yawning crater. The Haliburton people were there with waterlines and the Michelin mud experts were on hand to lend the benefit of their experience and advice.

And last, but by no means least was Bob Sayers himself, with his own ideas as to how the well fire should be "killed." Every conceivable method was considered, from dynamite and high explosives to directional drilling, even the possible use of the spectacular Reagan Latch—anything to douse the flames and save the huge rig from total destruction. After interminable discussion, these arcane theories were considered impractical, and dismissed. Bob Sayers decided that the more conventional way of pumping mud and steam into the drill hole would probably do the trick.

There was one drawback to his theory, and it was a big one. The "kelly swivel" on the rig had become disconnected somehow in the middle of the roaring fire, and had to be hooked up again before the drilling mud could be pumped into the well hole. This was what Bob Sayers was prepared to rectify.

By this time, all hands were exhausted and went to bed ready to deal with the problem at first light.

In the early morning, Sayers went to work. The RCMP had arrived on the scene and were busily taking pictures of the roaring inferno. Shell's production manager had retired to the safety of a nearby hill and was watching events unfold through his field binoculars. Charlie Arndt, the Cactus drilling superintendent, surveyed the scene from a nearby cement truck and took careful note of everything that went on.

The lion from Red Deer was busily engaged in connecting the kelly swivel to the Haliburton lines so that drilling mud could be poured down the hole. He first kicked in the tin door of the tool shed and made himself a blowout shield (protection against the flames) and inch by inch worked his way towards the kelly. By now he had a swedge reducer that enabled him to connect the kelly to the water lines. With this indispensable task accomplished, he returned to take charge of the steam and drilling mud operations.

At this point less than 380 litres (100 gallons) of water and drilling mud were poured into the drillhole and the fire was out. Bob Sayers went back to the cookhouse, delighted with the success of his efforts. He threw his hat in the air to celebrate the victory and presented his bill to Shell officials for a job well done.

Judge Peter Power was a model judge, patient, firm and courteous at all times. Under his expert guidance, the long-delayed trial proceeded with dispatch. In all, testimony was heard from 11 witnesses, four for the plaintiff and seven on behalf of the defendant. Thirty-three exhibits from both sides were tendered for the consideration of the court. Great photographs of the actual fire were displayed for the benefit of the judge and jury and enormous drawing pads showed in full detail how a typical oil rig was constructed.

It was all very impressive. The star witness for the plaintiff was Bob Sayers himself. As he described in graphic detail the frightening story, I called compelling and convincing evidence to prove how expensive and dangerous it was to be a blowout specialist in the world of oil and gas, and the jury was given a crash course on blowouts and what it cost for specialists from Texas like Red Adair to bring an oil- and-gas fire under control.

Intriguing as those charts and schematic diagrams might have been, the bottom line for the jury to consider turned on one basic issue: what was fair and equitable payment for the work that he had done? This was the vital question at which I hammered away and it would appear to have been grasped and fully understood by the jury. Among many other things, this was what I said to them.

"I suggest to you ladies and gentlemen, that Shell Canada Resources Limited haven't been very nice to Mr. Sayers. Look at the memos when you go back to your jury room. The memos contained in exhibits 19, 23 and 24, a nasty piece of business. To treat a man like that and disseminate those memos God knows where, saying that he is deceitful and tricky and that you shouldn't give him any business. What is his sin? What's his heinous crime? That he wants to be paid. That's all he asks.

"I did a job, I did it well, I want to be paid." They haven't done it. Would you put out that fire for $2 000, or $4 000, any one of you? Would you expose yourself to danger and risk of life and limb like he did? It is not a game for babies, it is a game for somebody with courage and intestinal fortitude, somebody who is prepared to risk his life and do a very dangerous job. I am suggesting that he did something he should be well compensated for."

The trial lasted for ten days. After listening attentively to the submissions of counsel and a thorough and comprehensive charge by Mr. Justice Power, the jury retired to true deliverance make and answered the four questions put to them by the Court, as follows:

Q.: Did Shell Canada Resources Limited employ Robert Sayers?

A.: Yes.

Q: Did Robert Sayers perform the work requested by Shell Canada Resources Limited?

A.: Yes.

Q.: Was Robert Sayers present when the gas well was brought under control?

A.: No.

Q.: If Robert Sayers performed work on behalf of Shell Canada Resources Limited, how much should he be paid for those services?

A.: Sixty thousand dollars.

When asked by the Clerk of the Court if the jurors agreed, if five out of six jurors had agreed to the foregoing answers, the foreperson indicated that the answer was yes. The trial was over.

As the former Chief Justice of Alberta, His Lordship McGillivray once remarked to me, "There is no place for oratory or eloquence in the Court of Appeal." And we have no jury in the Federal Court of Canada which addresses its attention to such vitally important matters as income tax and trademarks. But in the Sayers case, there *was* room for eloquence and compassion. We had gone back to grass roots. We had been in a people's court, where natural justice could be done, and the black letter of the law would take second place to equity and human decency.

In the sanctuary of their jury room, six people—four women and two men—made their own decision and cut his bill from $180 000 to $60 000. True deliverance was rendered on what they conceived was the right and proper thing to do.

Only a jury could have done that and in their inscrutable wisdom they must have felt that Bob Sayers was truly a brave man and had earned his money.

Shell Canada was anything but pleased with this turn of events and promptly launched an appeal in the Alberta Court of Appeal. Their Lordships, without having seen or heard the witnesses, reversed the verdict of the jury, and reduced the award to what they felt was a more reasonable sum of $12 500.

Sayers then sought leave to appeal to the Supreme Court of Canada, but his application was rejected. Even so, $12 500 was not bad pay for a couple of days work, at that. It reminded me of the expert who was called to the Hoover Dam site in Nevada, to start the turbines running again after they had come to a stand still. With one blow from his hammer, the expert smote the engine and the turbines were immediately in motion. The dam commissioners were aghast at his bill for $500 for professional services rendered and requested particulars of his account. Back came the bill in short order.

Professional services rendered:
Striking turbine with hammer . . . . $ 1
Knowing where to strike $499
Total fee $500

And so with Bob Sayers and the fire at Wabasco, Shell paid him for his expertise and his know-how, even if they did not feel that his courage and his mettle were worth very much. *C'est la guerre!*

Mitzi Dupre, the Ping-Pong Queen

When Mitzi Dupre danced her way over the Rockies and into my life, it was an exciting moment for me. In days gone by, in some parts of this continent, she would have been described as "high yeller," or possibly a "quadroon" but whatever the description, she was an impressive-looking lady. She had come over to Alberta from British Columbia, where the heat was on, notwithstanding her triumphant acquittal in Kamloops for taking part in an immoral performance contrary to the Criminal Code of Canada.

Why would the police want to harass so talented a dancer as Mitzi Dupre? Quite frankly, I don't think their hearts were in their job, and they did not pursue this alleged criminal with the vigor that they saved for thieves and the more common criminals. And besides, just what had she done that was so terribly wrong?

I blush to report that I never attended a performance by this talented young lady, and I only had it from her own lips and some of her more ardent supporters as to the kind of entertainment she provided an enthusiastic and admiring public. From all accounts, her dance, if so it can be called, was a terpsichorean combination of dancing and gymnastics, all done to music with the aid of props such as ping-pong balls, drinking glasses, flutes and other musical instruments.

The fact that she was dancing in the nude was incidental to the main performance. I was told that Miss Dupre was an athlete of great renown and after she had disrobed, she could carry out incredible feats of dancing and gymnastics never before seen in Alberta.

Her most celebrated *tour de force* was to place a ping-pong ball in her private orifice and then propel it with unerring precision to land in a glass of water a distance of some 20 metres (65') away. This amazing performance would be accomplished solely by manipulation of her anatomical muscles and was invariably attended by thunderous applause, as no one in the audience had ever seen anything quite like it. Even Isadora Duncan, in her revolutionary dance of the Rites of Spring, had never done anything as difficult as this!

This breathtaking performance was followed by a demonstration of her musical talent. Still completely naked, she would insert a small flute in her vagina and give a rousing rendition of "Mary had a Little Lamb" with the well-known round "Frere Jacques" for an encore. At the time of her appearance in Calgary, it was already the Christmas season, and to display her versatility, she would get into the spirit of things by playing "Jingle Bells" or any other Christmas carol that came to mind. Like the ping-pong balls, her musical sounds entirely emanated from the lower regions of her body and her muscular manipulations apparently intrigued her to the watching throng.

In Calgary at the Beacon Hotel, her audience was entirely male. The members of the Calgary morality squad, impressed as they were by her accomplishments, felt she came too close to some of the watching patrons and that at such times her movements were sexually offensive, rather than artistic, and made entries in their notebooks accordingly.

In some ways, Alberta is still a red-necked place. Mitzi's troubles really began down in Lethbridge, where a jaundiced blue-stocking was determined that the immoral sexual entertainment put on by Miss Dupre should not be allowed in her community.

This puritanically-minded person attended the hotel performance in Lethbridge and made detailed notes throughout the evening. Immediately following the show, as an indefatigable guardian of public morality, she reported the whole affair to the Lethbridge Police department, making a formal complaint in which she asked that Miss Dupre be prosecuted without delay. In due course, after similar performances at the Beacon Hotel in Calgary, two charges for unlawfully performing an immoral, indecent or obscene performance were laid against my client. The matter was underway.

Mitzi had a large and vociferous public following, so early on we decided that we would take our chances with a judge and jury, rather than with a judge alone. To advance her case one step further, we thought it would be in Mitzi's best interests if we could have an all-male jury, who would be likely to view Mitzi's acrobatics with a more favorable eye than would her female peers. I was aware that in years gone by provision had been made in the Alberta Jury Act for the empanelling of a special jury of six women to deal with issues of pregnancy and related female concerns, but to request an all-male jury to handle the charges confronting Mitzi was a different matter.

We went ahead anyway, and a preliminary motion was made to have an all-male jury for her trial. This application came on for hearing before Madame Justice Mary Hetherington, in the Court of Queen's Bench, as a preliminary motion to determine the mode of trial. To no one's great surprise, the application was not favorably received, and the trial was set down for hearing as an ordinary case.

It was far from an ordinary case, however. Shortly thereafter the matter was heard by Mr. Justice Bill Brennan, sitting with a jury, empanelled according to the provisions of the Jury Act of Alberta, and made up of 12 men and women.

Some years before I had been the prime mover responsible for changing the petit jurors in a criminal trial in Alberta from 6 to 12, to bring the Province in line with the rest of the British Commonwealth. This was one of the first acts carried out by Pierre Elliot Trudeau, who served for a brief term as Minister of Justice before becoming Prime Minister of Canada.

I was very pleased that the members of the jury panel had been increased to 12 persons, because I felt that the facts of the Dupre trial were eminently suited to be decided by 12 ordinary people from off the street, rather than a judge sitting alone, even a judge as fair and impartial as Judge Brennan was reputed to be.

But there was no acquittal in store for Mitzi Dupre, notwithstanding her narrow escape from the toils of justice in Kamloops, in spite of the novelty of her act. The whole case was just too much for the jury. The morality detectives recounted what they had seen take place in the hotels in Calgary and Lethbridge and Madame Blue-stocking underlined their evidence with her own complaint and litany of Mitzi's misdoings.

The jury, a mixed bag of men and women from Calgary and surrounding district, sat unmoved as witness after witness described with enthusiasm and admiration the *tour de force* performed by Mitzi Dupre. Expert evidence was called on her behalf from the sociology department of the University of Lethbridge to prove that what she was doing was simple erotica, and not obscene or pornographic in any way. Learned texts were quoted to show that simple erotica had no connection with violence and that there was nothing degrading to the female sex in Mitzi's performance.

It was all lost on the jury, however, who were not impressed by Miss Dupre's pyrotechnics, and who eventually concluded that her activities were not to be tolerated by the morality standards of the community of Calgary. In vain did I argue for free expression, comparing my client to the illustrious Isadora Duncan, who had the same immense vitality and flair for living—all quite unappreciated by a puritanical society.

The jury took a relatively short time to bring in a verdict of "Guilty" on both counts and Mitzi was fined the sum of $1 000 on each charge. As she had been released on bail for a similar offense in Edmonton, she concluded that Alberta was not the place for her to demonstrate her skills.

I followed her career with interest and learned that she eventually performed for the America Army in Guam in the South Pacific. I am sure she provided countless hours of entertainment and belly laughter for the members of the armed forces.

On her return to the U.S.A., she was murdered in Los Angeles at the age of 24, after supporting her widowed mother for years from the proceeds of her unusual dancing routine.

She was a tawny, lovely creature who walked as if a red hot poker were burning inside her. Like Isadora Duncan she has gone, but will be remembered for a long time.

My World of
Drunken Drivers

Drunken drivers played a prominent role in my years as a criminal lawyer. One of these was an artist of great prominence, now gone to his reward in the Great Courthouse in the sky. Quite apart from his prowess as a painter, almost everyone in Western Canada knew or had heard of Duncan MacKinnon Crockford. Duncan had survived the Battle of Britain with the RAF and flown spitfires over Egypt, emerging unscathed. His goatee beard and sturdy figure were always in evidence at the officers' mess at Mewata Barracks, where he would dominate every gathering by the sheer weight of his forceful personality.

Duncan was a law unto himself so it was only a matter of time before he was apprehended and charged with impaired driving. On the evening in question, Duncan was wending his way westward to his studio in Bearspaw Heights just outside Calgary when he had an unfortunate accident on 17th Avenue S.W., across from the Children's Hospital. At that spot, the concrete median took an unexpected 90° turn to the north and became a potential hazard to oncoming traffic, especially if a driver was not alert to changes in driving conditions.

A copious supply of the best Glenfiddich whisky did not help. Duncan collided with the concrete median and his station wagon ground to a halt. Naturally somewhat perturbed by this turn of events, Duncan emerged from his vehicle to take stock of the situation. On this particular night he was dressed in his long white greatcoat and with his imperial beard looked like a Cossack officer from the Russian steppes.

The police arrived on the scene just as Duncan was surveying the damage to his vehicle and relieving himself by urinating on the side of the road. Unfortunately, his aim was not true and he made great yellow stains on his beautiful white coat.

This unfortunate episode, coupled with his unintelligible Scottish brogue, was too much for the attending police officer and Duncan was promptly arrested and charged with impaired driving. Happily for Duncan, all this occurred before the breathalyzer law was passed. He was not obliged to furnish a sample of his breath, which might well have had incriminating results.

Shortly thereafter the case came on for trial before Provincial Court Judge John Harvie. The judge was an artist of considerable talent himself and listened to the sad story of Duncan's nocturnal escapade with sympathetic attention. Until, that is, he heard the police evidence about the urination on the coat.

At that point it was game over. The judge threw down his pen and literally turned his back on the rest of the proceedings. Such a performance by a fellow artist was hardly professional. "Guilty as charged" and Duncan was fined and punished according to law.

"Duncan," I said, "this is awful. What, what are we going to do?"

"Laddie, it's very simple," replied the great man, "file an appeal and do it right now!"

The Master had spoken. An appeal was launched forthwith, and on we went to the District Court to appear before His Honor Harry Rowbotham, who was reputed to be an authority on things mechanical and the rules of the road.

Judge Rowbotham was singularly unimpressed by the misadventure with the beautiful white great coat. To the court, it was a matter of complete indifference as to whether Duncan's coat was white or black or whether the act of urination had or had not taken place. Judge Rowbotham put the engineering department of the City of Calgary on trial. They were the real villains in the piece. They had caused the accident by creating a trap with the unusual position of the median.

Appeal allowed!

I was elated. As the Court cleared, I congratulated the artist on his narrow escape from the toils of justice.

"Duncan," I whooped, "we did it! we did it! You are not guilty. Go and sin no more."

"Ach, Web," replied the great painter in a brogue so thick you could cut it with a knife. "The whole thing was nothing but a damn bore."

I looked down at the sheaf of papers in his hand. There was a motley collection of caricatures of all the key players in the courtroom scenario; the Crown Prosecutor, stern and forbidding in his black robes, the rugged features of Counsel for the Defense and the shining bald pate of Judge Rowbotham himself, all actors in a drama of trifling importance to an artist who lived in another world.

Then there was Captain Michael William Scott, master-mariner, who as man and boy had sailed the seven seas of the world, coming finally like a fish out of water to Calgary. Here he stayed for almost 30 years until he made his way back to the sea where he rightfully belonged.

Michael and his outrageously irresponsible behavior were a lawyer's dream. In many ways he was probably the most entertaining client I ever had. Michael was born in London, England, within the sound of Bow Bells, which technically made him a Cockney; but he prided himself in being a Scouse, as he was brought up in Liverpool and knew Merseyside better than the Thames.

How many clients could regale you with an impassioned oration of the cremation of Sam McGee, or plan an arm-wrestling contest on the top of the world at the North Pole. That would be an international arm-wrestling contest with the Russians, of course!

How many clients would seek your advice on the purchase of Dead Man's Island off the coast of Puntarenas, Costa Rica, or on the niceties of Admiralty law in salvage at sea as he rescued an unseaworthy vessel from foundering with all hands?

The only client of this kind I ever had was Captain Scott. He was talented and fearless. How could you fail to admire the man? Like Blondin sailing over Niagara Falls in a barrel, he descended on a steel wire cable from the Husky Tower to the top of the Bank of Montreal during the Calgary Stampede, supported only by a flimsy leather belt, amid admiring cheers from astonished onlookers.

Small in stature, but big in heart, Michael was always in trouble of one kind or another, or engrossed in hare-brained schemes that never seemed to get off the ground. Needless to say, his track record as a stable man of marriage left much to be desired. Maybe it takes one to know one, or perhaps we were kindred spirits, but I felt irresistibly drawn to this unconventional nonconformist and did everything in my power to help him on his merry way.

My first service of a purely legal nature was to pilot Michael through the shoals of the Alberta divorce court. His Lilliputian wife tearfully told the judge that although Michael was a charming fellow with many sterling qualities, he was an impossible man to live with and their marriage was hopelessly and irreconcilably at an end. As this was unquestionably a marriage breakdown, the judge granted a decree absolute, *a vinculo matrimonii,* immediately.

Matrimonial confrontation was only the beginning. From there we moved to the legal perils of drunken driving and the preservation of Michael's driver's license from the all-seeing eye of the Registrar of Motor Vehicles up in Edmonton. Not that for a moment I condone the heinous offense of drunken driving with its often lethal consequences. Poor Michael never hurt anyone. He merely viewed driving and drinking as an ongoing merry battle with the men in blue. Sometimes Michael was the winner; more often the prize went to Calgary's finest, as they established that Michael was not a fit person to operate a motor vehicle on the Queen's highways in Alberta.

For Michael, his never-ending "gargles" were an expensive pastime. Biochemists with impeccable professional credentials would appear on Michael's behalf to convince the trial judge that the breathalyzer readings were suspect and could not be relied upon.

But more often, Michael's own personality was his best defense. Witness the time that he was acquitted of impaired driving by "Fearless Freddy" Thurgood, when the court heard evidence that Michael had made the night air of the police cells dance and sing, as he practised his operatic arias in solitary confinement. His Honor Judge Thurgood concluded that such a quaint personality could not possibly be guilty of drunken driving and for the first time in living memory applied the doctrine of reasonable doubt and acquitted the accused!

But as the venerable Indian philosopher would have us believe, the pitcher that goes too often to the well gets broken, and eventually Michael's luck ran out. The axe fell when he was haled before that pillar of the criminal law, His Honor Judge John Harvie, and charged with impaired driving of a motor vehicle on Acadia Boulevard with more than 80 mg of alcohol in his blood.

"There he was, Your Honor, weaving on the highway, and waving his arms while he was conducting some imaginary orchestra. I asked the accused what he was doing? Conducting *Cavaliera Rusticana.*"

In broad daylight on a busy Calgary street in heavy traffic! This was too much for Judge Harvie, who promptly convicted the accused of impaired driving.

Some time later the Judge met Michael and me while playing tennis on the indoor courts at the Glencoe Club.

"It was too, too bizarre," said the Judge. "If he had told the policeman he was listening to country and western music, I would perhaps have believed him and let him off, but Cavaliera Rusticana, that was too much! I had no choice, I had to convict him." Of such weighty considerations are judicial decisions made!

When the Calgary peace officers apprehended Michael, in full Highland Scottish regalia, on the night he presided at a Robert Burns Memorial Dinner and delivered the Immortal Memory to the Scottish Bard, an unsympathetic policeman rejected Michael's expostulations as to his sobriety and arrested him for the same offense. But this time it was Michael against the breathalyzer machine and Michael threw in the sponge rather than challenge the forces of modern technology.

Months later, when Michael moved across the mountains to Vancouver, his impairment problems came with him. It was not long before

Michael's driving habits were of more than passing interest to the Vancouver police. In short order he was convicted again of his old bête noir, but the British Columbia gendarmes had a method all of their own to deal with my irrepressible client. Placing him under house arrest, they fastened an electronic device to his ankle to alert the constabulary every time Michael left his office.

Big Brother was indeed watching him. For several weeks they made sporadic visits to Michael's home to let him know they were keeping an eye on his every move. This involuntary supervision proved very successful and Michael graduated with honors from his period of probation. Today he is teaching hundreds of sailors and fishermen the basic rudiments of coastal navigation and safety at sea. As the Captain of a luxury motor vessel in the Queen Charlotte Islands, Michael is a reluctant teetotaler. In the rain and mists of the B.C. coast he is ready for his last hurrah as one of the great master mariners of our time.

Over the years, as a criminal lawyer I had more than my share of drunken drivers. In some ways they were a breed apart, especially in their protestations of innocence and their determination to beat the most unjust charge brought against them.

Most colorful of these defiant miscreants was an RCAF officer named Fred Wetherall. It may well be that the conviction for drunken driving carries with it a certain social stigma to be avoided at all costs. In any event, almost all my clients were prepared to go to any lengths to escape conviction, but perhaps not as far as Fred Wetherall.

After all appeals and adjournments had been exhausted and Fred was convicted of drunken driving, he decided to pack it in. All alone on a hot summer afternoon in July of 1979, he soared in his private airplane at a level of 3 048 metres (10 000 feet).

Who knows what thoughts went through his mind high above the city and threw open the throttle, plunging towards the flat plain three kilometres (two miles) below. Only a spot was left of one of the great aerial fighters of our time. Those who knew him best would have you believe that he never got over his criminal conviction and that the outcome of the case played a major part in his decision to bring his life to an untimely end.

Michael Scott and Duncan Crockford reacted quite differently to the charge in question. Outwardly it did not seem to bother either of them at all. But then, there really are different strokes for different folks!

Plagiarism and the Stampede

When the last post was blown for Fred Kennedy, Alberta had lost a great journalist and Calgary an outstanding public figure. His sturdy presence and abrasive pen had been a familiar part of the newspaper world for many years and his searing diatribes on the immorality and permissiveness of present-day society will be sorely missed.

He was a reporter of the old school. His column "I write as I please" was a fixture of the *Albertan* for many years, and delighted his legions of friends and supporters while throwing his enemies and detractors, of whom there were just as many, into paroxysms of anger and disgust.

Fred Kennedy was not a person to be ignored. You either loved him or hated him, but you could not be oblivious to his presence. His views were simply and directly expressed and his message was never in doubt. To a host of people he was the red-neck to end all red-necks, an Archie Bunker personified, who used the power of the Fourth Estate to discipline and flay the slack and decaying culture he saw on every side.

There was never any question as to where Fred stood on any of the great issues of the day. He was for capital punishment and against abortion on demand. He became apoplectic on the subject of drugs and the "permissive behavior" of high school and university students.

Of all the things he championed, from the veterans of the First Great War to sulky racing and thoroughbreds, one of his most cherished and abiding loves was the Calgary Stampede. It had been dear to his heart since that wandering cowboy, Guy Weadick, had come up to Alberta from Wyoming in 1912 and made the Calgary Stampede the greatest outdoor show on earth.

One of his early books was entitled *The Calgary Stampede*. Over the years it had become a classic and a source of considerable income to Fred. The book, which was a magnificent chronicle of the colorful events the Stampede had offered each and every year since 1912, was a recognized authority on the history of the Stampede and of the "Big Four" founders.

Imagine, then, the anger and astonishment Fred Kennedy felt when in the late summer of 1980 he found virtually the whole of chapter 12, entitled "A Cowboy's Dream," reproduced in the pages of *Sports Illustrated*—under the same title, but with no credit or recognition attributed to Mr. Kennedy. After reading the story in *Sports Illustrated* from start to finish, and comparing the sports story with the original version as set out in Fred's Calgary Stampede, there was no question as to what had happened.

It was not a matter of striking or substantial similarities or anything of that kind. It was Fred's story from sternpost to gudgeon, to use a naval metaphor. Every word was almost the same in the article and in the book. It was literary theft, blatant and undisguised and to say that Fred Kennedy was upset would be an understatement of the grossest kind. He steamed into my office, showed me the offending article and the original book from which the purloined story had been taken and instructed me to sue.

Sports Illustrated at that time was a subsidiary of Time Incorporated, out of New York City, but its Canadian office was in Vancouver. We sued everybody on the masthead of *Time* magazine and the material that flowed into Calgary concerning this literary contretemps was beyond belief. The only weak spot in the Kennedy armor was that Fred had never registered his copyright with the copyright office in Ottawa, but this did not deter Mr. Kennedy in the slightest.

He knew he had copyright of some kind by virtue of the fact that those were his written words. He knew that a court would protect him against the infringement of whatever copyright he may have had. By the time he sued the officers of *Sports Illustrated* and the entire New York office, the defendants to the action were in double figures. The case never went to trial, for after protracted negotiations, the matter was settled out of court at a figure which need not be disclosed. Suffice it to say that Fred Kennedy made more money out of his copyright litigation than he received from the royalties of his book.

Justice was done. Fred was paid and the Stampede and Guy Weadick's dream get bigger and more successful every year.

The Man from the Black Forest

In Calgary in the 1960s, the German community was 50 000 strong and the most powerful and influential of the new ethnic groups that made up the cultural mosaic of a vibrant, growing city. One of my early clients was Gerd Topsnik, who had come to Canada as a farm boy of 16 from the Black Forest country of South Germany. Weighing in around 93 kgs (250 pounds), he was a large order in more ways than one, physically and emotionally a powerful and dominating figure of a man. East and West Germany are joined together again, and every time I see the huge form of Helmut Kohl on the television screen, I am reminded of my years with Gerd Topsnik.

It is not often you have a client for whom you batted a thousand, to use a baseball metaphor. Gerd Topsnik was one of them. Looking back on his legal and business problems, Gerd would not have settled for less. We won every case we touched.

He was the Teutonic personification of Germanic *arbeitslust*. Finding life on his uncle's farm north of Red Deer too uneventful, Gerd decided to become a wrestler in Calgary under the watchful eye of the great Stu Hart. In spite of a successful and innovative technique, where he would use his head as a battering ram against his unsuspecting opponents, he felt there were quicker and less painful ways of making his fortune. And so he went into the night club business with a vengeance.

In short order he opened a night spot called the Blind Onion. Immediately his problems began with the Alberta Liquor Control Board and the morality squad of the Calgary Police Department. The Calgary police were nothing if not ingenious and resourceful and when the city by-laws proved ineffectual at shutting down Mr. Topsnik's operation on one pretext or another, the men in blue sought the assistance of the Alberta Liquor Control Board.

By this time the German farm boy and former wrestler was a successful restaurateur and running a profitable business with a strong appeal for the haut monde. Until Gerd arrived on the scene, the denizens of the night had been restricted to such unsavory haunts as The Cellar, The Isle of

Capri and the Chicken Inn, which were really a thin veneer for prostitution and the drug trade. Gerd quickly expanded the Blind Onion into a thriving business for ladies of pleasure and even moved into the Lethbridge area, where he opened a nocturnal establishment called the Pink Panther.

The police, however, were not to be denied. When all other avenues of attack had been explored in vain, a charge was laid against big Gerd under the Liquor Act for unlawfully keeping liquor for sale in a public place. In due course the matter came on for hearing before His Honor Judge Turcot of the District Court of Southern Alberta. When the murky evidence was subjected to judicial scrutiny, His Honor quickly ruled that there was no proof beyond all reasonable doubt to establish any criminal intent on the part of Topsnik. Charge dismissed.

Shortly thereafter Gerd disposed of the Blind Onion and the Pink Panther and concentrated his Teutonic energy on a new venture he called Dino's Hideaway Cabaret. This flourishing establishment was in the centre of Calgary's business district and as the Roaring Sixties came into their own, it gave the German entrepreneur his long-awaited opportunity. He began by having his ladies dance in the nude, which at that time was a daring and outrageous thing to do.

The detectives of the morality squad of the Calgary Police Department viewed this new departure with anger and misgiving; anger, because Topsnik had thwarted all their previous attempts to bring him to justice and misgiving because they were not quite sure of their legal grounds.

Gerd was tireless in the pursuit of his business activities. He was not a neo-Nazi by any means, but he felt that the police were fair game and he was not afraid to take them on, no matter what it cost him.

The new star performer at Dino's Hideaway was a sweet young girl with auburn hair and freckles named Kelly Johnson, from a farm near Okotoks. I always thought of her as the corn-fed girl from Okotoks, just stepped off the farm. She was very young and quite demure, as if dancing in the nude was not something she did every day of the week; but neither was it something of which she was ashamed.

The performance came off as scheduled, shortly after lunch in a club crowded with regulars. Unknown to Mr. Topsnik, there was an undercover detective from the Morality Squad seated in the audience, busily taking notes for future reference. As the lights dimmed and the blaring music softened, young Kelly made her appearance. Her copper hair hung down over a full-length sable fur coat—her only other attire were her high-heeled shoes, on which she pirouetted before an admiring audience as if she were at a fashion show. She was like a tiny burlesque queen and in a matter of minutes she doffed her mink coat, tossed it aside and was down to the bare buff.

She revolved in the nude around the miniature platform amid thunderous applause and stamping of feet. The whole incident could not have taken more than three minutes, just long enough for the assembled throng to feel that they had been given their money's worth. Miss Johnson, clad again in her opulent fur, disappeared from view through a beaded curtain and the lone detective retired to consider what action should be taken.

The wheels of justice turned quickly and Dino's Hideaway found itself facing a charge under the Criminal Code of Canada for conducting an indecent theatrical performance in a public place.

Then began a series of legal manoeuvres that carried the corn-fed girl from Okotoks all the way from the Provincial Court of Alberta to the Supreme Court of Canada.

Her initial trial was before the late Judge Fred Thurgood of the Provincial Court. Fred Thurgood had come out to Alberta from St. Peter's on Cape Breton Island. He acted as solicitor for the City of Calgary, became a Crown prosecutor and eventually a judge of the provincial court. It was a unique trial in that the total evidence took less than five minutes, with the legal submissions at the end of the case lasting for almost two hours.

Under cross-examination I asked the morality detective two questions:

Q.: Detective, did you find the performance offensive or disgusting in any way?

A.: No, I did not.

Q.: As a matter of fact the whole thing was rather beautiful, was it not?

A.: Yes, it was.

With that terse but illuminating evidence, we moved into argument which was edifying to say the least. This was in 1973, almost a decade before the new constitution became the supreme law of the land. I argued for the defense that this was a landmark case and that books such as *Lady Chatterley's Lover* and *Ulysses*, among countless others, proved conclusively that important, fundamental principles like freedom of expression and censorship were involved in this case and the rights of the individual were at stake.

Judge Thurgood was only mildly impressed as to the basic principles involved and reserved his decision until morning. It has since come to my attention that he was genuinely perplexed as to what he should do with this great case. How could he explain his position to his brothers in lodge if he were to acquit the corn-fed girl from Okotoks. And so he compromised.

"I'll find her guilty," he must have said to himself, "but only a little bit guilty and give her a fine of fifty dollars."

"Detective, did you not find it rather beautiful?"

This Solomon-like resolution was pleasing to everybody except Mr. Topsnik. "On to appeal" were his instructions to me. We immediately applied by way of a stated case on a point of law to the Supreme Court of Alberta and in due course the matter came on for hearing before the late Mr. Justice Riley. In characteristic fashion, the great Riley cut through the murky morality that surrounded this area of law and found that by prevailing moral standards, as they existed in Calgary and Canada in 1973, Kelly Johnson had done nothing indecent or improper and quashed the charge.

The Queen did not appreciate Mr. Justice Riley's decision and the Crown asserted an appeal to the Appellate Division of the Supreme Court of Alberta (as it was then called) and shortly thereafter *Regina v. Johnson* was fully considered by the highest court in the province. The late Mr. Justice McDermid wrote the decision for the court. In his opinion he found that Miss Johnson's theatrical performance was indeed improper and illegal and he restored Judge Thurgood's finding of guilty.

Most people would have rested at this stage and turned their attention to something else, but not Gerd Topsnik.

"Webster, he said to me, I want this case to go to the Supreme Court in Ottawa, so get moving!" I did just that and after the usual delays in the legal system we found ourselves in Ottawa to argue the watershed case of *Regina v. Johnson* and determine a new code of morality for Canada.

I had been to the Supreme Court of Canada only twice before and this was an awe-inspiring experience for me. It was in the late spring of 1973 and to my astonishment we were to have a nine-man court, which was an indication that their lordships conceived this case to be a matter of national importance. The case, although the evidentiary material was minuscule, turned on some important principles and was an early attempt by the highest court in the land to lay down guidelines in the legal quagmire of obscenity and pornography.

It was an impressive and unforgettable sight. The Supreme Court building stands like a grey stone fortress above the Ottawa river, off to the west of the Parliament Buildings. Nine of their lordships, in their scarlet and ermine robes, solemnly arrayed themselves to rule on the fate of Kelly Johnson. It was not a lengthy submission and there was no time for eloquence or legal pyrotechnics. As Acting Chief Justice Fauteux quietly explained to me, in his firm French-Canadian accent:

"Mr. Macdonald, on the facts of this case, there was perhaps no indecent theatrical performance by Kelly Johnson."

But the court was unwilling to lay down any moral standards for the country as a whole. Perhaps wisely, for what may be morally acceptable in Montreal may be completely out of order in a rural hamlet in northern Ontario.

I was outside Athens at the shrine of the Delphic Oracle in September of 1973 when I received the astonishing news that the Supreme Court of Canada, in a 6-3 decision, had ruled that Kelly Johnson had not taken part in an indecent theatrical performance when she danced in the nude for a few brief seconds at Dino's Hideaway Cabaret in Calgary. At the time it was considered a landmark decision, a great blow for freedom from censorship and the blue-stocking prudes who were attempting to set puritanical moral standards in a free and liberal society. And perhaps it was!

My own observation is that the wheel has not only come full circle in matters of this kind, but has gone too far in the opposite direction. It would seem that the Crown now has the virtually impossible task of having to prove beyond all reasonable doubt that gross acts of sex simulation do offend contemporary standards.

Almost twenty years have passed since Kelly Johnson's demure performance. What could have been presented as a graceful and dignified exhibition of the female form divine has now lapsed into something sordid and degrading. It is now very clear that there is a commercial market for this kind of pornography. Those who do not wish to view these tasteless performances have only to stay away. There appear to be different strokes for different folks!

And so, on a very narrow and restricted interpretation of the law, Section 170 of the Criminal Code of Canada, as of 1973, was Kelly Johnson acquitted. Justice had triumphed. Mr. Justice Riley had been vindicated and Kelly Johnson danced off into oblivion never to be seen on the public stage again. Gerd Topsnik was elated and returned to Calgary more determined than ever to carry on his battles with the morality detectives of the Calgary police force.

For the next few years, Gerd was flying high and moved on from being a small-time wrestler and burlesque operator to the world of real estate and foreign investment. He acquired a silver-blue Mercedes and wore enormous ornate rings on his fingers, set off by a heavy gold chain and crucifix over his massive chest. He started work on a multimillion dollar house, just off Diamond Head in Hawaii and owned 16 condominiums in Waikiki with all the trappings of a merchant prince. He had come a long way from his uncle's farm in Stettler and the days when he bred Welsh ponies and helped his father-in-law run a pig farm.

The backbone of it all, the source of his working capital, was Dino's Hideaway, where the money arrived in small amounts but on a frequent and regular basis. The real problem with the Dino operation was that it required constant supervision, most of it from midnight on. For Gerd this was not a matter of deep concern. His extremely attractive Dutch wife Carla and his two daughters were safe at home and there was always his best friend and crony of many years standing, Jurgen Wolfe, to look after his interests on the homefront. Gerd and Jurgen were both German immigrants and like Damon and Pythias of old, they were always together. Jurgen had a highly successful business making concrete blocks. He spent the evening hours at Gerd's house, which notwithstanding that he was a married man himself, he found to be more attractive than his own home.

As the years went by and Gerd spent more and more time at Dino's or with his German friends at the Gasthaus Restaurant, Jurgen and Carla were left by themselves. The inevitable happened—they fell in love. Carla moved out of the matrimonial home into an apartment of her own but even at that stage Gerd did not suspect that Jurgen, his best friend, was having an affair with his wife.

On a bleak winter's night close to Christmas 1977, Gerd left the night club early and drove down to the Canyon Meadows area where Carla had her apartment. There to his great surprise, he saw his friend's car parked on a sidestreet. Jealous and upset, Gerd stormed up to his wife's abode.

"It's Gerd," Carla cried out. "Jurgen, go out the back way."

Jurgen slipped into the backyard to make his escape. Unfortunately for him a metre of new snow had fallen and he could not quite get to his car in his dash for freedom.

Gerd was a man of action. Armed with a steel hammer from his snowmobile, he caught up with Jurgen, who could not climb over the garden fence. With two mighty blows from his hammer, Gerd split open his former friend's head. Jurgen fell bleeding and unconscious on the snow. Gerd departed in great haste and left his friend behind in the expectation that he might not have killed him after all. He threw the murder weapon into the Glenmore dam and went over to Jurgen's apartment to await his arrival. Jurgen, badly beaten, was far from dead and belatedly made his way home. There Gerd bathed his face and bandaged his wounds and the pair returned to Carla's apartment to await the arrival of the police.

The Calgary police took a statement from Jurgen Wolfe and in due course Gerd was charged with attempted murder. For reasons still unknown, Jurgen declined to testify against his friend, notwithstanding his statement. Without Jurgen's vital evidence, the case collapsed and Gerd walked out of the courthouse a free man.

The angry Calgary police charged Jurgen Wolfe with perjury. He was promptly convicted and sentenced to 18 months imprisonment. Gerd and

Carla were divorced shortly thereafter. After his release from prison, Jurgen and Carla were married.

Gerd eventually moved to Hawaii and went into the sausage business with great success. Today he is an international businessman with connections all over the world. His meteoric rise to success comes as no surprise to me.

An Irishman's Dream

George Murphy grew up on a hard-scrabble farm on the Alberta-Saskatchewan border near a whistle-stop called Youngstown. From earliest times, as one of seven children, he had visions and plans of being an industrialist or a member of the landed gentry.

As a young man, he claimed to be a pugilist of some renown and in his more expansive moments would tell me he was known as "One Punch Murphy" or "One Round Murphy," whichever you preferred—the terror of the ring. George was a man of volatile temperament and at times given to strong drink, which only enhanced his exuberant behavior. Childless himself, George devoted himself to his grandiose business schemes and set out to build an empire without any money and only his boundless energy and native cunning to help him along the way.

After a disillusioning experience in Thunder Bay, Ontario, when his friend and partner in the coal business departed unexpectedly for the United States in the middle of the night (with the Royal Canadian Mounted Police in hot pursuit), George returned to Alberta undaunted and determined to make a fortune as a housebuilder.

As early as 1965 he set his sights on the Town of Canmore, a tiny mountain hamlet on the edge of Banff National Park. For years the village fathers had planned to build a thriving town along the banks of the Bow River, but much of the proposed development was in the flood plain and no one would venture into such a hazardous project, until One Punch Murphy arrived on the scene.

In many ways he was years ahead of his time, with the vision and intestinal fortitude to enter places where more cautious souls would fear to tread. From the Stoney Indians he learned about the river bottom lands and that the prospect of river flooding was remote. He figured the odds were in his favor, if he could only get the stamp of approval from the Canmore Town Council to build the first fifty houses he had in mind. But the real carrot lay in the option he secured on 18 hectares (45 acres) of beautiful land on the other side of the railway track on the northern boundary of the town. It was a glorious plan, but subject to one fatal Achilles' heel. The whole development had to be completed to the satisfaction of the town. One Punch had no money to work with and in short order the entire project was bogged down in a mass of caveats and builders' liens that brought everything to a standstill.

George instructed me to sue the Town and force them to honor the option that he held on the 18 hectares north of the railway line. After years of battling with the bureaucrats in the Alberta Department of Municipal Affairs, the case came on for trial before the late Mr. Justice Steer of the Court of Queen's Bench of Alberta. When the court learned that One Punch's work had to be completed to the satisfaction of the Town of Canmore, it was game over for George. All of his labor went down the drain and his magnificent vision of an idyllic townsite in the Rockies had to be finished by other hands. But he was the pioneer who saw the potential and the possibilities a quarter of a century before anyone else. Canmore came into its own during the Winter Olympics of 1988 and today the Three Sisters mountains look down on a burgeoning community, the dream in George Murphy's eye so many years before.

The Canmore disaster only spurred One Punch Murphy on to other plans. He had visions of a rustic empire in the Kicking Horse river country of eastern British Columbia. Once again George had no money, but as usual this did not deter the one-time pugilist.

His was a tremendous scheme of epic proportions. The "Kicking Horse" ranch was to be a self-contained magnificent spread with a five-star hotel, its own super garage and service station, a helicopter airport, horses for trail rides, tennis courts, camping and swimming pools, a hunting and fishing lodge, rustic cottages, private trout pools and all that went with these facilities. The mighty CPR was to reopen an abandoned railway station below the lodge and the Trans-Canada highway would twin its road allowances to accommodate the traffic that George envisioned coming to the ranch.

The most exciting skiing in North America was to be developed at Seven Tooth Mountain next door. Heliport skiing was also close at hand. The possibilities were boundless. The hydro power of Kicking Horse Falls, only eight kilometres from the ranch, was to provide electricity. I was instructed to set up an ecumenical foundation like the Barbara Scott trust in Toronto, so that homeless children everywhere would have an opportunity to enjoy the wonders and pleasures of the Kicking Horse ranch.

The bureaucratic hurdles that had to be overcome before this wilderness paradise could be created were awesome. In far-off Victoria, I secured for George the last Land Use Development Contract from the then Social Credit government and after a 40-hour drive on winter roads through the Rockies and the Kootenays, I filed our Land Use Contract with the Municipal authorities in Nelson, B.C., with only minutes to spare.

Grit and ambition, however, could only carry George so far. Like his efforts in Canmore, the entire project foundered for lack of working capital. All the people who had contributed their time and labor to what was undoubtedly one of the great wilderness dreams in North America watched helplessly as the Kicking Horse Ranch moved into receivership and George's plans collapsed like a house of cards.

The loss of the ranch killed George Murphy. In the end, he lost his wife, his home was sold and he became paranoid and deranged. His spirit finally broke under pressure from every side as his hopes and dreams disappeared forever. One Punch had lost his final fight and he went down for the count, a broken and despondent man.

Crowfoot's Heirs

I will not soon forget that hot July day in 1960 when the great artist Nick de Grandmaison introduced me to Chief Clarence McHugh of the Blackfoot (Siksika) Indian band at the Stampede Grounds in Calgary. Clarence was an impressive figure in his blue serge uniform, provided free of charge to him by the Department of Indian Affairs, with the yellow stripes down his trousers to indicate he was a chief.

It was a fortuitous meeting as far as I was concerned and the beginning of a labor of love. I came to learn first-hand the story of one band of Canada's native people, the Blackfoot tribe of Gleichen, who reside some 100 km (sixty miles) east of Calgary in Alberta.

From that first meeting it was clear that Clarence and I were kindred spirits. As soon as he recognized a sympathetic and understanding listener, he poured out the story of his people at the hands of the government of Canada. In the words of Chief McHugh, the Blackfoot reserve had been carved up "like a Christmas turkey" since the mighty Chief Crowfoot had entered into Treaty No. 7 with the British Crown in 1877.

It was one long and tragic story of shabby treatment and neglect. I was mindful of a similar tragic account in a famous American book, *Century of Dishonor*, which describes the tragic fate of the native people south of the border. But this was not a story in a book—it was a true story of how a people die. Night after night I heard from this wise old man how the spirit of his people had been destroyed.

Clarence had never gone past Grade IV. From 1939 to 1945 he had served his country overseas with the Canadian Army. It was now 1960 and he was pressing the Canadian government for recognition of the harm done to the Blackfoot people and for some measure of compensation and redress.

For weeks we met in my little office down on First Avenue S.W. until piece by piece we assembled a Statement of Claim in what was then known as a Petition of Right. This monumental effort, when completed, formed a formidable indictment of abuse and neglect on the part of the federal government towards the people committed to their care. Up to this time, the Blackfoot pleas had fallen on deaf ears. Retired army officers in Ottawa ran the Department of Indian Affairs like a military operation, and the Indians of Canada were treated as if they were wards in a state of pupilage.

Since 1850 a consistent policy of assimilation had been followed by the central government, and Section 91 (24) of the British North America Act had placed Indians and Indian lands squarely under federal jurisdiction. With the might of the Indian Act behind them, faceless bureaucrats in Ottawa could pursue this policy of paternalism that would in time extinguish the Indian way of life completely and force them to enter the Canadian mainstream. With no money and 4 000 km (2 500 miles) between him and the nation's capital, Clarence McHugh was a lone voice crying out in the western wilderness.

A criminal lawyer always goes to the scene of the crime if at all possible to have the proper feel of the problem. Clarence was only too happy to show me how, over the years, the Blackfoot reserve had been chopped to pieces by successive administrations in far-off eastern Canada. Never before had I seen the squalor and abject poverty I witnessed on the Blackfoot reserve.

After Treaty No. 7 had been signed by the Indians of Southern Alberta with Queen Victoria's representatives on September 22nd, 1877, the once nomadic Blackfoot people had been relegated to a strip of land on either side of the Bow River. Here federal policies tried to convert them as quickly and painlessly as possible from a nomadic race of hunters to a nation of farmers and tillers of the soil. They became essentially a tribe under trust. For almost a century their affairs were conducted by an absentee landlord in Ottawa, as the Blackfoot moved from a Stone Age culture into the twentieth century.

The Blackfoot reserve was a bleak, windswept place across the CPR railway track from the town of Gleichen. Bisected by the Bow River, the reserve formed a rectangular block of land roughly 32 km (20 miles) long by 12 km (eight miles) wide. Down in the bottom lands, in the cottonwood trees along the river, were scattered Indian shacks that the Blackfoot humorously called "Washington" and "Little Chicago."

Clarence showed it all to me: the random highways crisscrossing the reserve; the Old Sun school; the ramshackle hospital; the open-pit coal mines where the tribe dreamed of great profits from royalties that never seemed to materialize; the oil and gas jacks and pumpers busily at work just *outside* the boundaries of the reserve; the huge dam built by the CPR to provide water for the nearby town of Bassano and the Eastern Irrigation District.

This was the Blackfoot Indian reserve. Clarence and his people felt that their resources had been squandered and pillaged by the Canadian government and the white settlers, who had surrounded their lands ever since Treaty No. 7 entered their lives so many years ago.

Their main grievance was the sale of their best land by the Crown and the failure of the government to compensate them adequately for the loss sustained. Huge land surrenders had taken place in 1911 and 1917 in what has been described as two of the biggest real estate sales in Canadian history!

When these land sales were over, the Blackfoot had lost the whole southern half of their reserve across the Bow River. The original owners felt that they had never been fully paid for these surrenders. Furthermore, they took the position that the surrenders themselves were carried out under fraudulent and illegal circumstances and could be set aside in a court of law.

To add insult to injury, the Blackfoot alleged that in 1893 they were deprived of their timber limit on Castle Mountain, up the Bow River from Banff, which had been set aside for them by the Department of Indian Affairs because they did not have an adequate source of timber on their reservation proper to build houses.

How much is a mountain worth? Clarence McHugh always claimed that the government was supposed to replace the Blackfoot timber limit on Castle Mountain with a similar timber lot in the Highwood River country, south of Calgary, but this had never happened.

The whole unhappy story was set out in the Petition of Right I duly prepared for Clarence McHugh, and filed for the Blackfoot in the Exchequer Court in Ottawa. Particulars of the claim, demanded by the Department of Justice, were supplied by us as best we could, considering the meager material at our disposal. It was like a ward suing his trustee when the ward is illiterate, and all the material documents are in the hands of the trustee. We pressed on for years, and the federal government never delivered a defense, although they were fully aware of the claims and grievances of the Blackfoot people.

Throughout the 1960s there was considerable discussion about the appointment of an Indian Claims Commissioner to deal with the situation. Both the Diefenbaker and Pearson administrations worked on statutes that would have made a five-man Indian claims commission the law of the land, capable of dealing with the complex Indian problems of land entitlement and aboriginal claims. But every time the proposed legislation was about to be passed, it would die on the order papers and the question of an Indian claims commission would be quietly shelved and forgotten for other "more important" matters.

And then Pierre Elliott Trudeau entered centre stage on the Canadian political scene.

I have it on reliable information that Canada's most controversial prime minister was dealing with some pressing political matters in Yellowknife in the Northwest Territories in the winter of 1969. Seated across from him at the dinner table was Dr. Lloyd Barber, a leading educator and president of the University of Regina in Saskatchewan. After a broadranging discussion of matters affecting the Canadian body politics, including the aboriginal peoples of the Far North, the great Trudeau stopped in mid-conversation and posed a direct and completely unexpected question to Dr. Barber.

"Lloyd," said the new prime minister. "Now would you like to be a one-man Indian Claims Commissioner for Canada?"

Somewhat surprised and taken aback by this unexpected inquiry, Dr. Barber sat silent for a moment. "Pierre," he replied, "I don't know whether I am the right man for all this, but it is an extremely important job and if you feel that I can handle it, I will take it on and do my very best."

That was all Trudeau needed. With a stroke of the pen, he signed an order in council appointing Dr. Lloyd Barber Indian Claims Commissioner for Canada. In a few brief moments he accomplished what the two preceding prime ministers of Canada had attempted to do for a decade with no success.

Dr. Barber was a happy choice, not only for Canada, but for the approximately 450 000 "Status Indians" of the country as well. I must confess that Barber's sleight-of-hand appointment by Trudeau had not come as a complete surprise to me. In the early winter of 1971, I had driven out to the airport to meet with the Honorable Jean Chretien, who then served as Minister of Indian Affairs with the Trudeau government. In the airport coffee shop, I was quick to question the minister about the appointment of an Indian Claims Commissioner, which was of great importance to my clients.

"Chimo," he replied as he raised his coffee cup in a gesture of greeting. "I am just back from the Far North, and 'Chimo' means 'You are my friend.'"

From this happy introduction he went on to assure me that the Indian Claims Commissioner would be a *fait accompli* within the next few weeks. Little did I know that the historic meeting between Trudeau and Lloyd Barber had already taken place and that a new world for the Indian people of Canada had already begun!

In a very short time Dr. Barber arrived at my office to discuss the strategy of the Blackfoot claim. The word for the new commissioner was "solid." He sat there impassively like a German junker, with heavy jowls in his square-cut face and a massive skull with hair cropped to the bone, and carefully read over the Petition of Right that Clarence McHugh and I put together so many years before. Apparently our claim was the first to come to his attention in writing. He approached the problem with the vigor and enthusiasm of a mechanical engineer with a demolition problem on his hands. After several hours of discussion, as he analyzed the claim point by point, he finally came to a decision.

"Webster," he said, "the best way to go about this is to keep it as simple and concrete as possible. Especially when you're dealing with the federal government. Otherwise you'll get lost in a mass of details and they won't see the forest for the trees."

"I've gone over the case you've put together, and the 30 specific claims you've made. It seems to me the one claim you are advancing that is capable of quick mathematical calculation is your contention that the Crown had an obligation to provide 'ammunition money' to the five bands which signed Treaty No. 7, as long as the sun will shine and the rivers flow, in the amount of $2 000 a year after 1877."

"This has never been done. It really is quite a straightforward matter. This is 1972, and by my reckoning the Crown has to pay the Indians under Treaty No. 7 $2 000 a year for 95 years, which if the money has not been paid, makes a total of $190,000."

"This whole matter of Indian claims is like a huge log jam. All we need to do is pry this one log loose and the whole thing will come apart. Let's go after Ottawa right away and tell them the Treaty No. 7 Indians want their ammunition money!"

It was so pleasant to have someone come up with a beautifully simple and pragmatic solution to a heretofore impossible conundrum. I felt that the first step had been taken on the long path back to the repayment of the terrible debt Canada owed her native people.

It was indeed a long path back and was not made any easier by the fact that the ammunition money was owed to all five tribes who had signed Treaty No. 7, not just the Blackfoot band alone. With Dr. Barber easing the way, innumerable meetings were held between the government and the Treaty 7 Indians, comprised of the Blackfoot, Sarcee, Peigan, Stoney and Blood bands.

From government records it appeared that an attempt had been made by the Crown to honor their obligation by payment in one form or another for a period of about eight years following the signing of the treaty. Payments of any kind ceased in 1885 with the outbreak of the second Riel rebellion. After that year there was no record to indicate that bullet money had been sent to the Indians of southwestern Alberta.

The mighty Crowfoot, like a Winston Churchill of the western plains, had held his people firm to the British Crown but back in Ottawa, no ammunition, or money in lieu thereof, was sent out to Alberta. In short order, the Riel rebellion was suppressed and the following year in 1886 the first far-reaching Indian Act was passed that was designed to assimilate the native people into the mainstream of Canadian life.

In a watershed decision in 1973, the federal government agreed to pay the Indians their long overdue ammunition money, but this was the beginning, not the end of the case. Here we were with the first acknowledgment in the history of the country, that Canada was to honor a solemn treaty with her native people and the Indians could not agree among themselves just how the money was to be distributed!

There was the award from the government, unquestionably suffering from pangs of conscience, and the recipients of the Crown's bounty could not agree how to cut up the bonanza. From the very beginning there was controversy and dissension as two schools of thought had diametrically-opposed opinions.

Was the money to be allotted on a per capita or a per stirpes basis? This was no mere academic distinction or semantic play upon words. The smaller bands, the Sarcees for instance, had a band roll of only 500 members, and quite naturally they insisted on a straight five-way split (per stirpes) of the ammunition money, while the more populous bands, like the Bloods (almost 3 000) and the Blackfoot (about 2 500 bodies) wanted the division to be made on a per capita basis, or so much per person. The fight was on.

For five years the battle raged, and came no closer to an agreement. It is said that justice delayed is justice denied, but in this case, no blame could be attributed to the trustee. It was the beneficiaries who could not resolve the issue amongst themselves, and for five years the whole matter was in a state of suspended animation, until the problem was finally laid to rest by Mr. Justice Pat Mahoney of the Federal Court of Canada. His Lordship carefully perused the provisions of Treaty No. 7 and concluded that the whole arrangement with the Indians was that everything was to be carried out on a per capita basis and on that basis the distribution was eventually made. The "bullet money" was paid over to the Indians, as agreed upon, with interest, and the Blackfoot were left to pursue their remaining claims against the Crown.

For years there was no consensus within the five bands, however, and the Peigans and the Sarcees, spearheaded by Chief Nelson Small Legs Senior, stonewalled the final payment until their abortive attempts at appeal had lawfully run their course.

By the time the ammunition claim was settled, over 20 years had passed since Clarence McHugh had first launched his epic crusade against the Indian Affairs department, and the Blackfoot patience was running low. Expert help was brought in to appraise the land surrenders of 1911 and 1917, and the timber limit taken from them on Castle Mountain. Research was made into their rights under the Lame Bull Treaty of 1855 when the Blackfoot Confederacy had relinquished title to the American Bureau of the Interior, covering a vast tract of land east of the Rocky Mountains and running southerly from Red Deer in Alberta to Yellowstone Park in Wyoming.

Settlement had been made with the American Blackfoot in 1935, but at that late date the 49th parallel of latitude marked the international boundary between western Canada and the United States, and so no American money was set aside for the north Peigans or Canadian Blackfoot, as they were outside the jurisdiction of the continental United States. The Canadian Indians were like forgotten heirs, quietly left out when the American Blackfoot claim was settled.

During this period the Blackfoot at Gleichen engaged the services of Father Charon, an Oblate priest from northern Alberta, who spent many years on the Blackfoot reserve gathering data on the land surrenders and the documentary evidence surrounding the loss of their timber limit on Castle Mountain. The good father was a French Canadian and he worked tirelessly for the Blackfoot people.

We made a good team as month after month we dug through tribal documents and government papers to show that the land for the Bassano Dam had never been expropriated lawfully by the Crown and the water rights of the Indians had never been lost. Their claim for water rights was extended to the irrigation system and ditches run across their land causing irreparable loss and damage.

All in all, it was a gigantic claim and when allegations of mismanagement of their schools and hospitals, gravel pits and road allowances were added to the claims that had been festering for almost 100 years, it was clear that the Blackfoot grievances were to be taken seriously. At the moment, the Canadian government is attempting to piece together this incredibly complex matter, and a branch office in Vancouver has now got the unenviable task of quantifying the Blackfoot claim. It is late, late in the day, but it is hoped there is still time to deal with this whole matter in a fair and equitable manner.

Early in 1977 I was first exposed to the dynamic energy and single-minded purpose of Hanne Marstrand, known to her Indian friends as "Hurricane Hanne." She waged her own private war with government at all levels for the amelioration of the lot of Canadian Indians in general and the Cree Indian people of Hobbema in southern Alberta in particular.

Prior to our first meeting, she had dispatched the incredible Maurice Strong (who later became her husband) to make a preliminary reconnaissance into the work I was doing for her favorite people. Hanne Marstrand was a fireball of energy and she used Maurice Strong's high connections with the Liberal power base in Ottawa to achieve her ambitions for her Indian friends in every possible way. She always moved at the high port, and with a single-minded intensity carried on a non-stop crusade for native rights.

She was especially devoted to the battle being waged by Chief Robert Smallboy, who like a modern Moses was determined to lead his people back into the wilderness to their traditional way of life. Smallboy was one of the four Hobbema chiefs, whose bands of Cree Indians had enjoyed huge profits from the oil and gas royalties flowing from deposits on their reserve.

Drugs and alcohol abuse were rampant among the Hobbemas, and Chief Smallboy felt that the only answer to the Sodom and Gomorrah surrounding his people was to set up an isolated camp somewhere in the eastern foothills of the Rockies, far removed from the vices and temptations destroying his band. He only wanted a modest tract of 259 sq. km (100 sq. miles), so that his people could trap and fish as they had done since time immemorial. There would be no drugs or alcohol of any kind in his camp.

Unfortunately, the lands they yearned for were under the provincial jurisdiction of the Alberta Department of Lands and Forests, which had no desire to create a precedent by granting title to even as modest a tract as the one requested, and refused to relinquish a square inch of land to Chief Smallboy.

To Hurricane Hanne this was like waving a red flag at a bull. To continue the metaphor she locked horns with the entire government hierarchy, both federal and provincial, in an attempt to acquire the campsite for these unfortunate people. With unrelenting Scandinavian tenacity she strove to bring the government bureaucrats to their knees and have them bend their rules in her favor, so Smallboy's people could have the Shangri-La they so desperately needed.

It was not to be. Notwithstanding my valiant efforts to help her, and the influence in high places of the ubiquitous Maurice Strong, the Crown refused to cede title.

Undaunted by the bureaucratic iceberg that blocked his way, Chief Smallboy gathered his flock together and marched off into the Alberta forest lands and set up his camp in defiance of government authority.

While his great trek was taking place, a gathering of the indigenous people of the western hemisphere was to be held in the old League of Nations building in Geneva, Switzerland, under the non-governmental auspices of the United Nations. There Hanne hoped to obtain a formal resolution that she would present to the land officials in Edmonton when she returned to Alberta.

We were all in Geneva for the moving and unforgettable experience. In the spring of 1977 aboriginal peoples had gathered in force from all over the western hemisphere. I met the formidable Mike Meyers, from the Seneca Nation of the Iroquois Confederacy, who had cleared Swiss customs with a passport of his own making, duly granted to him by the Seneca Nation in New York state. The most vocal Indians came from the Rosebud Sioux reservation in South Dakota. Their virile and young leader limped around the gathering, exhorting everyone within hearing distance to stand up against the "multinational" oil interests and the evil Bureau of the Interior of the American government. His name was Russell Means and he cut a dashing figure as he addressed the throng.

"Why does he limp like that?" I asked a bushy-haired young reporter from an Indian newspaper in St. Paul, Minnesota.

"You'd limp too," the journalist replied, "if you had as much FBI lead in you as he has."

I thought back on the skirmishes between the Sioux and the U.S. government, fought off and on ever since the Battle of Wounded Knee in 1890. These battles had been synonymous with Indian repression and I knew exactly what he meant.

Hanne got her resolution supporting Chief Smallboy and his efforts, but the Alberta Crown was obdurate and remained unmoved. In due course, Hanne was adopted by Chief Smallboy and moved down to Southern Colorado where she fought her Indian battles from afar. Chief Smallboy has since died. Although some of his followers have made their way back to the Hobbema lands and all their evil ways, the Smallboy camp remains in the wilderness, a symbol of Chief Smallboy's faith in a way of life that is no more.

The year 1977 was also significant to me, as I was introduced to Hurricane Hanne. My clients, the Blackfoot of Gleichen, were well aware of the significance of the year 1977 for another reason. It marked the centennial of Treaty No. 7 which had been signed at Blackfoot Crossing.

Those were tempestuous times for the native peoples of Canada. South of the border American settlers moved westward to the Pacific. Following the Civil War the U.S. cavalry conquered and destroyed the native people of the United States to the point of extinction.

In 1877 Canada was in between the Riel rebellions, and Sir John A. Macdonald dispatched the North West Mounted Police to suppress the whiskey traders from Montana and to keep Canadian Indians friendly to the British Crown. The mighty Crowfoot was a pivotal figure in these negotiations, and only his prestige and eloquence prevented hostilities from breaking out.

With the disappearance of the buffalo, the culture and age-old traditions of the Indians were soon to be forgotten. In a series of treaties, the Canadian Indians ceded vast tracts of their territory to the Crown. A new era had arrived.

On September 22, 1877, Indians from all over southern Alberta gathered at Blackfoot Crossing to sign Treaty No. 7 as an indication of their peaceful intentions and to enter into a binding relationship with the British Crown. After several days of negotiations this memorable document was executed. The government was represented by Lieutenant Governor Laird and Colonel James MacLeod of the North West Mounted Police. Chief Crowfoot of the Blackfoot spoke for the Indian people. A half-breed scout, Jerry Potts, acted as interpreter and to the booming of cannons and the beating of drums, Treaty No. 7 became a part of Canadian history.

The treaty meant different things to each side. To the Crown it was an affirmation that the Indians would become peaceful subjects of Canada. To the Indians it was a solemn pact between two sovereign peoples whereby the Indians ceded title to a vast tract of land to Her Majesty Queen Victoria of Britain, on the solemn undertaking of the Queen that she would look after her Indian children forever.

What a memorable day September 22nd, 1877 must have been! For five long days and nights, Crowfoot, the Chief of Chiefs, had been torn with indecision. Finally he decided to cast his lot with the Queen's Cowboy and the mounted police as the most effective deterrent against the whiskey traders and "long knives" who were pouring into Indian country from the United States and destroying the buffalo forever. His lean figure and aquiline features made him an imposing presence as he described the problems of southwestern Alberta.

> I hope you will look upon the people of these tribes as your children now and that you will be charitable to them, who have protected us as

the feathers of the bird protect it from the frosts of winter . . . I wish them all good and trust their hearts will increase in goodness. I am satisfied. I will sign the treaty.
– from *Fifty Mighty Men* by Grant MacEwan, Modern Press, Saskatoon, Saskatchewan 1958, p. 27

The Winston Churchill of the western plains rested his case. In his eloquent words a sacred covenant had been made between the Great White Mother and her Indian subjects to last "as long as the rivers run and the grass will grow," and for over 100 years the Indians of Canada have waited patiently for those promises to be carried out.

As the summer of 1977 approached, word spread like a prairie fire that Prince Charles, the direct descendant of Queen Victoria, was coming in person to Blackfoot Crossing to assure the Indians of southern Alberta that the promises were alive and in good standing, and that they would be honored as solemn undertakings of the Crown.

With royalty coming to Gleichen it was only fitting the visit should be recognized for the historic occasion it was, by delivering to the heir apparent to the British Throne a gift to commemorate the royal visit.

At this point I contacted my friend, Professor Cal Orton of the Nickle Arts Museum in Calgary, and asked him to prepare a replica of the Treaty 7 medal that I would present to his Royal Highness on his arrival at the Blackfoot reservation.

The good professor proved equal to the assignment. In short order he had produced an exact replica in plaster of Paris of the great silver medal struck a century before and given to each of the chiefs who signed Treaty No. 7. The medal showed in bas-relief Her Majesty Queen Victoria wearing the royal crown and on the obverse side, the stalwart figure of Lieutenant Governor Laird, shaking the hand of an Indian chief who had the unmistakable features of Chief Crowfoot. The medal hung from an impressive multicolored ribbon. I was delighted with this facsimile of a medal—an ideal present for the Prince of Wales when he came to visit his subjects.

Prince Charles appeared at the Blackfoot Crossing shortly after lunch on July 6, 1977 and roughly 3 000 people were on hand to witness the great event. The festivities were marred by a raging sandstorm that blew with such vigor it threatened to bring down the enormous brown tent erected in case of rain. The tent was packed to the breaking point, as everyone pressed inside to escape the sandstorm with its blinding dust. I managed to get under cover with my present for the Prince safe and sound in my breast pocket, and stood alone in that mass of surging humanity, waiting patiently for peace and quiet to prevail.

To my astonishment, I saw a wooden scaffolding at the far end of the tent, and there seated all by himself on a wooden chair was Prince Charles

A present for Prince Charles

in khaki dungarees, waiting for the proceedings to begin. There was no time for delay. I made my way along the side of the tent towards the platform, past Indians and stern-faced members of the Royal Canadian Mounted Police, who were there to maintain law and order and to provide the Prince with security from violence should it be needed.

I made my way to the back of the platform and climbed up the trestles until I reached the top. There was no one on the platform but the Prince and myself. Holding my medal firmly in my hand I approached His Royal Highness. It was a golden opportunity, almost too good to be true.

"Hello, Prince," I said, "I'm the lawyer for the Blackfoot people and I've brought you a present."

"Very nice of you," replied His Royal Highness. "And just what have you got?"

"I've brought you a replica of the Treaty Seven medal," I replied.

The Prince was wearing an open-necked cowboy shirt and no tie. To my intense disappointment and chagrin, I observed that he was already wearing a medal around his neck—the real thing.

"But I see you've already got one," I stammered. "Where on earth did you get it?"

"They gave it to me, of course," replied Prince Charles. "Why, do you think I pinched it?"

"No, of course not," I answered. "But they are very hard to come by, and I was wondering what you are going to do with it."

"Do with it?" was his quick reply. "I'll take it home with me to Buckingham Palace and wear it every time I have a bath."

I gazed in anguished discomfiture at the thick medal hanging around the royal neck and was about to carry on with this entertaining conversation when an air force officer arrived on the scene and spirited away the Prince of Wales to more important matters awaiting his attention.

Earlier that day Prince Charles had publicly assured the Indians of southern Alberta that the promises given to their ancestors when Treaty No. 7 was signed would be honored and upheld in the spirit with which they were made, and the Indians firmly believed the Great White Mother and her representatives would keep their word.

And so, one might well ask, whither the plight of the Indian in Canada today?

The Mohawks and the Lubicons and other Indian militants such as the Peigan activists, with their unending battles over the Oldman River dam are far from dead. Native problems and aboriginal rights are high profile and topical at the moment. This was vividly drawn to my attention when I was on top of Signal Hill in St. John's, Newfoundland in November of 1988, waiting for the arrival of the Olympic Torch from Athens.

Never have I been so cold. The ocean dampness crept through the soles of my shoes and chilled me to the bone. The torch was late and the only active group in a mass of freezing humanity was a throng of Lubicon picketers, who had come all the way from northern Alberta to tell the world about their problems with the multinational oil companies and to gain sympathy and support for their plight. On its arrival, the Olympic torch was to be carried across Canada. The Lubicons well knew the eyes of the world would be on Newfoundland that morning and the Olympic torch would be obliged to share the limelight with the Lubicon claim.

The recent events at Oka have been disturbing and upsetting. The demands of the Lubicons will just not go away. Elijah Harper and Ovide Mercredi are permanent fixtures on the Canadian landscape. The Cree Indians in northern Quebec continue to scuttle the sale of electric power to New York state. The aboriginal claims of the native people in the Naas Valley, British Columbia, cry out for settlement.

It is obvious that only a few very wealthy bands of Indians have the resource base that will enable them to make "self-government" and "sovereignty" a viable *modus vivendi*, and until then the Department of Indian Affairs in some form or another will have to be maintained as a necessary evil.

The recent settlement between the Canadian Inuit and the Canadian government is a beautiful case in point of what can be done when both sides have resources and goodwill working for them. To suddenly scrap the Indian Act and abandon native reserves overnight would be brutal and inhumane.

In the last analysis, the Indian problem of Canada is quite similar to the race problems in South Africa. Time and understanding, and decency on both sides, perhaps will settle a painful problem that has been disturbing this country for 150 years.

The Indian people of Canada have come a long, long way since the pleas of Chiefs like Clarence McHugh and Leo Pretty Young Man fell upon the deaf ears of an uncaring Ottawa.

A Conflict of Interest

It is sometimes said that a police officer's lot is not a happy one. A similar observation could well be made about a solicitor in what is commonly known as a "conflict of interest." For centuries lawyers have been expected to conduct themselves with absolute impartiality towards their clients, never allowing their respective interests to overlap in any way. But the dividing line between the two spheres of interest are not always crystal clear. There can be difficulties of the subtlest kind; where, say, there are property problems and the client's solicitor unintentionally crosses the line to a conflict-of-interest position.

When "Baldy" Morkin came in to tell me he had lost his farm, and outlined the circumstances of his sad case, I perceived what to me was a conflict of interest. Baldy had read about the victory of the Treaty 7 Indians forcing the federal government to pay them their "bullet money" and he thought, rightly or wrongly, that I could do something similar for him.

It was to be no easy job. The Morkins had been farming down in the Claresholm country south of Calgary since the turn of the century, and Baldy had been growing grain on family land just outside the town boundary as long as anyone could remember. It was prime land for mixed farming, but if the town were to expand, this property was sure to be annexed, and Baldy would make himself enough money so that he would never have to work again. Unfortunately for Baldy he had lost control of his farm and his back was to the wall.

Things had not been going well financially on the Morkin property. Baldy was a reasonably good farmer, but a poor businessman, and for many years it was all he could do to stay afloat. He had no children, and he watched with some degree of envy the successful farming operations of his brother Tom and his nephews on the farm next to his own.

The ugly threat of mortgage foreclosure seemed to be always hanging over his head. In the autumn of 1979, with winter coming on, he was at his wit's end as to how to save his farm. He had over a section of choice farmland. Apart from the usual problems of drought, dust storms, falling commodity prices, adverse freight rates and everything else a farmer has to face, Baldy was a survivor, and in this "next year country," he knew he could weather the storm. But his mortgage was being foreclosed and he had nowhere to go. So he turned to his lawyer, John Boras down in Lethbridge and asked for help. It was then that the problem of conflict of interest arose.

Baldy was really up against it. He would lose everything unless John Boras and his friends could save him. So they formed a game plan. They would incorporate a company to be known as Western 5 and Baldy Morkin would transfer his farm to the new group. The equity in the new company was to be split five ways, with Baldy to have 20 percent of the common shares and John Boras and his three client friends in Lethbridge holding the other 80 percent. A new mortgage was to be obtained by the Boras group and the proceeds would be used to retire the existing mortgage and thereby avert the foreclosure that was approaching its final stages.

The way would then be clear for a subdivision of the Morkin farm and everyone, including Baldy Morkin, stood to make a handsome profit. The pivotal figure in the whole transaction was John Boras. He was a prominent Lethbridge lawyer and the solicitor for the three friends he brought into the Morkin deal. He was also the solicitor for Baldy Morkin and Mr. Boras was to have 20 percent of the equity in the farm himself. There is an old Irish proverb that "no one can drive three mules at the same time," or, in Biblical parlance, "no man can serve two masters."

This thorny question did not seem to have disturbed any one in the Western 5 group, except Baldy himself. He was a quiet, soft-spoken, stubborn man, and hard of hearing as well. With only a limited grade school education, he was not really interested in the finer points of mortgage financing, unless it was a means for him to hold on to the farm that had been in the Morkin family for generations. Silent and morose, he attended the meetings of the new company, but took very little part in their grandiose plans to break up his farm and get the necessary approvals from the municipal district so that the land could be subdivided.

The one point that he did grasp firmly and clearly was that he was not going to farm anymore. The mortgage foreclosure was not going to happen, but the end result was not going to be all that different for him. He had been a farmer all his life and if Baldy had his way, he would be a farmer until he died.

Deep down in his heart he just wanted out of the whole affair. He would find a new mortgage of his own and carry on as he had always done.

The only way out for him that I could see was to set the transfer aside as a voidable transaction, and appeal to the equitable jurisdiction of the court that the parties were in a conflict-of-interest position, which would invalidate the whole sale.

It was easier said than done, and the actual trial in the Supreme Court of Alberta took 11 days. For the late Mr. Justice Cameron Steer, there was no great problem with the facts or the evidence; it was the ethical and moral principles that seemed to cause him considerable mental anguish.

The prestigious Calgary firm of Fenerty and Company, presumably as the solicitors for the insurers of Mr. Boras, took the lofty stand that this was a straightforward and bona fide transaction, and that any considerations of conflict of interest were completely irrelevant and just did not enter the picture. Early on, Mr. Boras was represented by the present Mr. Justice Brennan, who following pretrial discovery, was elevated to the bench of the Supreme Court of Alberta. He was succeeded by two energetic young lawyers, David Tavender and Bill Pieschel, who fought tirelessly to give their client a full and complete defense. I was all alone on this one, as usual.

I never ceased to wonder at the painstaking and beautiful preparation with which David Tavender presented his case. With the ease and grace of a ballet dancer, he wove his way back and forth through the thick black binders containing his briefs on the evidence and examination and cross-examination of numerous witnesses, with the important passages underlined in transparent yellow ink. Amongst that vast volume of paper and exhibits he could invariably find the document or passage he was looking for. It was a highly professional and unforgettable display.

I argued that Baldy Morkin had been pressured to convey his farm to the Western 5 group, and submitted that the whole affair should be set aside on grounds of undue influence, as well as the fact that the gentlemen from Lethbridge were in a conflict-of-interest position that could not be supported by the court.

Mr. Justice Steer was obviously having great difficulty with this aspect of the case. His great bristling moustache made him look like a British cavalry officer marching with Gordon to Khartoum. At the end of this long and hard-fought trial, he reserved his decision as he pondered over his reasons for judgment.

Eventually, in a carefully reasoned decision, he set the transaction aside and Baldy Morkin went on to farm again. It was a precedent of great importance to the legal profession, for it reaffirmed that no man, let alone a lawyer, can serve two masters, and where there is indeed a conflict of interest between a lawyer and his client any transaction flowing therefrom cannot be allowed to stand.

The North American Gypsy

I had worked off and on for Kenny Popow for many years. Of Ukrainian stock, he had come down to Calgary from Edmonton and seemed always to be on the periphery of the law, with intricate automobile transactions that caused him frequent trouble but from which he invariably seemed to emerge unscathed.

He was a stocky, owl-like fellow, but behind the bifocal glasses and placid features there lurked an iron will. He was always a fighter and a survivor, and the word "surrender" was not in his vocabulary. I had not heard from Kenny for a long time, when he called me unexpectedly to say that this time he was in trouble far afield and needed my help.

In the early 1970s he had been busily engaged in acquiring old buses and obsolescent streetcars in Canada and taking them down to California for overhauling and repairs. When the remedial work was done, he either disposed of the refurbished vehicles in the United States or Mexico, or brought them back to Canada for sale. There was just no question he loved cars and everything connected with them. They were meat and drink for him.

Needless to say, his activities were of more than passing interest to the customs officials. When he ran afoul of the customs people in 1974, the object of his affections was a Mazda car of doubtful vintage he had acquired in the United States. After reconditioning it until it was as good as new, Kenny drove his Mazda across the country to the Lakehead area of Thunder Bay in Ontario. He planned to take his car back into the United States and make a profitable resale.

Expecting to clear customs at the border crossing of Pigeon River, some 50 km (30 miles) southwest of Thunder Bay, Kenny then planned to make his way across Ohio to the lucrative markets of the eastern seaboard. Unfortunately, the customs officials did not see it the same way. A close examination of the documents left these worthies less than satisfied as to the title to the car and Kenny found himself arrested and charged with contravening the Customs Act of Canada.

This was serious trouble indeed, for as only a few people know, the Customs officers have more sweeping powers in Canada than any other arm of the government and it is no easy task to challenge their jurisdiction.

Kenny found himself a stranger in a strange land. Undaunted, he decided to defend himself. His case came on for trial in the court house in Thunder Bay before a court composed of judge and jury. The axe fell and he was sentenced to six months in prison. At this stage he made his *cri de coeur* and called me in to defend him. He was far from home and it was foreign country to me as well, as I was not a member of the Ontario bar.

By this time Kenny was out on bail, pending his appeal, which he implored me to file. His fate hung in the balance while I did my best to expedite matters to bring his appeal on for hearing.

The first order of the day was to get called to the Ontario bar for this one appearance. This was a technicality but an absolute necessity. In due course I made my way to Osgoode Hall in Toronto and appeared before some 30 Benchers of the Law Society of Upper Canada.

This solemn gathering was presided over by the Treasurer of the Society. This was strange nomenclature to me, as I was not sure whether there was a president in absentia, who would normally have conducted proceedings, or whether the Treasurer was indeed the head man of the Benchers and this was the way things were done in Ontario. The matter was over in a few minutes, and with the proper credentials, I had the required standing before the Court.

The Ontario Court had courteously placed the Popow appeal as number one on the list, because we had come all the way from Alberta. However, a necessary formality had not been complied with and our appeal could not be heard. Under Ontario rules the appellant, who was at large on appeal bail, was required to surrender himself to the sheriff of the judicial district of Thunder Bay, the place of his conviction. From there he would be conveyed to the Court of Appeal in Toronto. So we lost our position as the number one appeal on the list and were bumped down to second place, while an interminable case involving an $8 million fraud occupied the attention of their Lordships.

The three-man court that eventually heard the appeal wasted no time on window dressing. They took judicial notice of the fact that Pigeon River was in the territorial jurisdiction of the trial court at Thunder Bay and concentrated their attention on what they felt were the real issues before the Court; namely, whether the trial judge had properly considered the relevant sections of the Customs Act and the complicated regulations drafted pursuant to the act.

A review of the evidence revealed that the trial judge had not referred to the regulations in his charge to the jury. As I recall, the Appeal Court felt that if the trial judge had directed the attention of the jury to the material regulations, the verdict could well have been different. This dereliction was a serious error in law warranting a new trial for Kenny Popow.

Back in his Toronto hotel I bade farewell to my client. There I was introduced to his three-year-old boy, who had been given the interesting names of "Elvis" (after the great star of rock and roll) "V-8" (after the V-8 engine no less!) "Popow." By now that little boy is a teenager and with names like those, and a father like Kenny Popow, one can only surmise that automobiles and things mechanical are an important part of his life.

At one stage during the appeal, the sometimes irascible Mr. Justice Schroeder, who was acting as Chief Justice of the Appeal Court, described my client as "the North American Gypsy." Perhaps he was, but of this I am sure: wherever he is and whatever he is doing, he will never cross the border at Pigeon River again.

Wounded Birds
ళ్లళ్లళ్లళ్లళ్లళ్లళ్లళ్లళ్ల

I well recall a case where a coal miner in Pictou County, Nova Scotia battered his wife to a pulp with a pick-axe handle following a drunken Saturday night binge. This was 1946. "Case dismissed" the court decided. "In other parts of the world this behavior might be construed as physical cruelty, but not in Pictou County on a Saturday night."

The practice of law reflects the changes in social conditions surrounding us. It has come to my attention that in North America a decree for divorce is granted every 27 seconds of the day. This was not the case back in Halifax when I first acted for unhappy spouses, caught in the marriage trap, who wanted a divorce *a vinculo matrimonii,* so they could start their lives anew.

In Nova Scotia divorce was no jesting matter and the required corroboration of alleged adultery was sometimes very difficult to obtain. That province by the sea was not quite the same as other common-law provinces, in that physical cruelty, as well as adultery, was a ground for divorce.

In those dark days following the War, all Halifax divorce cases came up before the brothers Graham. The elder Graham presided as the Equity Judge and his younger brother acted as Watching Counsel for the Department of the Attorney General. I have seen divorce cases in their Court go on for three-quarters of an hour, while the Watching Counsel, in his high-pitched falsetto voice, harassed and badgered a female petitioner until the courtroom was flooded in tears. This is a far cry from the present day, when the average uncontested divorce is completed in about five minutes and on most occasions only the petitioner has appeared in court for the great event.

It was Kipling who described the Victorian women he knew in those unforgettable words:

> *And the female of the species*
> *Is more deadly than the male.*

Quite frankly I have never found them that way at all. If I had my way, every day would be ladies' day, and I am anything but distressed to see women finally coming into their own. They are flocking into the work-place and carving out careers in fields that were unknown before the war. Speaking as a mere man, I welcome them. Once again, in the immortal words of Fred Huntley, "They have raised the tone of the alley." But men and women being what they are, the battle of the sexes grinds remorselessly on—sometimes lightly, sometimes grimly, but always there.

Shortly after my arrival in Calgary, I was accosted at a dance following a law dinner by the buxom wife of a tiny English barrister, who had become one of the more prestigious figures at the Calgary bar.

"I say, Webbie," she said in her pleasant English accent, "do you take divorce cases?"

"Sometimes, my dear," I replied. "Depending on the circumstances, who the parties are, the merits of the case, and all that sort of thing. Now who are we talking about?"

"It's Michael," she said.

"But who is the alleged participant?" I inquired. In Nova Scotia the court was concerned with the corroborating witness who provided supporting evidence to establish adultery, but in Alberta the alleged participant was a most important party.

"It's his cello," replied Beryl in mock gravity. "Every morning he gets up at five o'clock and goes down to the basement and plays on his cello instead of playing with me!"

"Beryl," I said, "that's grounds for divorce. I'll take the case!"

At the other end of the spectrum are the wounded birds, the women who really have a hard time in the marriage game and have turned to other consorts in their yearning to be free.

In more euphemistic terms, it could be perhaps described as alienation of affection. But how can there be alienation of affection when there is no affection to alienate?

I had a classic encounter in the early 1960s turning on this very point. A prominent petroleum engineer, who shall remain nameless, felt that he had been cuckolded by an equally prominent orthopedic surgeon whose attentions to the engineer's wife had passed beyond the bounds of professional propriety. Candlelight dinners and clandestine trysts in wooded groves were many times observed by the jealous engineer, but all to no avail. Suspicion piled upon suspicion is not proof, and the court felt that a case for alienation of affection had not been made. Events took their natural course and eventually all parties divorced and the allegations of alienation of affection were forgotten.

Alienation of affection in the little town of Sundre, Alberta took quite a different turn from its counterpart in Calgary when the then-mayor of Sundre paid amorous attention to my client's wife.

Horst Malegowski was a Polish coal miner and the work that he did after coming to Alberta often took him far from home. The mayor of Sundre, when not dealing with his municipal problems, would spend an inordinate amount of time at the Malegowski farm, ostensibly for the purpose of repairing the furnace which frequently was not operating in a satisfactory manner.

On one such occasion, some time after the furnace had been long forgotten, the coal miner returned home unexpectedly and found the mayor in the kitchen in his stocking feet. Malegowski, who had been a prize fighter in his day, was anything but pleased to find the mayor as an uninvited guest in his home.

The mayor fled the scene to the safety of his municipal office with the enraged Malegowski (who by this time had picked up a firearm) in hot pursuit. At the municipal office natural justice was done and a badly battered mayor was taken to the hospital. Malegowski subsequently pled guilty to a charge of assault and was heavily fined, at which point the mayor decided to sue for damages.

Eventually the case of *Ceveny v. Malegowski* came on for trial in the Court of Queen's Bench at Red Deer, at which time the Plaintiff claimed damages for assault following the battle at the Townhall in Sundre. As the sordid details were laid out for all to see, it was patently clear that the mayor was up to no good in Malegowski's home. On the basis of *ex turpi causa non oritur actio* (from a bad source a good cause of action does not arise) the court dismissed the claim. Like the Calgary case referred to above, everyone was in time divorced and pursued the even tenor of their way.

As time went on, I encountered more and more wounded birds yearning to be free who turned to the courts for their release. Sometimes they had passed the point of no return and nothing could be done for them. Like the Dutch wife who was obviously deranged, and who came to me deeply upset, assuring me that her husband was plotting her death and she was not long for this world. True to her word, in a matter of days her dead body was found, filled with carbon monoxide, inside her truck in the garage behind her home.

The police investigation found it was death by her own hand. Obviously she had been in an acute state of mental depression. I recalled her recounting how her husband taunted her, how he had locked her in an iron cage and said he would never let her go. I went to her funeral on 17th Avenue S.W., and as the music played "Make the world go away, and get if off my shoulders," my heart bled for her. It is not only man's inhumanity to man makes countless thousands moan, man's inhumanity to woman is often just as bad.

And then there were times when it was a joy and a delight to open the cage and set free the wounded bird.

Victoria was such a case. She had come to Alberta from one of the outport villages of Newfoundland and was hopelessly trapped in a marriage to a realtor from which she yearned to be released. With luminous dark eyes and full-blown lower lip, she was Canada's answer to Sophia Loren.

I assured her I was her rod and her staff and could open the marriage cage and let her fly away. And I did just that. It is cases like hers that give a man the Messiah syndrome and make it all worth while.

I have defended many cases of rape, or sexual assault as they are now called, and have mixed feelings concerning the complainants of this unhappy offense. To my mind these cases fall into two broad categories.

First, there are bona fide victims who are quietly minding their own business, when without warning they are attacked and violated, most often by a criminal sexual psychopath. These innocent women are involved in a traumatic and harrowing experience from which they may never recover and should receive every protection the justice system can provide.

But so many of the wounded birds in the courts of law have been the authors of their own wrong. By their apparently promiscuous conduct they brought misfortune on themselves. When a woman has put herself in such a position that a sexual approach by a male is the inevitable result, can it be held that the man is solely to blame? Should he alone be punished, or is she not a willing participant and just as guilty?

The "rape shield" law has been replaced by a tough new standard for consent and cases of violence against women are at last getting the treatment they so rightly deserve.

Of all the wounded birds who arrived in my office for one reason or another, I felt most sorry for the unfortunate women injured by the insertion of an intrauterine device known as the Dalkon Shield into their bodies. There were roughly 22 of them with the same distressing story.They had submitted to the implantation of this horrific metal scarab in their respective anatomies as a sure-fire method of birth control that would effectively prevent the male spermatozoa from reaching its union with the female ovium.

On inspection, the Dalkon Shield was hardly a sinister-looking object. About an inch and a half in diameter and with outstretched arms radiating from a central area, it resembled a flat, golden spider from an Indian temple. To my untutored masculine eye, it did not appear particularly dangerous, but every female client had basically the same horror story to tell about the ghastly effects the shield had upon them.

Their injuries varied in the complexity of their complaints. Some women had become barren and attributed their infertility to the evil device. Others had violent headaches and severe abdominal pain they never had before. All of the complaints had one basic grievance; that their ills and problems were caused by the malfunctioning of the Dalkon Shield.

In almost every case, the victims had only partial or defective medical records to back up their claims. Over the years the medical evidence had been lost or disappeared, or was difficult to obtain, which made it virtually impossible to document their accusations.

It was immediately apparent that their claims could only be resolved in the United States, for that was where the multinational drug conglomerate which had produced and distributed the Dalkon Shield all over the world was located. If the claims were to be pursued, as well they should, an American attorney was essential. As the claimants increased, and the media across Canada took up their cause, I looked across the border to New York City. There in the Big Apple, a dynamic attorney named Paul

Rheingold was assembling the legal and medical data that was necessary to bring the A.H. Robins Corporation to its knees.

It was no easy task. According to Rheingold, the courts in some American states like Maryland and Virginia were more receptive and sympathetic to the Dalkon Shield claims than other more conservative jurisdictions. Like a giant snowball, the Dalkon Shield cases gathered momentum, and after months of almost token resistance, the A.H. Robins Company threw in the towel and sought refuge in the safety provisions of Chapter XI of the American bankruptcy laws.

The tale of woe is far from over. The medical plight of women, the most visible side of the sexual revolution, has shown beyond any possible doubt that women are still fourth-class citizens in a male-dominated society. Women's grievances about adequate condoms and breast silicon implants only underline their contention that medically, women have never really had the fair shake that is rightfully theirs.

Long before Anita Hill and Judge Thomas became household words across North America and trial by spectacle on TV was the order of the day, I came in contact with Bonnie Robichaud, the Canadian symbol of sexual harassment in the workplace.

This was one courageous woman, who dared to fight for principles that she felt had been violated in a man's world. When she came in to enlist my support in her struggle, sexual harassment was a well-understood fact. But nobody discussed the problem openly or did anything about it. Not so Bonnie Robichaud! By the time she reached my office she had been battling for years to prove her point.

She had been working as a toilet cleaner with the Department of National Defence at the Air Defence Command base in North Bay, Ontario, since 1977. By November of 1978, as a reward for her hard work, she had been promoted to the position of lead-hand, subject to a six-month probationary period lasting until May of 1979. Throughout this period she was subjected to the unwelcome attentions of the foreman of the Cleaning department, who sexually harassed her while she was engaged in the performance of her duties. And all of this under the supervision of the Base Commanding Officer of the Department of National Defence!

Bonnie Robichaud was not one to take this without fighting back. Over the following years she exhausted all legal manoeuvres open to her, through the Byzantine complexities of the Canadian Human Rights Commission and the Review Tribunals, the appellate mechanisms of the

Federal Court of Canada and, as a final resort, the Supreme Court of Canada itself.

By June 29th, 1987 she had won, establishing once and for all that a female employee could not be harassed with impunity by a male supervisor in the workplace. But was it a Pyrrhic victory? After dozens of court appearances and thousands of letters, Bonnie Robichaud had triumphed, but at what cost!

This was no wide-eyed female liberationist. Here was a woman who had single-handedly fought for her legal rights in the courts of this country. The question of her damages still remains to be determined, but her whole story is another glorious chapter in the history of women's rights in Canada, not unlike the five women from Alberta who persuaded the Judicial Committee of the Privy Council that women in Canada were "persons" within the meaning of the British North America Act and could therefore be legally appointed to the Senate.

Well done, Ms. Robichaud!

Terror Stalks the Deerfoot

I first saw Kelly Jacobson all swathed in bandages at the Calgary General Hospital after his almost fatal collision with a concrete buttress on the Deerfoot Trail in north Calgary. It was a miracle he escaped death, and an even greater miracle that his baby daughter had come out of the crash with hardly a scratch.

A dreadful accident, but Kelly Jacobson and his child had both survived. So I was at a loss to understand the sinister view the Crown attached to the whole affair. In the eyes of the police, my client was in dark, serious trouble. Their theory was that Kelly Jacobson, on the day in question, had driven his car on a death ride up and down the Deerfoot Trail. The Deerfoot is a main traffic artery leading north to Red Deer and Edmonton, south to Lethbridge and the U.S. The police contended that Kelly Jacobson, with criminal intent, had deliberately smashed his car into a concrete pillar on this freeway in order to kill his child and himself.

Kelly himself sustained a broken arm and head injuries in the accident. His car was a tangled mass of wreckage. His baby, however, was unhurt and he was puzzled and confused as to why the police were so angry about the whole affair. He and his wife were at the parting of the ways, and he knew how she, as the child's mother, felt about it all, but her bitterness and upset feelings should have been quite different from those of the police, or so he thought.

Because of his injuries, it was some time before the case could be set down for trial. Mel Brown, a balding, soft-spoken young lawyer, acted as the agent for the Attorney General in the case. I was constantly surprised at the hard-nosed position assumed by the Crown throughout the trial.

I was probably more than a little prejudiced towards my client, which may be a failing I have been guilty of on more than one occasion. As I saw it, the accident on the Deerfoot Trail had happened because my client had lost control of his car from some mechanical reason, or he had a momentary blackout, or he had temporarily lost touch with reality because he was under severe emotional stress. I could conceive how the collision had occurred for any one of the foregoing reasons, but could not understand the police theory that he deliberately set out to kill himself and his child by causing a fatal accident.

The police had reacted to the situation with speed and efficiency, and mounted a formidable case for us to meet. Immediately following the accident, homicide detectives had taken statements from Kelly's sister and brother-in-law, as well as from people who were eyewitnesses at the scene of the accident. Kelly's wife was called to give evidence about the events of the fatal day. Pictures of the child were produced, which only added to the tension and high emotions of the trial.

I had elected trial by judge in the Provincial Court of Alberta, as I did not view the case with the same gravity as the Crown. This was an error in judgment on my part. If I were doing it all again, I would have elected trial by judge and jury, with the reasonable expectation that I would be able to extract a sympathy verdict for the distraught father that I was unable to get from the trial judge sitting alone.

Assistant Chief Judge H.G. Oliver, the presiding judge, made it obvious from the outset that he felt he was dealing with a heinous crime of the deepest dye. His ruddy kindly face took on a most serious mien, and it was patently clear there would be only justice and no mercy when the time came for his decision.

It was an uphill battle all the way. Mel Brown, as Crown Prosecutor, was firm and fair, and no problem to deal with. The trial judge, however, was quite a different matter. It is a tradition of British law that the role of the presiding judge is to listen to the evidence, and at no time should he abdicate his judicial function and enter as a gladiator into the forum. Justice must not only be done, but abundantly be seen to be done. Not so in this case. By actual count the judge interrupted the hearing, mostly in argument with myself, 243 times, so that throughout the trial I was battling not one antagonist, but two, and they held all the cards.

At the conclusion of the evidence, the judge adjourned the case and reserved his decision. Court reassembled in a few days, and to my astonishment the judge had prepared about a dozen written copies of his decision to hand out not only to counsel, but to numerous members of the media; the Jacobson case was a high-profile matter of considerable public interest.

Then the court proceeded to read into the record Judge Oliver's written reasons for judgment. Shortly after the reading of the written reasons commenced, I heard the court describe my client's baby as "his precious cargo" and I knew it was all over. The judgment found Kelly Jacobson guilty of criminal negligence, with the requisite criminal intent to support the charge. The judge thereupon sentenced my client to 12 years imprisonment. I was shocked and stunned by this incredible turn of events and determined to file an immediate notice of appeal.

When the appeal came on for hearing, the Court of Appeal directed a new trial, notwithstanding my vehement criticism of the intervention by the trial judge during the course of the hearing. I described, as vividly as I could, how the trial judge had descended into the forum and assumed the role of advocate by interrupting the trial at every conceivable opportunity. Without giving written reasons, the court ordered a new trial forthwith.

When the matter came on for a new trial, before Mr. Justice Paul Chrumka in the Court of Queen's Bench, it was clear that my client was going to be found guilty of negligence of some kind and that the real issue was the question of sentence. After conviction, a finding of "Guilty" was entered and the court sentenced Jacobson to imprisonment for a term of 5 years, a substantial gain for him after the 12-year sentence imposed by Judge Oliver.

All in all, it was not a happy story. My client came from a broken home, where his alcoholic father beat him unmercifully. Loss of his house and a pending divorce had Kelly Jacobson on the verge of a nervous breakdown. On the day of the accident, he had driven back and forth on the Deerfoot Trail a number of times before leaving the highway and careening into the concrete abutment with terrible results.

Who knows what was on his mind at that time? Did he intend to end it all, or was it a frightful accident aggravated by slippery snow on the highway? Above all, did he intend to kill himself and take his child with him? Only he knows the answers to those questions. He has had psychiatric treatment and is now remarried and carving out a new career for himself. Life has not been all that great for Kelly Jacobson up until now. Good luck, Kelly. Hopefully there are better days ahead!

Ticket to Heaven

As the seventies gave way to the eighties, there was mounting discontent with mainstream religions, and with the advent of the Flower People, offbeat cults bloomed and flourished on all sides. One of the more aggressive of these groups was "The Moonies," who took their name from their Korean founder, the Reverend Sun Myung Moon.

On the surface they were dedicated, harmless people and only visible to most Calgarians at the entrance to liquor stores, where pale and sad-faced young ladies sold roses for a dollar apiece and forwarded the proceeds to the Reverend Moon and his Unification Church in the U.S.A.

Further investigation would have revealed that these flower vendors were part of a vast network across the continent, which produced a great deal of money for the Reverend Moon and his Unification Church. In earlier and unhappier times in Korea, the Reverend Moon had been persecuted unmercifully for his religious beliefs, but after his arrival in the United States, things improved immeasurably for him, and the dynamic leader soon had a huge estate on the Hudson River outside New York City and among other profitable ventures, a thriving fishing business based in Gloucester, Massachusetts. These flourishing business operations soon attracted the attention of the Internal Revenue Service and the income tax problems of the Moonies were about to begin.

Back in Calgary, the new movement had attracted a number of followers who had formed their own church and as a side line set up a rug-cleaning store, along with a picture-framing business. A quiet young man named John Abelseth was the spearhead of the local Unification Church. By hard work, John and his people had built up their business to be a going concern, as they would say in Nova Scotia, and everything in the garden was lovely—except for John's family.

His father and mother were hard-working, God-fearing Norwegian immigrants, who lived and worked at Seebee on the Bow River outside of Calgary, and they viewed their son's apostasy with misgiving and concern. He was a brand to be snatched from the burning, and they were determined to rescue him from the forces of evil before it was too late.

There was no alternative. John had to be kidnapped and "deprogrammed" without delay.

Just before the time of his abduction, John had visited the main Unification Church in San Francisco, and was supportive of what the church was trying to do. He was 35 years old and unmarried, and in no time became a dedicated follower of the Reverend Moon, wholeheartedly embracing the teaching and principles of the Unification Church.

On the night of April 27th, 1981, as John was coming out of the garage behind his picture framing business, he was captured by professional thugs, hurled into a van and taken away. Immediate attempts were made to de-program him. At that stage, his family planned to have him transported to a de-programming centre in Iowa called "Unbound Incorporated," where they hoped John would see the error of his ways and return to what they considered a normal way of life. He was held incommunicado for a week in Calgary before his captors set out for Iowa. In Great Falls, Montana, John was left unattended for a short period of time and made his escape. He fled to Colorado and from there he flew to San Francisco, and eventually back home to Calgary.

By this time the fight was on in earnest. John laid criminal charges for kidnapping and conspiracy against the de-programmers and sued them as well for damages. Witnesses and legal advisers came up from San Francisco to testify at the criminal proceedings, but between the preliminary inquiry and the trial, John was kidnapped again and this time detained against his will for 75 days. In a series of moves he was shunted to isolated places in southern Alberta and from there to his uncle's farm outside of Corner Brook in Newfoundland.

During these 75 days he was not left alone for a minute, and was subjected to relentless psychological brainwashing to compel him to renounce his support for the Reverend Moon and the Unification Church. It became a battle for the mind of John Abelseth. As the days wore on, John deluded his jailers into believing that he had repented and forsaken his "evil" ways and would sever all ties with the Moonies.

On his return to Calgary, John Abelseth knew that his family and captors meant business, so he decided to meet with the press and make a statement that would plainly outline his position for all to see. In a typed three-page press release, he clearly and persuasively outlined his reasons for supporting the Unification Church and made a strong and rational plea to his family and the public to understand his behavior and beliefs. He described in graphic detail how he had been abducted against his will by the de-programmers who had unsuccessfully tried to "brainwash" him and bring him back to reality.

He concluded with these moving words:

I felt then, as now, that I have no choice but to bring legal proceedings. Somehow the world—the public and the media, must listen. Human rights have been violated. My own family have been victimized by the biggest con job ever. I must do everything I can to stop this kind of thing from ever happening again. I must expose and prosecute those who take advantage of great people like my own family, so others are not subjected to the same kind of treachery. That is my determination.

At this juncture John decided to leave Canada permanently and work for the Unification Church in the U.S.A. From his sanctuary in New York he tried to have criminal charges enforced against the kidnappers, but the three main "bounty hunters" were in the United States and Calgary authorities were not very enthusiastic or sympathetic about bringing these people to Canada for trial. With John safely out of the country, the whole affair was quietly forgotten, especially as the Reverend Moon had more pressing and immediate problems in the United States.

By the summer of 1982, I put John Abelseth and the Moonies out of my mind and moved on to other things. Then quite unexpectedly I received an invitation from John to come to his wedding in New York city. This was to be no ordinary wedding and I was expected to be there as a legal observer for the Unification Church, though for just what purpose I was not quite sure.

Four thousand of the faithful had been hand-picked by the Reverend Moon to take part in a mass wedding. The whole of Madison Square Garden had been reserved for the great occasion on a hot Saturday in July. Great banners extolling the principles and doctrines of the Unification Church hung from the ceiling of the Garden, and the colorful flags of participants from 58 nations were more like an Olympic gathering than a religious ceremony.

Outside the Garden, noisy picketers marched up and down the street, loudly protesting the whole affair, castigating the Reverend Moon and the Unification Church and all they stood for. But the Reverend Moon had done his homework. All the necessary municipal permits had been obtained and the mass wedding proceeded with clockwork precision.

Two thousand couples took part in this unusual ceremony. The men were all dressed in dark grey tuxedos and the brides in floor length snow-white gowns and gloves, which gave them a virginal appearance. At one end of the Garden was an elevated dais with two raised platforms, where stood the Reverend Moon and his wife, flanked by two fonts of holy water to bless the faithful as they marched by.

The whole thing was incredible to see. The participants ranged in age from 17 to 63, men and women of every color and race. Young Caucasian girls were paired with Orientals, and blacks with whites. The great doors

Ten thousand years of happiness!

at the end of the Garden opened at 11 a.m. and out marched the happy couples, eight abreast, to mount the steps leading to the dais where the Reverend Moon and his wife waited.

It is not only the Pope who can sprinkle holy water on true believers. In a low Korean incantation, the Reverend Moon blessed each group of eight bodies as they passed before him, and he and his wife sprinkled holy water on their bowed heads. In the background an unseen orchestra played the wedding march from Lohengrin.

After the blessing, still eight abreast, the entire throng descended the platform and went out into the well of the Garden. It was like watching a great white caravan moving across the floor with almost military precision. On reaching the appointed spot, the group would turn around and face the platform until the entire Garden was completely filled with 4 000 people waiting to enter holy matrimony. They gazed with upturned expectant faces at the Reverend Moon on the dais, who was about to pronounce them husband and wife.

This of course was only a presumption on my part, for the whole wedding ceremony was conducted in Korean and there was no interpreter on hand to translate exactly what he said. The assembled throng, however, seemed to understand what was going on, because at the conclusion of his benediction, the Reverend Moon shouted a word that sounded like "Bonsai," whereupon 4 000 people shouted "Bonsai" in return and a great cloud of white gloves and flowers were thrown in the air by the lovers to show they were well and truly married. (I think a literal translation of "Bonsai" means "long life and 10 000 years of happiness," or words to that effect.) They kissed and embraced. The solemn marchers who had first entered the garden were now ecstatic with joy.

The great marriage match was over and 2 000 couples were now ready for lives of married bliss. It would be interesting to know how many of these prearranged marriages have survived. In many centres of the world, especially in Asia, prearranged marriages, in which the betrothed see each other for the first time on the wedding day, are the accepted way of doing things. Some people contend that when properly carried out, these arrangements give a more solid and lasting foundation to the institution of marriage than the more romantic, haphazard approach favored in the West.

By 1982 the American public in general and the Internal Revenue Service in particular, were very distressed with the Reverend Sun Myung Moon and the profits flowing to the self-proclaimed Prophet of God and his Unification Church. My mind went back to the conviction of the mobster Al Capone in the 1920s, when the U.S. government finally put him away for income tax evasion, after finding it impossible to convict him on a host of more serious charges.

The same prosecutorial net was thrown around the Korean religious leader with a similar result. The Reverend Moon had been extremely successful in his business ventures since coming to the U.S.A. In 1982, the same year that I attended the mass wedding, the charismatic religious leader was found guilty of filing false federal income tax returns, and was sentenced to 18 months in prison, and fined $25 000 for his failure to pay $162 000 in taxes on income from a bank account and an import company.

The Reverend Moon was free during the appeals from his conviction. He had originally requested a "bench" trial by judge alone, rather than a jury trial, due to the unfavorable publicity. He retained the services of the celebrated constitutional lawyer, Lawrence H. Tribe, a professor at Harvard Law School. The law professor, who had a national reputation as a defender of civil rights and feminist causes, took the position that the Moon case did not involve religion alone, but was concerned with the issue of how minorities were to be protected against oppression.

Tribe felt that the entire prosecution was an unwarranted intrusion by the government and the jury into church affairs. He argued that the religious leader was unfairly prosecuted for financial practices common among the larger established churches, and that the time-honored principle of separation of church and state threw a shield of immunity around his client. All to no avail!

As far as I know, John and his farm-girl wife from North Dakota have five children and are living happily in the U.S.A., where John does proselytizing work for the Unification Church through the National Council of Churches and travels all across the country imparting the holy word to anyone who will listen. Perhaps by now he, too, has earned his ticket to heaven.

Under the Golden Bell

It all happened during my winter holiday of 1982. When I returned to my vacation base in San José, Costa Rica, after a beautiful day of flying out over the Pacific and the desert country of Guanacaste, the telephone rang. Captain Michael Scott had tracked me down in Central America to discuss an important business proposal. The details of that great venture have long since disappeared, but the telephone conversation is vividly etched in my memory.

It was a long way from Calgary, Alberta to Costa Rica, but it was as if Michael were in the next room. It soon appeared that the real purpose of his call was to introduce me to his old friend Sandy Cruickshank, and in a matter of seconds, I spoke to this dynamic and entertaining little Scotsman who was to leave an indelible mark on the inhabitants of my adopted city.

It appeared Sandy and Michael wanted to purchase Deadman's Island, though for what reason I am not sure. The telephone conversation lasted about three-quarters of an hour and there was great excitement at the other end of the wire when I told Michael and Sandy I had flown over Deadman's Island, close to Puntarenas, that very afternoon. They wanted me to buy the island sight unseen; I advised them that I would brief them fully about this venture as soon as I returned to Calgary.

Nothing came of all this exciting talk about Costa Rican real estate, but it was an appropriate introduction to the colorful world of Sandy Cruickshank and his nonconformist ways. How Robert Service would have loved him. I know the poet would have found a special place for him as one of the men "who don't fit in."

Sandy is approaching 50 by now but it must have been an unforgettable day when, at the age of 18, he told the venerable bankers in Aberdeen, after two weeks service in one of the leading financial institutions of the Granite City, that he was setting out for the new world of America to seek his fortune. Sandy had a restless and mercurial disposition. So Sandy, who had been sent to one of the more prestigious schools in the north of

Scotland, gave the banking world of his native land the back of his hand and set out for Canada to carve out a career all his own.

It might be said of Sandy that he suffered from the small man syndrome. At just over 152 cm (5' tall) his head seemed to be disproportionately large for the size of his body. Clear blue eyes gleamed out from under a thick mass of grey hair, and with his beard he reminded you of some bright gnome from another planet. Before arriving in Calgary he had covered a lot of ground, from the outports of Newfoundland and Labrador to the sun-drenched islands of the West Indies, where he had peddled life insurance and any other saleable commodity he could lay his hands on. His stay in Trinidad came to an abrupt conclusion when he made some disparaging remarks about the color of the premier's skin.

Sandy was very quickly back in Canada, where he immediately turned to building houses and collecting pit props for the coal mines of Europe. Not one to stay too long in any one place, Sandy made his way across the country and found work in the Doukhobor country of Grand Forks, British Columbia, only to leave the Sons of Freedom forever as he set out to ride a horse from British Columbia down to San Francisco. With these adventures behind him, Sandy worked his passage back to Calgary, where he knew people like his old friend Captain Scott, and set himself up in the house construction business again.

Sandy was a talented fellow in many ways. One of his chief delights was to own a restaurant business and all the sidelines that went with it. His ranging eye never forgot the West Indies and yearned to have his own establishment in one of the exotic islands off the coast of South America.

Closer to home in Calgary, he became interested in a restaurant called the Bistro Pigalle. There he attempted to put together a consortium that would take over a fantastic hideaway in Grenada, where for very little money he could be master of a restaurant quite unlike anything yet seen in the Caribbean. Unfortunately, or perhaps fortunately, events political and otherwise completely beyond his control put this venture out of the question. Sandy decided he would achieve his ambition closer to home.

At that time I was working with one of the brightest lawyers who had ever left Toronto for Alberta, one Sandy Wetmore, to wit, and Sandy Cruickshank retained Sandy Wetmore to acquire a lease for a proposed restaurant on 17th Avenue S.W., next to where the Alazar Temple used to be. The great Wetmore, in a period of aberration, overlooked the matter of the restaurant lease, and Sandy Cruickshank's wrath knew no bounds.

At 9:01 a.m. he arrived at my office and accused Mr. Wetmore of abdication of duty and allowed he was prepared to drive the Torontonian's earring down his throat with a trophy awarded me by the Calgary Secretarial Association. Things became heated to an alarming degree, at which point I decided that discretion was the better part of valor, and retreated to quieter and more salubrious surroundings. It was an ill wind that blew Sandy Cruickshank a lot of good, for though he missed the lease on 17th Avenue S.W., he was able to pick up the site of the old Calgary Public Market down by the Bow River, which was a much more suitable place for his purposes. The Sandy Wetmore contretemps blew over and in short order the irrepressible Cruickshank was ensconced in spacious quarters that had once housed the Calgary Public Market. He was what he had always wanted to be, a restaurateur in his own right, with all the space he needed to make it a thriving and going concern.

And he did just that! In an opulent and almost decadent metropolis like Calgary, Sandy Cruickshank's restaurant landed like a bomb. It was an unconventional establishment, to say the least. The thick carpets and ornate cutlery that graced the conventional restaurants of Calgary were nowhere to be seen. There were no curtains in the windows or carpets on the floor and the resplendent waiters and waitresses found elsewhere in the restaurants of the city were conspicuous only by their absence. Everything was cut to the bare bone—except the food! The cooking was done on open stoves, plain for all to see. The Boat People from Vietnam, who comprised the kitchen staff, carried out their culinary miracles silently and skillfully under the watchful eye of Sandy himself. A truly unique place.

Liquor was on the honor system. Patrons would help themselves or settle up with the custodian at the door before they left the premises. Tablecloths were quite unknown and the strains of classical music were lost and overcome in the jangle of glasses and dishes on the table tops during lunch time at the Kingfisher Restaurant.

It was not a restaurant or eating place in the ordinary sense of the word, but more like an inn or a tavern, where Sandy also carried on a thriving fresh fish business. Great chests of seafood and blocks of ice moved in and out of the restaurant while the Kingfisher guests and patrons partook of their delightful seafood meals.

The eating area was on the ground floor. Thick iron bars across the windows gave a rather sinister air to the whole place. Just outside the main entrance stood the good ship *Kingfisher*, authentically rigged by Captain Scott himself, with "Kingfisher" in great white letters proudly painted across the dark-blue hull. When occasion required, such as a street dance at the time of the Calgary Stampede, announcements would be made or prizes given away from the poop aft of this imposing vessel. Sandy had imported the *Kingfisher* from the Fraser river in British Columbia, to provide appropriate nautical atmosphere for a seafood restaurant. The most outstanding appurtenance of the *Kingfisher* was her great golden bell, which had been taken off the vessel and hung just outside the kitchen area, and whose solemn tones produced the necessary silence when formal announcements were to be made.

It was not very long before the Kingfisher was more than just an unusual seafood restaurant. In addition to being a first-class gourmet cook and a lover of good wines, Sandy was a keen observer of the political world about him. Every facet of public affairs was of the greatest interest to him. It was a simple task to transform his seafood restaurant into a miniature Hyde Park, a Speaker's Corner, where interesting and colorful people could come to express their views on any subject they pleased and entertain the supper guests if they should choose to listen. By this time Sandy and I were close friends, and the Kingfisher was an oasis in a cultural desert. Immediately I saw the restaurant as a lodestar to attract unusual personalities as guest speakers. At first I was going to call this entertaining pastime "Webster's Wonderful World," but Sandy felt this was too much like Walt Disney and we settled for the more prosaic title of "Tuesdays with Webster."

It was a great and immediate success. Calgary had never seen anything quite like it before. The unique features of the restaurant, coupled with the outrageous behavior of the proprietor, made it the talk of the town.

By this time I had been practising law in Calgary for almost 30 years, and had a great list of potential speakers to draw upon, from safecrackers and ladies of the night to the leading industrialists and socialites of the city. When I invited people to come speak to us on a Tuesday night, the refusals were few.

"How would you like to attain immortality?" was my stock inquiry.

"You too can join the ranks of the immortals by addressing the Kingfisher Adventurers Society next Tuesday night on a subject of your choice!"

They jumped at the opportunity. We had some unforgettable Tuesday evenings as one outstanding personality after another would talk about a favorite topic and then field questions and insolent inquiries from every quarter of the dining room.

We heard from the most interesting people on a wide assortment of subjects. Captain Michael Scott regaled us with his days before the mast in the far corners of the world.

Roy Farran, soldier, novelist and newspaper man, fought again his army campaigns in Italy and North Africa.

Miles Smeeton (now deceased), a gallant cavalry officer, author and seaman, took us around the Cape Horn as he told us in unforgettable detail that "Once Was Not Enough."

Jay Straith, a barrister and solicitor by vocation, but a mountaineer by avocation, scaled for us the mountain heights of the Himalayas.

Patrick O'Callaghan, then editor of the Calgary Herald, educated us on the world behind the scenes of the modern newspaper.

Hans Macej, the spearhead of the oil and gas industry in Western Canada, explained the arcane complexities of the price of oil.

His counterpart from the field of gas exploration, Jim Grey, unfolded his plans to force the Mulroney government in Ottawa to reform the Canadian Upper House and give the country a Triple E Senate, which would be elected, equal and effective.

Marvin McDill, now gone to his reward, enlightened us on his tireless labors for the entry of *Canada II* in the race for the America's Cup.

Dr. Ernie Johnson described how he had performed 95 cataract operations a day in India following the Bhopil disaster.

Oh they were stirring and exciting times!

But best of all, Sandy enjoyed the unending political battles that go on in a democracy such as Canada. It made no difference to the little Scot whether the problem was on a municipal, provincial or federal level, it was all grist for the mill. Early on he had discerned that Ralph Klein was a wonderful choice for mayor, and when that incredible populist phenomenon was still an unrecognized investigative reporter, Sandy launched him into public life. Ralph Klein became the most popular mayor Calgary had ever known, even more popular than the legendary Don MacKay of white hat fame.

After the civic election, Sandy was ready to open his Kingfisher restaurant. When the bureaucrats at City Hall gave him administrative static, to which he was not accustomed, he threatened his erstwhile friend the mayor that if he did not have his building permit within 24 hours he would hire a Sherman tank and blow out every window in City Hall! Within 24 hours he had his permit, but his relationship with the Mayor was never quite the same.

On the provincial level, Sandy gave his support and energies to the charismatic Calgary lawyer Ron Ghitter, who sought the leadership of the Progressive Conservative party when Peter Lougheed decided to call it a day. Sandy threw himself into the fray with vigor and enthusiasm and raised $7 000 dollars to support the Ghitter cause. Unfortunately for Mr. Ghitter, red-neck Alberta was not quite ready for a man of his Semitic background, and talent and ability notwithstanding, Ron Ghitter was not chosen to lead his party.

When the sun shines on Ralph Klein

Sandy was at his best in the federal arena, where matters of concern to the whole country were at stake. When Free Trade was a prime issue in Canada, the Kingfisher was a natural forum to debate the pros and cons of this contentious issue, and who more fitting to present the federal side of the case than the great Jean Chrétien himself. He came willingly to our café and in his fractured English interspersed with Francophone asides, the streetfighter from Shawinigan mesmerized his audience with his prophetic forecast for a strong and truly federal Canada.

Both before and after Chrétien we lured a beautiful speaker in the person of Tom Axworthy to talk about the future of Canada. Hailing from a prominent Liberal family in Winnipeg and former principal secretary to none other than the great Pierre Elliott Trudeau, in the words of the immortal Fred Huntley "he raised the tone of the alley" and gave us all much food for thought.

In the mid-1980s the problems of South Africa were of interest and concern to the whole world, and we were delighted when Glen Babb, the South African ambassador to Canada, came to our restaurant on one of my Tuesday evenings to discuss the plight of his native country and the affect of apartheid and economic sanctions on South Africa. It was an unforgettable evening. We were not surprised to learn that shortly after his visit to the Kingfisher he had been recalled home to take over the prestigious post of the Africa Desk for South Africa.

Before he left Canada, he made some pointed remarks about the deplorable conditions of Canada's Indian reserves. On the question of Canadian sanctions against South Africa he stated quite bluntly that we in this country were like people in glass houses throwing stones, and it was not fitting or appropriate to assume such a holy position when our own situation was hardly above reproach.

Of all the speakers who came to our café, probably the most controversial was the Victoria lawyer Doug Christie, who in the spring of 1986 was up in Red Deer defending Jim Keegstra on whether the holocaust had ever existed, and whether or not the Eckville schoolteacher was guilty of teaching heinous and reprehensible matters to his unsuspecting pupils.

On a hot Tuesday evening in early spring the media was present, and the sprinkling of survivors from German concentration camps were listening with interest to what the lawyer had to say in Keegstra's defense. The air was thick with tension. The usual hubbub and clangor completely ceased as Doug Christie warmed to his subject. Standing stiffly erect with his back to the bars of the restaurant windows, his features entirely devoid of humor, Keegstra's lawyer piled statistic upon statistic to prove that the holocaust had never happened and that the whole story was an international conspiracy and a figment of the Jewish imagination. Before he departed for Red Deer, he parried a host of penetrating questions from his unsympathetic audience, singling out the well-known civil libertarian lawyer Sheldon Chumir and a prominent member of Calgary's Jewish community as a target for his remarks.

"I see you sitting there, Mr. Chumir and I see, too, you are flanked by the *Globe and Mail* and the Southam Press. I know that my remarks this evening will be misconstrued and taken out of context when they appear in the newspapers tomorrow morning. But the truth is the truth and I defy you to refute anything I have said here tonight."

On this happy note, the Great Defender returned to Red Deer to carry on with unabated vigor his one-man battle for freedom of expression in a democratic society, no matter how distasteful or unpleasant the doctrines may be to the vast majority of the population.

At the Kingfisher restaurant there was never a dull moment. If feminists wished to address us, they were more than welcome, and we heard from interesting and exciting women like Martha Cohen, who described in fascinating detail how she and her cohorts put together the multimillion dollar Calgary Centre for Performing Arts, while at the other end of the spectrum, Nancy Luxford told us of her incredible stay with the aboriginals of Papua New Guinea.

All of this was in keeping with Sandy's attention to anything and everything of interest to the people of Calgary, male and female alike. No chauvinist he, and the Kingfisher was not to be a hangout for bar flies and male beer drinkers, although a special brand of Calgary's Big Rock Beer was one of Sandy's favorite promotions. Belly dancers, exotic cooking schools, fashion shows, street dances and carnivals were all part of the Kingfisher fare and made his bistro quite unlike anything the city had seen before.

Any matter of immediate importance was meat and drink to Sandy. As the 1988 Olympic Winter Games approached, they took on great significance to him. Bill Pratt, a CEO for the Games and Mayor Ralph Klein outlined plans for this sporting extravaganza to spellbound audiences. The Kingfisher and its assorted activities were swept along in a great burst of civic pride that was to make Calgary a city of international fame and importance.

Some celebrations, of course, were more memorable than others, such as the Robert Burns dinner on January 25, 1986. This is the time when true Scots all over the world gather together to pay homage to their great ploughboy poet and have an evening of revelry and song. The Robert Burns party at the Kingfisher was to follow this great tradition and elaborate preparation had been taken to make this a truly unforgettable occasion. The guests arrived in proper Highland dress and the haggis was piped in by a lone Scottish piper, who filled the old public market with his stirring Scottish music. It was a bizarre scene. Sandy himself was in his usual blue jeans and behind the golden bell, the boat people prepared the evening meal on open fires.

The whisky flowed like buttermilk and Scottish jokes and stories were the order of the day, as everyone joined in the toast to the haggis and got ready for the traditional Scottish meal, prior to the recitation of the Immortal Memory in honor of the Bard. Suddenly to the astonishment of us all, there was a great outburst from the kitchen, followed by an unmistakable declaration of war.

Sandy: "The potatoes aren't cooked enough."

The Boat People: "This is how we cook potatoes!"

Sandy: "No goddammit, this is how you cook potatoes, you cook them my way or else!"

The Boat People: "We quit!"

Sandy: "No, you're fired, the whole lot of you!"

Whereupon the Boat People, every last one of them, put on their coats and marched out into the freezing January cold. Confusion reigned supreme. What to do? Much liquor had been consumed, the haggis had arrived, but the main course had not been served. Never at a loss, Sandy requisitioned all the guests to lend a hand. The ladies donned aprons and with Sandy in charge the potatoes were cooked in Cruickshank fashion. The meal proceeded, even if not quite as planned.

In due course I delivered the Immortal Memory and all hands invoked a toast to the Scottish poet that he would have been proud to receive. That night, all over the world, from Dunedin in New Zealand to the North British Society in Halifax, Nova Scotia, tributes were paid to the immortal Burns, but none I wager with more vigor and enthusiasm than in the Kingfisher Restaurant in Calgary!

As Bob Blair, one of our great gas industrialists said to Sandy one night, "Sandy, you've got a world-class restaurant here—you've cut out all the bullshit!"

When I heard of this remark, I knew he was right. The intellectual content of the restaurant, where people could meet and exchange ideas and swap insults, were more important than the bare floors and windows with iron bars and no curtains. When the restaurant first started, the handsome young manager of one of the big international hotels told Sandy that he was doing something very important and not to let it die.

It was brash and exciting and different. Sandy would put on a sales dinner for Allan Fotheringham to help the sale of his book, *Capitol Offenses.* He had a fund-raising party to stop the golden handshake for a city commissioner who had his snout deep in the public trough and Sandy took it upon himself to launch a *pro bono* public lawsuit to stop such improper proceedings.

But finally the bureaucracy got to him. The provincial government terminated his lease, and when the Department of Health decided to prosecute him for allowing cockroaches to run at large in his restaurant, Sandy decided it was time for fresh fields and pastures new.

Sandy had left behind him a great track record in the criminal courts of the province. The charges had all been the same—assault occasioning bodily harm and threats of one sort or another to people who had incurred his displeasure. He had won, with some help from me, acquittals on them all and left an indelible mark on the criminal courts of the province.

Legacy of a
Secret War
❦❦❦❦❦❦❦❦❦

Down in the rattlesnake country of southeastern Alberta, there is a military base known as Defence Establishment Suffield. It sits near the Alberta-Saskatchewan border in the middle of a bleak and forbidding desert. Notwithstanding the isolation, it has flourished as a training ground for British soldiers, and for half a century Defence Establishment Suffield (DES) has been a pivotal centre for international experiments in chemical and biological warfare.

Some time before the outbreak of the Second World War in 1939, Canada had been working closely with the United States and Britain to build up both defensive and offensive weapons to protect the Allies against germ warfare and attacks from the enemy using poison gas. Canada's leading medical figure, Sir Frederick Banting, was extremely active in this military endeavor, and by virtue of the fact that he had won the Nobel prize for his pioneer work in the field of diabetes, lent Canada considerable prestige in the whole affair. The Americans had the money and the British the expertise needed for this vital war work; but Canada had the territory, and the vast expanse of the Suffield training grounds was ideal for this program.

The war came to an end in 1945, but the military establishment at Suffield carried on, and by 1984 was a thriving defense base for military training of all kinds. In addition to the military personnel who used Suffield for war games in the summer time, there was a large contingent of scientists and civil servants who did defense work for the Department of National Defence the year round.

Dr. Celso Mendosa had migrated to the United States from the Philippines. After advanced studies in chemistry and agriculture he graduated from the University of Iowa with a Ph.D. in agricultural science and came to Canada in 1983 as a biological researcher with the Department of National Defence in Ottawa.

In due course, he was transferred as a civil servant class III to Defence Establishment Suffield and moved with his family to Medicine Hat, Alberta, a few miles distant from Suffield. Dr. Mendosa was a scientist, first, last and always, but the inner hierarchy of the defense establishment did not take too kindly to Dr. Mendosa and his ways. He was not quite the same as his colleagues. His skin was dark, which gave him a swarthy, almost oriental appearance. He had come to Canada via the United States, but as a Filipino, English was not his native tongue, and his language and grammar did not always measure up to the high expectations of his confreres.

In short there was professional jealousy insofar as Dr. Mendosa was concerned. He was subjected to harassment of subtle and various kinds in the workplace and ridiculed by his fellow scientists. They made it increasingly difficult for him to carry out his experiments with snakes and animals in highly sensitive areas. This harassment went on insidiously and relentlessly. Equipment for his experiments would mysteriously disappear. Thinly-veiled insinuations were made to the effect that his experiments with rats and snakes served no useful purpose.

Pressure was brought to bear on him to improve his English, despite the fact he had already published many scientific papers and travelled all over the world attending lectures and seminars on chemical and biological matters. He was forced to take a course in English, supposedly to correct and improve his grammar and composition. In short his whole lifestyle and professional competence were viewed by his colleagues and his immediate superiors with jealousy and a jaundiced eye.

Within the structure of his department, overt attempts were made to make him toe the "official line," whatever that may have been, and to crush his spirit. Worst of all, he found himself relegated to an inferior level in the department, accompanied by a substantial cut in pay.

A mild person, and a gentleman to his fingertips, Dr. Mendosa fought back as best he could against the monolithic power of the federal government, namely the Department of National Defence.

There were prescribed avenues for venting his grievances and he took them all. His paper war with the faceless bureaucrats of the defense department went on for years. He filed grievance complaints with his union of professional workers. He sought help from the ombudsman. He lodged complaints with the Canadian Human Rights Commission. All to no avail.

To determine what the Department was saying and doing behind his back, the doctor used every weapon at his command, including the new Access to Information Act to get at secret documents affecting his case.

In due course, his plight attracted the interest of the New Democratic Party in Ottawa and the matter was aired on the floor of the House of Commons. This publicity, in turn, made him a subject of interest to the RCMP. A special investigator was detailed to inquire into whether Dr. Mendosa was a threat to the national safety. The doctor's work had been cleared by an independent outstanding biochemist at McGill University and as might be expected, the special investigator of the RCMP found absolutely nothing detrimental to my client.

He then came to see me, as under the new Constitution and Charter of Rights and Freedoms he could eventually find relief through the courts. The quickest and most effective attack was to bring action for defamation. I issued two statements of claim in the Court of Queen's Bench of Alberta against two different groups who had made defamatory remarks about my client and the nature and quality of his work.

Most insulting was a letter published and circulated among the scientific fraternity at Suffield, describing a biological paper given by Dr. Mendosa at a defense seminar on the base as "an international embarrassment"and otherwise holding up his lecture to hatred, ridicule and contempt. Litigation solicitors of the Department of Justice were brought into the fray and the battle was on.

By this time the federal Crown realized that they were dealing with no ordinary man and that Dr. Mendosa would exhaust every recourse open to him in order to show he had been wronged. Settlement overtures were quickly forthcoming. Dr. Mendosa was restored to his rightful position and received adequate compensation for the damages sustained.

The Mendosa case had already achieved considerable notoriety. The matter had been aired on Canadian national news and the doctor was interviewed on the Sunday night program W-5.

In a different matter, Defence Establishment Suffield had been whitewashed and cleared by a supposedly impartial investigator from Ottawa as to whether or not there were still enormous stockpiles of poisonous gases on the base. Now, at the time of writing, there is a hue and cry with respect to "volunteer" soldiers who had been injected with highly toxic chemicals at Suffield—supposedly in the national interest—and who may well develop cancer as a result.

As for Dr. Mendosa, he has departed from this unhappy scene, and is putting his life back on track.

The Primrose Path to the Everlasting Bonfire

Of all the really serious crimes in the Canadian Criminal Code, arson is probably one of the most difficult to detect and prove. Generally speaking there is no smoking gun to assist the police, and as the arsonist usually carries out his work in secrecy without any witnesses to watch him, convictions for arson are relatively rare. The evidence is almost always circumstantial. Unless someone is there to see the accused apply the lighted match, generally suspicion falls short of the "proof beyond all reasonable doubt" required in a criminal case. But if the circumstantial evidence is strong enough, a conviction can follow.

Many times a "successful fire" is followed by a claim against a fire insurance company, which naturally arouses suspicions on the part of the company and the police. Payment is made only after thorough and meticulous investigation.

Or there can be open and blatant arson, like the fire set by a Polish client of mine as an act of revenge against her brutal husband. Among other things, he ejected her from the matrimonial home and forced her to sleep outside the house in a dog kennel in Calgary's sub-zero weather. My client must have been an ardent feminist, for things had come to a head when the husband told her to keep on working while he lolled in the sun, drinking wine and strumming his guitar.

"In Italy," he said, "women do all the work, and men drink wine and sleep all day in the sun."

"That," said Mrs. Kaminski, "may be okay for Italy, but not for Polish women in Canada, and this is Canada."

Back to the dog kennel she went. Hell hath no fury like a Polish woman scorned. My client vented her rage on her husband by burning an abandoned building across the street from her home, where she suspected her husband of marital infidelity. She set the shack ablaze and placidly awaited the arrival of the police.

When the police appeared on the scene, they found my client in an advanced state of intoxication, trying, in her stocking feet, to stamp out the fire she had set. The court found there were mitigating circumstances and tempered justice with mercy by sentencing her to a nominal fine.

As an arson case, the sad story of Nori Lott, a Portuguese client of mine of long standing, was quite bizarre.

By dint of long hours and unrelenting work, Nori had built up a thriving business as a picture framer. He had moved into palatial quarters in southwest Calgary. Nori had come up the hard way, and he did not waste his money on unnecessary employees like bookkeepers and accountants. This made more money for Nori, but like everything else it had its price. The federal government and their various minions, like the Income Tax department and the Sales and Excise division, were his unseen partners. They insisted that proper books and records be kept, and appropriate returns on various aspects of his business be made on a regular basis to Ottawa.

These were normal requirements for every business in Canada, large or small, and Nori's picture-framing business was no different in this respect. A part-time bookkeeper or accountant would have taken a load off his shoulders, but Nori was determined to avoid what he felt was a totally unnecessary expense. He was battling a paper enemy and the mountains of government forms and returns with their endless inquiries for statistics and information finally got to him and drove him to the verge of a nervous breakdown.

Things came to a head in the spring of 1982, when Nori felt he was drowning in a sea of government records and corporate returns, and he decided to put an end to the whole hopeless situation.

By this time he was carrying on his business in brand new quarters, quite unlike anything he had known in the backbreaking struggle he had gone through in climbing up the business ladder. At 5:35 p.m. he sent his son and only helper on home. Then he found an empty beer bottle, inserted a candle in its neck, piled a mass of hated government forms around his improvised torch and set it all ablaze. Nori locked the door and left the building. In half an hour the whole office was on fire and quickly burned to the ground. His business, which he had so laboriously built up over the years, was no more. Gone also were the returns and records that had driven him past the point of no return.

His framing business was a labor of love and the building his pride and joy. I listened to this story with compassion and some understanding. He had been destroyed by a paper tiger, a tiger with an insatiable appetite and never-ending demands. It was just too voracious an animal for Nori Lott. I could not help but think of these moving lines of Oscar Wilde's:

> *Yet each man kills the thing he loves*
> *By each let this be heard*
> *Some do it with a bitter look*
> *Some with a flattering word*
> *The coward does it with a kiss*
> *The brave man with a sword*

Nori did it with a match.

Provincial Court Judge Cioni understood the problem, and punished the accused with a nominal fine.

After all these people who for one reason or another have set illegal fires, you suddenly find yourself defending a client charged with arson, who is completely innocent.

Such a one was Donna Quasnick. This dynamic lady was struggling to set up her automotive business in a man's world. She had an automobile parts franchise down in the Brooks area of southern Alberta, on the way to Medicine Hat. She was a feisty and meticulous person and after three years of hard work was just beginning to break even and put the business on its feet.

Not being averse to hard work, on the Saturday morning in question Donna had gone back to her shop to satisfy a customer's request for a truck part. After a quick search, she realized she did not carry this item. At 1:25 p.m. she locked the door behind her and set out to return home. At 1:30 p.m. her whole plant was ablaze and the Brooks volunteer fire department was on its way. By the time of their arrival, the fire was completely out of control and the building burned to the ground.

Brooks is a town of approximately 50 000 people and the headquarters of the Eastern Irrigation District. The Quasnick automotive building was right in the centre of town. As a growing and prosperous farming centre, Brooks was the main office for a detachment of the Royal Canadian Mounted Police. They investigated the case with their customary thoroughness and impartiality. Statements were taken, polygraph tests administered, and an examination was conducted by a fire expert from the fire marshall's office in Edmonton.

Donna Quasnick remained the prime suspect, but 16 months went by and no indictment had been laid, until finally the RCMP charged her with willfully setting fire to her business premises, thereby committing arson contrary to the Criminal Code. Brooks is not a huge metropolitan centre and the whole town was aware of the police investigation. For almost a year and a half Donna was under the shadow of suspicion.

It was true she was the last person to leave the business premises, but in a realistic analysis of the whole situation, she had no motive and stood to gain nothing financially from the fire. To be sure, there was a fire insurance policy, but the loss was payable to the mortgagee of the company's business and there would be nothing left for my client after the proceeds from the insurance were turned over to the mortgagee. She was indebted to the local bank for a small amount and her business, after years of hard work, was far from bankrupt.

All of this may explain in part why it took the authorities so long to lay the charge in this case. There was no apparent motive. At best it was a case built on the fact that Donna was the last person to leave the building and the fire had broken out only minutes afterwards.

It was a serious matter. Donna was really a client of my friend the late Alf Harris, and we felt from the beginning that she was innocent. She was a woman with a great talent for detail, so the first thing I asked her to do was to make a model of the entire premises, as best she could remember. Her model was a thing of beauty, showing every room and piece of furniture to scale. She prepared in minute detail the windows and shelves for the automotive parts, and most importantly, the oil furnace. This was in a direct line with the front door and the sliding door at the rear of the premises.

After 16 months of meticulous investigation, it was the theory of the police that Donna Quasnick had gone to her business in broad daylight and scattered what they termed an "accelerant," namely gasoline, all over the woodwork before setting the place on fire.

Following the fire, the police had taken innumerable photographs of flame damage. It was their belief that the burn patterns left by the flames proved their theory indisputably. I found a professor of chemical engineering from the University of Calgary, who in the weeks before the trial conducted numerous tests to establish the cause of the fire in the automotive plant.

Professor Tollefson's tests were based on a different hypothesis. According to our expert, the fire had started from gas fumes created by the mixing of automotive paint, and these fumes had been forced back against the furnace when the front door of the building was opened and closed. The firebox in the furnace was only 10 cm (4") off the floor, so it was reasonable to conclude that the highly-flammable paint fumes had rolled back as a vapor from the front door and ignited when they came in contact with the firebox in the furnace.

As presiding justice, His Lordship Peter Power accepted the theory of the defense expert as a reasonable explanation. In addition, he accepted the accused's denial that she had started the fire, and finding her a convincing and credible witness, acquitted her.

Imagine then her distress when she read the account of her trial and acquittal in the *Calgary Herald* the next day. It was implied in no uncertain terms that she had only been acquitted on a legal technicality which had allowed her to escape the toils of justice and a conviction for arson she so rightly deserved.

She immediately sued the newspaper for libel and defamation and the case was settled out of court. Donna Quasnick has left the business world of Brooks for Calgary, but it will probably be a long time before she tries to earn her living again in a "man's job" in a man's world.

Masters of Deceit (and Others)

Some of the most intriguing and delightful criminals I have encountered in almost half a century at the bar have been the confidence men who prey on human cupidity and by one ruse or another induce their victims to part with hard-earned dollars. For the most part, they are pleasant personalities—indeed that is almost always their stock in trade—and the gulled parties are often reluctant to press charges. More times than not they are left holding the bag, appearing very unlike the shrewd and sophisticated investors they would like to be. How true the adage, "A fool and his money are soon parted!"

Over the years I have never ceased to marvel at the rapidity and eagerness victims hand over their money to pursue the most hare-brained schemes. These schemes were ultimately to give them pie in the sky and the life of luxury for which they yearned. The con men and sharpies, who live a precarious existence on the dark side of the law, have preferred to remain nameless. I am obliged to respect their desire for anonymity and refrain from identifying them too closely. Suffice it to say that their methods appealed to a great many people and kept the "paper hangers" and other purveyors of "get rich quick schemes" alive and well long after the emptiness of their schemes had been revealed.

It was not my lot to defend any of the great criminals of our time. For the last 15 years of my practice I acted for minor petty criminals, the fraud artists and their like who prey upon an unsuspecting public and relieve them all too quickly of their surplus cash. I would appear for the NSF cheque people (of whom there were many) the stock manipulators and "paper hangers," who by deceit or other fraudulent means, defraud the public or any person of any property, money or valuable security, contrary to the Criminal Code of Canada. Over the years the legal noose has tightened and all that is necessary for the Crown to prove is that "deprivation" has been suffered by the victim—that is sufficient to support the charge.

And so they went their merry way, the cheque "kiters," the purveyors of the South Seas bubble technique, the Elmer Gantrys and Jimmy Bakkers of the Calgary scene. Last, but by no means least, was "Jimmy the Con," with his incredible record of 455 convictions before he saw the error of his ways and ran for the respectable position of mayor of Calgary.

They were all colorful, interesting people whose only sin was their propensity to cut corners and take short cuts not allowed by law, in their pursuit of the almighty dollar.

I also represented young men in their hard-up days, before they climbed to the top of their career ladder and became famous, each in his own way. I think in particular of Bert Messier, the "Little Napoleon of EZE Brew Coffee," who reached the pinnacle of his success during the 1988 Winter Olympics; and Larry Ryckman, who bounced like a rubber ball from moving pictures to three-dimensional sound and as his supreme accolade carried his Calgary Stampeders to football triumph by bringing the Grey Cup home to Calgary.

And then there were the battling Sikhs, newcomers to Canada, who would rather fight than eat and the Portuguese immigrants from the Azores, who wanted to promote a bloodless bullfight in Calgary, notwithstanding the resistance of the Canadian Customs officials. To say nothing of Fernando Ricaforte and his Filipino friends, embracing Canada and a new way of life after they had fled from the Marcos' tyranny in their native land.

And last, but by no means least, was Dean Preston, the "Ewok" man, with his black slouch hat, tatooed arms and enormous belt buckle displaying the stars and blue cross of the Confederation states. He told an intriguing story about a battle in outer space between his "Space Pets" and the Olaks and an alleged infringement of copyright that has yet to be determined.

I loved them all, these colorful clients I have known. Their innumerable problems just naturally became my own.

The Troubles of Doc Fingers

The role of defense counsel is fraught with heavy responsibilities and one of the gravest, in my opinion, is the task of saving a man's career. Such a case was "Doc Fingers" Szapko, who faced charges of sexual assault against a young boy, which if substantiated could have ruined his reputation and career.

The lot of a chiropractor in North America has not always been a happy one. "Doc Fingers," with his sometimes innovative chiropractic techniques, was often misunderstood by his fellow practitioners, to say nothing of the medical profession. Born and raised in a Ukrainian family in the Edmonton area of Alberta, he studied chiropractic in the most advanced schools in the United States. He was convinced that a great many human ills can be traced to nonalignment of the spine and its detrimental effects on the human body therefrom.

Dr. Szapko had returned to Alberta from the United States and at the time of his legal problems, had set up an office in Strathmore, some 50 km (30 miles) east of Calgary. He also had a branch office in Beiseker, an area of about 5 000 people, settled mostly by German farmers on the way to Drumheller. An intensely serious bachelor just turning 40, Dr. Szapko was a man dedicated to his profession and the alleviation of human suffering wherever it was found. As a younger man he had shown considerable talent as a pianist and he entertained at public malls and shopping centres across the province, where his proficiency at the keyboard earned him the name of "Doc Fingers." This sobriquet was most apt, for not only was he adept with his fingers on the piano keys, but he was equally gifted in the use of his fingers to manipulate the human spine. Quite apart from the piano, he owned an airplane and derived a great deal of satisfaction and entertainment in flying solo around the countryside.

While in Beiseker, Szapko had performed chiropractic work on a young boy whose parents were on welfare. He offered to take the boy flying on one of his weekly visits to Beiseker after the day's work was done. Then to his horror he found himself charged with sexual assault of this same boy, whom he had known for only a few weeks and for whom he had done some beneficial chiropractic work.

By the time Doc Fingers came in to see me, his preliminary inquiry was over and he had decided to change lawyers. It may well be that his previous counsel had been more concerned with the law (as perhaps he should have been) than with the finer points of chiropractic science that were of paramount concern to Dr. Szapko. I would have to familiarize myself with the new chiropractic techniques as followed by Dr. Szapko; not only to defend the case properly, but to satisfy the learned doctor, to whom the methodology of his profession was more important than the law.

Looking back on it now, it seems that Dr. Szapko was almost paranoid about the whole affair. He hotly protested his innocence and laid the blame for his prosecution squarely at the feet of the Strathmore RCMP with whom he had an ongoing vendetta for parking violations. I gave all these competing distractions the importance they deserved and tried to zero in on what I felt was the real defense in the case, the groundless complaint of the boy who laid the charges in the first place.

Why had he done this to the doctor and what kind of a boy was he? These questions could not be answered satisfactorily without making an extensive visit to Beiseker and Strathmore and a full investigation of the complainant's background and his family. I was awash in a sea of speculation when I tried to pinpoint the motive in this case. It was true there had been financial problems between the doctor and the father of the boy. It was also true that the boy had amorous designs on the doctor's receptionist at the same office. But these were matters of pure conjecture and would not stand up in a court of law.

In the last analysis, the case turned on the issue of credibility. It was the word of a 17-year-old boy with doubtful background against the sworn testimony of a dedicated professional with an unblemished criminal record. The Crown endeavored to impugn the doctor's credibility by bringing out problems the doctor had experienced in his professional background, but I argued that these did not affect his credibility.

Cross-examination of the informant showed that he was an unstable personality given to drug and alcohol abuse. It was also shown that he was an exhibitionist who disrupted the school in Beiseker by planning to leap off the schoolhouse roof and by acts of sexual exhibitionism that were to say the least in very poor taste.

Dr. Szapko, on the other hand, was a model of professional competence and decorum. He called colleagues from Edmonton and Lethbridge who without exception extolled the ability and expertise of Doc Fingers. They explained to the court that what had happened to the boy, if indeed it had happened at all, was at worst an accident and an occupational hazard that could have happened to any chiropractor in a like situation.

As Madame Justice McFadyen presided over these contentious proceedings the air was thick with tension. Dr. Szapko, with his professional reputation at stake, was taut with nervous suspense and uncertainty. On the vital question of credibility, the court found in his favor. The charge against him was dismissed, whereupon the doctor entertained us all at the Baldwin Piano Centre by playing a selection of classical variations on a magnificent grand piano to celebrate his victory. As far as Alberta was concerned, he felt that the damage had been done. A relieved but melancholy man, he departed to the U.S.A. and is doubtless practising his own brand of chiropractic somewhere south of the border, with the success and recognition he deserves.

In a case like this the work is its own reward, with satisfaction that knows no bounds in saving a man's career and returning a useful member to society.

The Crown Never Wins, Never Loses

Our judicial system has come a long way since our ancestors settled their more serious problems through ordeal by fire or trial by combat. On the lengthy march to civilization, the settlement of disputes took longer to work out than most things. Our constitutional safeguards were shaped and formed by trial and error until we finally arrived at a system of which we are sometimes inordinately proud and hold up as a model for less fortunate people to follow.

Over the centuries we have come to believe that in the search for truth, which is what a trial is supposed to be all about, the adversary system as we know it has played an extremely important part in making the Anglo-American judicial system the envy of the entire world.

Sometimes even the best systems that human ingenuity and experience can devise do not always work with the perfection and efficiency we would like, but for the most part justice is generally done, and even better is abundantly seen to be done.

The Hamnet case, in my experience, was one of the exceptions which proves the rule that the adversary system is a tried-and-true method for arriving at the truth—in a given set of circumstances. The adversary system generally works best in a criminal trial, where the accused person is presumed innocent until proven guilty beyond all reasonable doubt, and the burden of proof is upon the Crown. In a British country the Crown is represented by the Director of Public Prosecutions, or the Attorney General, and in the administration of justice, the prosecutor holds a very special place. Under our judicial system, the Crown never wins and never loses a case.

As the Crown's representative, the prosecutor is expected to present the evidence fairly and impartially, and to lay all the evidence before the court, whether it is harmful or beneficial to the prosecution. Justice is done on the facts disclosed by the evidence. Behind all this, of course, is the prosecutorial discretion which purports to act like a screen to ensure that only proper cases are brought for trial in the first place, and that frivolous and unnecessary prosecutions do not occur.

R. v. Hamnet was a puzzling case in more ways than one. Doug Hamnet was a welder of many years experience in the oil and gas industry. On June 19, 1987, he was working on an oil pipeline west of Innisfail, in the foothills of the Rockies. He had his own welding truck, a beaten-up old relic with a welding tank and hose mounted on the rear of the vehicle behind the driver's cab.

At the end of a long, hot day, Hamnet and his Indian helper had driven in from the worksite to Innisfail to have supper and quench their thirst with a few beer. Apparently Hamnet drank not wisely, but too well, and as closing time approached, decided that his helper would be the designated driver. He tossed the keys for the welding truck on to the table, so that his friend could drive them home.

The way back to the forestry camp, where they were to spend the night, was over Highway 17, a long, dark and dangerous section of road. Highway 17 was not clearly marked, there were hazardous grades on the curves and deer had been known to spring out unexpectedly on the roadway, causing serious accidents. Just past the intersection of Highway 17, with the crossroad marked as 17A, the highway going west bends into a sharp curve. No one knows at what speed the pair were travelling along the darkened highway, but tire marks on the road and along the grassy shoulder gave mute evidence.

The welding truck had left the pavement, crossed over to the grass shoulder and then come back on to the road again before lurching into a deep ditch. The vehicle dropped down below the shoulder, rolled completely over and landed on its roof, breaking tree branches and a wire fence in the process. Hamnet was thrown clear of the vehicle and was found by the RCMP in a semiconscious condition some five metres (17') from the truck. His helper was not so lucky. Hamnet was charged with criminal negligence causing death. This was an extremely serious matter requiring a full and complete investigation before the charge was laid.

Following his preliminary inquiry in Innisfail, Hamnet was committed for trial in Red Deer, although the Crown's case was circumstantial at best. An RCMP expert was there as a key Crown witness to testify that in his considered professional opinion, the death truck had been driving at a speed of at least 160 km (100 miles) per hour, which was criminal negligence of the grossest kind considering the road conditions.

But there was no case unless they could put the accused behind the wheel, and as one of the two suspects was dead, it was imperative for the Crown to prove that Hamnet was the driver, no matter what the speed of the vehicle.

Hamnet had been taken by ambulance to the hospital in Innisfail, where his wife drove up from Calgary to see him. On his arrival at the hospital the RCMP interviewed him as to the circumstances surrounding the accident. The statement he gave to the interrogating constable was never produced by the Crown at the preliminary inquiry. Why not? If the Crown has a duty to come up with all the evidence at a criminal trial, whether prejudicial or beneficial to their case, one would have anticipated that his first statement would have been produced at the preliminary inquiry and the question of its admissibility argued at that time.

As Doug Hamnet lay shocked and semiconscious in his hospital bed, the RCMP from Red Deer had arrived on the scene and taken a *second* statement from the injured man. On this occasion there was some indication that Hamnet, and not his Indian friend, was the driver of the truck, and that Hamnet had no clear recollection of leaving the highway or how the accident had taken place. At the outset this was a formidable hurdle for the Crown to overcome, for it was mandatory for them to show that this incriminating statement was given of Hamnet's own free will.

With the accused in a battered state of shock, it could hardly be said that the second statement was freely and voluntarily given. The court ruled it clearly inadmissible. Game over. Without the statement identifying the accused as the guilty driver, the Crown had no case, let alone proof beyond all reasonable doubt. The accused had no need to present a defense at all and the carefully prepared case we had mounted was not required.

Later on Hamnet carried out his own investigation. He discovered that residents close to the scene of the accident, upon hearing the fatal crash, rushed over to see what had happened. They found the Indian, quite dead, half in and half out of the truck on the driver's side. None of those witnesses had been subpoenaed to give evidence at Hamnet's trial. No evidence was called by the Crown as to who was actually driving the truck at the time of the accident or where the body of the Indian was found.

Hamnet had ready an engineering expert from the University of Calgary who could have proven categorically that the death vehicle that night could not have been proceeding at more than 100 km (65 miles) per hour. By this time he also had the evidence of an on-the-spot witness, who had dragged the injured Indian driver out from behind the steering wheel of the vehicle. There was his faithful wife, who had gone down to far-off Manitoba to see the deceased's body resting in his coffin with the large dent still on his forehead where he had come in contact with the windshield. Hamnet and other members of his family would have testified as to the restricted speed of the beaten-up old welding truck. Best of all, there was the first statement where Hamnet said it was the helper and not he who drove the truck that night.

Although he was ready to do battle, it was unnecessary. The system had performed as it was supposed to, and justice was well and truly done. The safeguards of our jurisprudence, with its checks and balances, had operated to give the accused a full and complete defense.

There are, however, unanswered questions in this case. Why weren't all the witnesses called who could have proven who the driver was that night? And why was the first police statement not shown to the defense before the trial? And why were the actual road tests used by the police to calculate the supposed speed of the Hamnet vehicle not made available to the accused?

The adversary system, properly used, is a safeguard and guarantee of a fair trial. But if all the cards are not laid on the table, the whole procedure can become a meaningless charade and lead to an abuse of prosecutorial discretion and police power. It then becomes a mockery to say that the Crown never wins and never loses, for the fine impartiality expected from the prosecution is no longer present.

I Lay all my Cards on the Table

As I looked back across the years, I knew the Hamnet case (see "The Crown Never Wins, Never Loses") was my last criminal case. I still had civil appeals to complete and the Ewok wars with George Lucas were far from over, but Hamnet was my final exit insofar as my criminal work was concerned. When my client was finally cleared of the indictment of causing death by criminal negligence, he heaved a great sigh of relief. Then I was able to take stock of my own situation.

Now I was about to pack it in as a criminal lawyer and defender of the great unwashed. I'd had 40-odd years at the bars of Nova Scotia, Alberta, Manitoba and British Columbia as champion of the underprivileged, defender of the damned. Was it worth it? If I had my druthers would I do it again? Perhaps I have no imagination, and only limited talents, but given the same opportunity I would.

My mind goes back to a cocktail party I attended shortly after arriving in Alberta in 1957. It was a legal function. I cannot recall the name of the senior counsel who was giving me sage advice and the benefit of his vast experience, but I can still see his earnest face as if it were yesterday.

"Young man," he said. "You are new in this town and about to go into some legal firm and start the practice of law. I have only one thing to tell you, and please remember this. The role of the criminal lawyer is often misunderstood by the general public. They cannot understand the presumption of innocence—that every person is entitled to a full and complete defense. But this is the work that criminal lawyers do. They are the last bastion of freedom between the government and the people. You have never really practised law until you have defended a man on a serious criminal charge."

Thirty-odd years later I know what he meant and how true his words were! It is almost half a century since I first read about the doctrine of "Scienter" in *Underhill on Torts* and started on the thorny road to law. I still remember the last Mr. Justice Doull's admonition that grey day in 1946 in Halifax when I was admitted to the Nova Scotia bar.

"Never forget, Mr. Macdonald," said the judge. "The law is a jealous mistress. She brooks no rivals and demands your unwavering faith and allegiance." And so it was!

It may well be that I had the wrong attitude toward this challenging profession. To me it was always a battle, and I never tired of the contest. Some of my colleagues took me to task by saying, "Macdonald, what's up with you? They say that sometimes you even take cases for nothing!"

It was true. And in addition to the cases you wanted to take, if you happened to be in the courtroom on arraignment day, you might find yourself a court-appointed counsel, without fee, as Chief Justice McLaurin or some other presiding justice went through the trial list and set down the cases for hearing. All this of course was before the days of legal aid. Under the prevailing system, all accused persons have the opportunity to obtain defense counsel provided by the Crown.

For more than four decades I watched the criminal world of Canada come and go. I wish I could say that I acted for some of the great criminals of our time, but such was not the case. I did, however, appear for a host of colorful and interesting people, minor figures on the fringes of the law, who made my life different and entertaining.

People like Louie Gatowski, for instance, charged with carrying a weapon dangerous to the public peace. The "weapon" in question was a bayonet from World War I, 56 cm (22 ") in length, a formidable-looking object. When I described this frightening blade to the Court as a "family heirloom," and submitted that the accused was not guilty of the offense as charged, my perennial rival E.P. Adolphe (senior prosecuting agent for the Attorney-General of Alberta) turned white with dismay at such a perfidious suggestion. I thought I had brought about a heart attack on that worthy gentleman. Needless to say, Gatowski was convicted, but the $20 fine perhaps indicated that the Court that day was prepared to temper justice with mercy in disposing of this contentious matter.

And there was the baffling case of Jimmy Liscomb, one of my early Calgary cases. Liscomb was an assumed name and I vow he was one of the toughest characters I have ever encountered. Unfortunately for him, he appeared without counsel before Chief Justice McLaurin, who towards the end of his long tenure on the bench was sentencing criminals before he even found them guilty. In this case, Liscomb was charged with being in possession of a tape-recorder, knowing it to have been stolen. Of course my client claimed it was part of a police frame-up, and that the tape-recorder had been planted on him in order to obtain a conviction. Following his trial before the inscrutable Chief Justice McLaurin, he was sentenced to six years of the best in Prince Albert Penitentiary, a maximum security prison, and a penal anachronism going back to the turn of the century.

When Jimmy arrived at Prince Albert his shoulders were so broad that two uniforms had to be stitched together to accommodate his burly frame. Probably the Court was right in giving him six years, for he had a lengthy criminal record covering everything from attempted murder to assault causing bodily harm. His eyes of watery pale blue were set in a broad Ukrainian face and his favorite *modus operandi* was to fire a rifle at the feet of a prospective witness, coming closer and closer to his target until the reluctant victim capitulated and promised to provide evidence in his defense.

Somehow he found me and I agreed to take his appeal. I well remember the Calgary detective who told me he had Liscomb in the palm of his hand like a beetle and if he chose he could crush poor Jimmy to death.

I travelled over 240 km (150 miles) to Prince Albert Penitentiary, standing stark and forbidding on the bleak Saskatchewan prairie, to get my briefing for the Liscomb appeal. In that frightening antediluvian prison, I met with Jimmy Liscomb for the last time. He was profusely grateful that I should have come so far to see him and he proudly presented me with his retainer, a hand-tooled Mexican leather briefcase I call the "Jimmy Liscomb bag" which I have carried with me all over the world. The evidence against the accused was entirely circumstantial, but the Appeal Court had no difficulty in upholding the conviction and sentence.

After his release from prison, Jimmy repented of his evil ways and went to the oil fields of Libya to earn an honest living. But the leopard cannot change his spots, and shortly after his return to Canada, Jimmy was murdered in an attempt to extort money from a wealthy farmer on the outskirts of Edmonton. He was one tough and unforgettable character.

The ladies of the night were minor but memorable clients in the justice system I knew. Like the Butterfly Girl, who came into my office one hot summer afternoon in her abbreviated shorts with her tiny Pomeranian dog on a leash. Before we addressed her legal problems, she wanted to know if I wished to see her butterfly, which was apparently tattooed on some obscure part of her anatomy. Just as we were to have a visual demonstration of this esoteric subject, in came my secretary and ruined what promised to be a most edifying consultation!

To say nothing of the welfare bum driving over to see me in her enormous Cadillac to engage me to release her prize poodle from the clutches of an avaricious dog parlor, whose only crime was wanting their bill paid before turning over the canine to its rightful owner.

"Have you no shame?" I enquired of this grasping female. But answer there came none as she drove off in her high-priced limousine to retrieve her expensive animal.

Many of the petty criminals I defended were unfortunate housewives, who, bored to distraction or in the high passion of the holiday season, descended to shoplifting for things they did not need, and then faced immediate criminal charges from the security officers of the city's department stores. The usual defenses of amnesia or accident or mistake were generally quite ineffective and the only hope was to mitigate the offense and keep them out of jail.

When I told Provincial Court Judge John Gorman that the two Dutch sisters I represented had acted in a spirit of whimsy when they picked up hundreds of dollars worth of Christmas gifts, including some bulky musical instruments, I thought the judge would fall off the bench— whether from amusement or apoplexy, I am not quite sure!

They were all part of the day's work. As time went on, I missed the drug lords and masters of organized crime spawned in the larger cities. Somehow, the "Crook of the Century" and gentlemen of that ilk passed me by.

It was not the greatest criminal law practice that ever came down the pike, but it was a passing parade of human frailty and fallen men and women. Where else would I have met people like Jimmy the Con, who despite a criminal record of 485 convictions, ran for mayor of Calgary twice on his populist ticket and garnered a large percentage of the popular vote?

To me, law was the most exciting game in town.

Whose Ewoks are They?

I must make passing reference to a highly colorful court case that may possibly go on for years.

As the matter is before the Federal Court of Canada, and sub judice, it would be inappropriate for me to discuss the facts or issues of this alleged plagiarism case, which before it is laid to rest will determine some vital questions of intellectual property law in Canada for years to come.

So I merely raise the question: did my client, Dean Preston, create the Ewoks when he wrote his script *Space Pets* in 1978, or were they produced quite independently by the George Lucas organization down in California for his final film in the Star Wars trilogy, *The Return of the Jedi*?

Time alone will tell. Round One concludes that the furry little creatures emanated from Lucas Films Limited but there are years of appeals ahead. The final outcome is in the lap of the gods.

Be Jubilant My Feet

There is no question but that lawyers are a misunderstood lot. It was a character in Shakespeare's Henry VI who allowed that "The first thing we do, let's kill all the lawyers." And there you have it. Are we reptiles or saviors? Speaking for myself, as the judges would say, lawyers are a necessary part of life. The world would be in a sorry state without them.

One by one, virtually all segments of our society in North America have fallen before the new despotism of the modern state, which controls and regulates every aspect of our lives. Only the justice system, with its trial by jury, remains intact. Even now, state-administered legal aid has begun to make inroads that threaten to take over our profession as well.

At times lawyering has been a lonely task. But I have always known that perseverance and a leap of faith will find the key to open a thousand doors. Was I fated to be a rebel without a cause, a misunderstood Don Quixote tilting forever at non-existent legal windmills? Or were there some underlying principles to be defended and upheld? Now that it is all behind me, I have absolutely no doubts or misgivings on this score.

Over the years I have been constantly asked, "If you believe a person is guilty of a serious crime such as murder, how can you possibly defend him?"

It has not been for me to judge the guilt or innocence of my clients. A host of people were prepared to do that. All I knew was that I believed in the system, and had only one duty: to provide my client with a full and complete defense according to law. The rule of law was paramount. In the eyes of the law, all men are equal and entitled to an impartial trial. The Anglo-American adversary system of jurisprudence, with all of its flaws, in my opinion stands unsurpassed anywhere in the world. And only the lawyer is left to pursue the elusive quest for justice in the courts of the land.

Law *is* and always will be the most exciting game in town. So be jubilant my feet and lead me down the paths of justice. The prize is there for the taking.